HOW TO READ THE BIBLE AND STILL BE A CHRISTIAN

HOW TO READ THE BIBLE AND STILL BE A CHRISTIAN

STRUGGLING WITH DIVINE VIOLENCE FROM GENESIS THROUGH REVELATION

JOHN DOMINIC CROSSAN

HarperOne

An Imprint of HarperCollins*Publishers*

HarperOne

HOW TO READ THE BIBLE AND STILL BE A CHRISTIAN: *Struggling with Divine Violence from Genesis Through Revelation.* Copyright © 2015 by John Dominic Crossan. All rights reserved. Printed in the United States of America. No part of this book may be used or reproduced in any manner whatsoever without written permission except in the case of brief quotations embodied in critical articles and reviews. For information address HarperCollins Publishers, 195 Broadway, New York, NY 10007.

HarperCollins books may be purchased for educational, business, or sales promotional use. For information please e-mail the Special Markets Department at SPsales@harpercollins.com.

HarperCollins website: http://www.harpercollins.com

HarperCollins®, ♨ ®, and HarperOne™ are trademarks of HarperCollins Publishers.

FIRST EDITION

Image on page 239 of the author's design, rendered by Joan Olson. Used with permission.

Library of Congress Cataloging-in-Publication Data is available upon request.

ISBN 978–0–06–220359–5

15 16 17 18 19 RRD(H) 10 9 8 7 6 5 4 3 2 1

For
Anne K. Perry
&
Alan W. Perry

CONTENTS

PART I
Challenge

CHAPTER I

Ending

A HYMN TO A SAVAGE GOD?

We had fed the heart on fantasies,
The heart's grown brutal from the fare.
WILLIAM BUTLER YEATS,
"The Stare's Nest by My Window" (1922)

THIS BOOK'S TITLE—*How to Read the Bible and Still Be a Christian*—
imagines some serious tension within the Christian Bible, between
being a faithful reader and being a faithful Christian. But how, when,
and where I first saw this problem influences how, when, and where
I first saw the solution. Here, then, to begin with, are some autobio-
graphical details as full disclosure for what is at stake for me in the
problem I propose for you and the solution I offer to you in this book.

A disclosure is already implicit in my triple name on this book's
cover. "John Crossan" is the name on my driver's license, passport,
and TSA pre-check protocols. But in 1950, at the age of sixteen, I entered a thirteenth-century Roman Catholic monastery and became
"Brother Dominic." My new vocation was supposed to wipe out, as it
were, my past identity and give me only a future destiny—as in the
biblical, so in the monastic tradition.

Nineteen years later, having finally realized that celibacy was vastly overrated, I left both monastery and priesthood to get married. But even if the rules had changed to allow a married priesthood, I still would have resigned in 1969. What was my problem?

My monastic superiors had recognized that five years of Greek and Latin in an Irish boarding school could not be wasted so they decided I should become a professor of biblical studies after ordination in 1957. I was not, and did not expect to be, consulted on any of their plans. Under my vow of obedience I did what I was told, but to be honest, I loved their decision.

In the Roman Catholic tradition it was required, and wisely so, that a degree in theology should precede any degree in biblical studies. First, therefore, I was sent back to Ireland for a doctorate in theology, then for two years to the Pontifical Biblical Institute in Rome, and finally for another two years to the French Biblical and Archaeological School in Jerusalem. It was, quite frankly, a magnificent education.

What should be kept in mind is that I was a Christian before I became a scholar but also a theologian before I became an historian. In other words, I have always understood the Christian Bible through those multiple optics, but I could always speak or write while seeing through the specific lens expected by a particular audience or demanded in a given situation. I should also admit that I never found those divergent viewpoints either confusing or alarming because of one fundamental conviction I have had for a long time: that reason and revelation *or* history and theology *or* research and faith—by whatever names—cannot contradict one another unless we have one or both wrong.

I am not sure where the serenity of this assurance came from, but it has never left me. My courses in theology were heavily invested in the *Summa Theologiae* of Saint Thomas Aquinas—and that was, like the name "Dominic," another thirteenth-century gift. My monastic superiors emphasized Aquinas to teach us *what* to think, but I also absorbed his writings greedily for *how* to think. If Aquinas spent the morning reading pagan Aristotle and the afternoon writing Christian theology, and never found a conflict between reason and revelation spoiling his lunch or disturbing his siesta, there must be no conflict between reason and revelation or any other such disjunctive pairs. That, at least, was my conclusion forever after.

As it happened, my departure from both monastery and priesthood had nothing to do with history and the Bible but everything to do with theology and the Pope. In the fall of 1968 I said on PBS that the encyclical *Humanae Vitae* was wrong about birth control. That led to an immediate rebuke from the cardinal archbishop of Chicago. When the dust finally settled about six months later, Cardinal Cody was still the archbishop but Father Dominic was both an ex-monk and an ex-priest.

When I moved from seminary to university in the fall of 1969, my research focus was already established on the historical Jesus, that is, on the living, breathing first-century Jew proclaimed as Messiah/ Christ and Son of God by some of his contemporaries but crucified as rebel and alleged "King of the Jews" by official Roman power. That focus had actually started far back in September 1960 when my religious superiors sent me to be chaplain for a group of Americans on a Roman Catholic pilgrimage across Europe. We visited Castel Gandolfo for John XXIII, Fatima and Lourdes for Mary, Lisieux for Thérèse, and Monaco for Grace (honestly!). And since it was 1960, we spent a day at Oberammergau's Passion Play, performed every ten years in the foothills of the Bavarian Alps.

In 1634 and every decade thereafter the villagers have fulfilled their promise of a full-day Passion Play in thanksgiving for deliverance from plague. Something happened for me that day when I first saw as *drama* a story I knew full well as *text*. The play made me confront new questions. How had the *same* crowd that filled the huge stage that morning to welcome Jesus on Palm Sunday become changed by afternoon to cry for his crucifixion on Good Friday? It was for me a quiet but clear epiphany that something was missing from that story of Jesus's passion, something was wrong when acclamation became condemnation without any explanation.

The play I saw in 1960 was the same version that Adolf Hitler saw in 1930 and 1934 (the tercentenary year)—that is, both before and after he became chancellor of Germany. His review: "Never has the menace of Jewry been so convincingly portrayed as in this presentation of what happened in the times of the Romans. There one sees in Pontius Pilate a Roman racially and intellectually so superior, that he stands out like a firm, clean rock in the middle of the whole muck and mire of Jewry."

My interest in and focus on the historical Jesus started that day in Oberammergau. But its memory meant that for me history would have to be laced with theology and that I could never reconstruct the historical Jesus as dispassionately as I might, say, the historical Alexander. Only good, honest, and accurate history might save Christian faith from a theological anti-Judaism as the continuing seedbed for racial anti-Semitism. That was why, after my return to Chicago in 1961, I joined Rabbi Shaalman on a Sunday morning TV program called (from memory) *Deicide or Genocide?* It was also why my very first scholarly article was called "Anti-Semitism and the New Testament" (*Theological Studies*, 1965).

Starting with my 1973 book *In Parables: The Challenge of the Historical Jesus*, and for the next twenty years at DePaul University in Chicago, that subtitle was the heart of my scholarly research and professional life. During those years my emphasis was always on history rather than theology, and questions of personal faith were bracketed as irrelevant for academic discourse. I myself, however, was always very aware of them. All of that started to change in 1991.

In that year I published the *big* Jesus book I had been preparing in bits and pieces across those two decades. I actually wrote *The Historical Jesus: The Life of a Mediterranean Jewish Peasant* for my academic peers and intended to raise the question of sources and methods for historical Jesus research. That did not happen, but something else did, and as far as I am concerned, it was much more important in the long run.

Peter Steinfels, noting that two Roman Catholics—both of whom were educated at the Pontifical Biblical Institute in Rome but only one of whom was still a priest, the other being an ex-priest—had published books on the historical Jesus that fall, compared John Meier's *A Marginal Jew* and my *Historical Jesus* as the front-page Christmas story in *The New York Times* for December 23, 1991. His story "Peering Past Faith to Glimpse the Jesus of History" was reprinted by other papers nationally and internationally.

What happened next surprised me immensely. I might have expected invitations to speak at seminaries or universities, but instead I was invited to lecture in *churches*—weekends of three or four lectures as well as sermons at Sunday services. The historical Jesus had clearly become a question not just of history or even of theology, but of Christian faith and church life.

Church venues are not the same as academic classes. I never said anything different about the historical Jesus in either location, but Q&A sessions after church lectures *always* raised theological issues involving Christian faith and practice—especially my own. How had historical research influenced my Christian faith? What was at stake for me in the Christian Bible after all those years of biblical study? It was, therefore, through church lectures rather than scholarly debates that this present book was conceived, born, and matured.

"A Whip of Cords"

IN CHURCH LECTURES I located Jesus within his first-century CE Jewish homeland and especially within its matrix of both violent and nonviolent resistance to Roman power and imperial oppression. Remember that word "matrix" for the rest of this book. It means for me the background you cannot skip—like British imperialism for understanding Mahatma Gandhi—or the context you cannot avoid—like American racism for understanding Martin Luther King Jr.

Within the options of that matrix, I emphasized Jesus's own nonviolent resistance to both Roman imperial occupation and Jewish high-priestly collaboration with it. But in the Q&A session after every lecture, strong if polite objections were often raised to that historical interpretation of Jesus.

One objection that came up repeatedly asked about that incident in the Temple of Jerusalem when Jesus apparently violently attacked people with a whip.

That was an easy one to answer. Jesus's action in that case was a prophetic demonstration against worship in the Temple excusing injustice in the land—injustice exacerbated, of course, by necessary high-priestly collaboration with Roman imperial power and control. That is why Jesus quoted Jeremiah's "den of robbers" (Jer. 7:11; Mark 11:17). (Jesus was not accusing people of thievery in the Temple. A "den" is not the place *for* robbery and injustice inside, but the hideout *from* robbery and injustice outside.) Jesus was, in fulfillment of God's threat in Jeremiah 7:14, symbolically "destroying" the Temple by overturning its fiscal and sacrificial bases.

But *only* the version in John 2:14–15 mentions both money changers and herd animals. Notice, for example, the twin halves of these sentences (with the NRSV corrected from the Greek):

> In the temple he found people selling cattle, sheep, and doves, and the money changers seated at their tables. Making a whip of cords, he drove all of them out of the temple, both the sheep and the cattle. He also poured out the coins of the money changers and overturned their tables.

In other words, *only* in John is there any mention of a "whip of cords"—not for the money changers but for the herd animals. That was an act of religio-political demonstration or of nonviolent resistance, not an act of violence with a whip used against people.

Furthermore, I continued, we can plainly see that even Pilate recognized that Jesus was resisting Roman control *nonviolently*; Pilate executed Jesus publicly because of that resistance, but he did not bother to round up Jesus's companions because he judged the Kingdom movement—correctly, once again—to be *nonviolent*. He would have crucified all of Jesus's followers if Jesus had been leading a band of violent revolutionaries. Mark's Gospel emphasizes that judgment by his parable of the nonviolent Jesus versus the violent Barabbas (15:6–9), and John's Gospel underlines it in the parable of the nonviolent Kingdom of God versus the violent Empire of Rome (18:36).

This, however, simply led to another, far more serious objection from church audiences. What about that Apocalypse from John of Patmos, what about the book of Revelation, and what about the second coming of Jesus Christ? No matter what I said about the nonviolence of the first coming, questioners objected that the second coming was to be supremely violent, was to be a war to end all wars.

Put bluntly, the nonviolent Jesus in the Sermon on the Mount seemed annulled and dismissed by the later Jesus in the book of Revelation. I turn next to that far more serious objection to a nonviolent God and/or a nonviolent Jesus.

"The Great Wine Press of the Wrath of God"

THE CHRISTIAN BIBLE ENDS with the glorious image of a marriage made in heaven, a wedding of humanity and divinity. It is a serene conclusion that establishes a transformed world, a hauntingly beautiful vision not of an Earth ascending to heaven, but of a heaven descending to Earth. This is a sublime symbol of ultimate cosmic regeneration here below upon a transformed and transfigured Earth. (I call it the "Divine Cleanup of the World" or "Extreme Makeover: World Edition.") The New Testament's book of Revelation, by the way, expanded that vision from the Old Testament's book of Isaiah.

Here, first, is that visionary scenario from the prophet Isaiah of Jerusalem toward the end of the eighth century BCE:

> On this mountain the Lord of hosts will make for all peoples
> a feast of rich food, a feast of well-aged wines,
> of rich food filled with marrow, of well-aged wines strained
>   clear.
> And he will destroy on this mountain
> the shroud that is cast over all peoples,
> the sheet that is spread over all nations;
> he will swallow up death forever.
> Then the Lord God will wipe away the tears from all faces,
> and the disgrace of his people he will take away from all the
>   earth,
> for the Lord has spoken. (Isa. 25:6–8)

Our world will climax with neither bang nor whimper, with neither destruction nor extinction, with neither evacuation-to-heaven nor emigration-to-hell, but rather with a transformational feast "for all peoples." God is, as it were, no longer the lord of hosts but now the host of lords—and ladies.

Next, sometime in the 90s CE, a Christian seer named John borrowed Isaiah's visionary hope but elevated his great cosmic banquet feast into a great cosmic marriage feast:

> And I saw the holy city, the new Jerusalem, coming down out
> of heaven from God, prepared as a bride adorned for her hus-
> band. And I heard a loud voice from the throne saying,
>
> > "See, the home of God is among mortals.
> > He will dwell with them;
> > they will be his peoples,
> > and God himself will be with them;
> > he will wipe every tear from their eyes.
> > Death will be no more;
> > mourning and crying and pain will be no more,
> > for the first things have passed away."

And the one who was seated on the throne said, "See, I am making all things new." (Rev. 21:2–5a)

It would be hard to imagine a more magnificent consummation. The biblical story ends, as do most comedic stories and romantic narratives, with a wedding feast. *And yet, and yet, and yet. . . .*

The first "and yet" concerns the wedding scenario as climactic celebration. The problem is that you wade to that blessed event through a sea of blood. I do not exaggerate. We are dealing with metaphors and symbols, of course, but they are metaphors of massacre and symbols of slaughter. The Earth, for example, is imagined as a vineyard ripe for a harvest not of wine, but of blood—like this:

So the angel swung his sickle over the earth and gathered the vintage of the earth, and he threw it into the great wine press of the wrath of God. And the wine press was trodden outside the city, and blood flowed from the wine press, as high as a horse's bridle, for a distance of about two hundred miles. (14:19–20)

During the American Civil War, the "Battle Hymn of the Republic" referred to God's "trampling out the vintage where the grapes of wrath are stored," but not even the blood of more than half a million dead would have reached the height of horses' bridles for *two hundred miles.*

The second "and yet" concerns Jesus Christ in that climactic wedding of Earth and heaven. On the one hand, he is the "Lamb that was slaughtered" (5:6, 12), the nonviolent martyr of violent imperial authority who becomes the Lamb-as-bridegroom in that climactic marriage feast (19:7, 9; 21:9). But he is also the Lamb who unleashes those terrible four horsemen: the rider on the white horse is Christ the conqueror (6:2, compare 19:11); the rider on the red horse is War the slaughterer (6:4); the rider on the black horse is Famine the price-gouger (6:5–6); and the rider on the green horse is Death the destroyer (6:8). Those are, once again, metaphors and symbols; but

Revelation's four horsemen are images of human horror and divine terror, and it is Jesus who unleashes them.

The third "and yet" concerns that promised climactic war. There will be, the text says, a great final battle between the Kingdom of God and the Empire of Rome, with the latter repeatedly identified by the code name "Babylon," from Revelation 14:8 through 16:19 to 17:5 and climactically in 18:2, 10, and 21. Why Rome-as-Babylon? Because the Roman Empire destroyed Jerusalem's Second Temple in 70 CE as the Babylonian Empire had destroyed its First Temple in 586 BCE.

Among those just-cited places, Rome, as "Babylon the great," is the "mother of whores and of earth's abominations" (17:5) and is filled with "demonic spirits, performing signs, who go abroad to the kings of the whole world, to assemble them for battle on the great day of God the Almighty" (16:14). But Rome will eventually be reduced to "a haunt of every foul spirit, / a haunt of every foul bird, / a haunt of every foul and hateful beast" (18:2). Here is how that great final battle is described:

> Then I saw heaven opened, and there was a white horse! Its rider is called Faithful and True, and in righteousness he judges and makes war. His eyes are like a flame of fire, and on his head are many diadems; and he has a name inscribed that no one knows but himself. He is clothed in a robe dipped in blood, and his name is called The Word of God. And the armies of heaven, wearing fine linen, white and pure, were following him on white horses. From his mouth comes a sharp sword with which to strike down the nations, and he will rule them with a rod of iron; he will tread the wine press of the fury of the wrath of God the Almighty. On his robe and on his thigh he has a name inscribed, "King of kings and Lord of lords." (19:11–16)

As we saw above (6:2), the rider on the white horse is Christ the conqueror with the sharp sword in his mouth (1:16; 2:12, 16). But, for me, the book of Revelation was and is profoundly wrong about the fate of Rome. Wrong, in fact, concerning both time and Christ.

First, Rome's destruction was to happen "soon," that is, within the author's or at least his generation's lifetime. That word "soon" tolls like a death bell from start to finish of Revelation. It begins with "what must soon take place" in 1:1, continues through 2:16; 3:11; 11:14; and 22:6–7, and climaxes with Christ's declaration that "I am coming soon" (22:20). But the Western Roman Empire continued until the late 400s and the Eastern until the mid-1400s.

Second, the Roman Empire was not *destroyed by* Christ but was, for better or for worse, *converted to* Christ under and after Constantine in the 300s. There is not a glimpse of that actuality anywhere in the prophetic vision of Revelation. Destruction, yes; conversion, no. (Only Luke-Acts imagined the future correctly as *Roman* Christianity.)

Third, Rome's imminent destruction was envisaged by Revelation as the consummation of the world, the establishment of a new heaven and a new Earth in that wedding feast of divinity and humanity (21:1–5). That heavenly vision is still a consummation devoutly to be wished and very far from clearly imminent.

Finally, as we have seen, Isaiah had imagined a great final feast to celebrate God's establishment of a peaceful Earth. There is, indeed, a great final feast in the book of Revelation, but it is "the great supper of God" for the vultures of the air:

> Then I saw an angel standing in the sun, and with a loud voice
> he called to all the birds that fly in midheaven, "Come, gather
> for the great supper of God, to eat the flesh of kings, the flesh
> of captains, the flesh of the mighty, the flesh of horses and
> their riders—flesh of all, both free and slave, both small and
> great." Then I saw the beast [the mighty Roman Empire] and
> the kings of the earth with their armies gathered to make war
> against the rider on the horse [Christ] and against his army
> [the angels]. And the beast was captured, and with it the false

prophet [the divine Roman emperor] who had performed in
its presence the signs by which he deceived those who had
received the mark of the beast and those who worshiped its
image. These two were thrown alive into the lake of fire that
burns with sulfur. And the rest were killed by the sword of the
rider on the horse, the sword that came from his mouth; and
all the birds were gorged with their flesh. (19:17–21)

Furthermore, those questions and objections about the violent
Christ in that climactic book of Revelation were intensified by two
contemporary factors external to my lectures in church venues.

"Whatever Happens, Never Forget to Wipe Your Sword"

ONE FACTOR, BETWEEN 1995 and 2007, was the publication by
Tim LaHaye and Jerry Jenkins of the multiple books in the Left
Behind series. Those books, and their subsequent movies and games,
arranged multiple and discrete biblical images of cosmic consummation into a more or less coherent scenario. But in doing so, they made
one egregious expansion beyond even Revelation's divine violence.
The great final battle was to involve not just Christ and the angels, as
in Revelation, but humans as well.

Here is just one example, from *Glorious Appearing: The End of
Days*, the second-to-last book in the set. The human protagonist is
Montgomery Cleburn McCullum, known as Mac, a "former pilot for
Global Community [GC] Supreme Potentate Nicolae Carpathia [the
anti-Christ]" but now converted to "Christ" as the "chief Tribulation
Force pilot on assignment at Petra" (p. ix). The incident takes place at
Jerusalem's Damascus Gate:

"Lord, forgive me," he breathed, spraying his Uzi and drop-
ping at least a dozen GC from behind. He felt no remorse. *All's*

fair . . . It was only fitting, he decided, that the devil's crew were dressed in black. *Live by the sword, die by the sword.* (p. 27)

Notice how the authors (ab)use the warning of Jesus that "all who take the sword will perish by the sword" (Matt. 26:52). Jesus said "all," but Mac lacks any sense of self-criticism—or even the grace of irony.

Another external factor was the release of the film *The Chronicles of Narnia: The Lion, the Witch, and the Wardrobe* in 2005. That movie was based on C. S. Lewis's book of the same name published in 1950 to start his seven-volume series.

As in the Left Behind series, so in the Narnia series: humans participate in the great final battle between good and evil. Also, in the Narnia series, good is portrayed by a male character and evil by a female one: Christ, "the Lion of the tribe of Judah" from Revelation 5:5, becomes Aslan, the lion in Narnia; the great whore from Revelation 17:1, 15, 16, and 19:2 becomes the White Witch of Narnia.

Furthermore, before Aslan the lion/Christ kills the White Witch, Peter, oldest of the four children who are the human participants in this apocalyptic battle, kills the Wolf-Monster. Afterward, Aslan/Christ reminds him: "You have forgotten to clean your sword . . . whatever happens, never forget to wipe your sword" (chapter 12). Once again, I have to recall a different admonition to another sword-yielding Peter: "Put your sword back into its place; for all who take the sword will perish by the sword" (Matt. 26:52).

Both the Narnia series and the Left Behind series go beyond Revelation by having humans—children in the former case and adults in the latter—participate fully in the divine violence of apocalyptic cleansing. Both of those series generated questions and objections from my lecture audiences when I spoke of Jesus's nonviolent resistance to Rome's control of his first-century Jewish homeland. If I wanted to speak, as I did, about the historical Jesus, my audiences asked, as they should, about Revelation and its divine violence now at least fictionally supported by human violence.

Clearly, and whether I liked it or not, I had to widen my focus from Gospel to Apocalypse, from historical Jesus to apocalyptic Jesus, and so across the entire New Testament from start to finish. But that focus could not and did not stop there; it had to extend to the entire Christian Bible and discuss the very character of the biblical God.

The Vision of a Bipolar God

IN THOSE CHURCH LECTURES on Jesus I proposed that his attitude of nonviolent resistance to violence was programmatically based on his vision of a nonviolent God. In other words, Jesus's message proclaimed the nonviolent Kingdom of a nonviolent God. That came, by the way, from the Sermon on the Mount where the divine model for "loving enemies" is a God who "makes his sun rise on the evil and on the good, and sends rain on the righteous and on the unrighteous." Our earthly nonviolent resistance to violence makes us appropriate "children" of that heavenly Father who acts in similar fashion (Matt. 5:43–48 and Luke 6:27–36).

But, whatever about Jesus in Temple or Apocalypse, it was concerning the character of the biblical God that questions, objections, and contradictions mounted exponentially. Was not the biblical God every bit as bipolar regarding violence *and* nonviolence as was that biblical Jesus? Sometimes it was argued that the God of the Old Testament was a God of vengeance and punishment while the God of the New Testament was a God of forgiveness and mercy. That was how, it was suggested to me, to solve my problem with the twin aspects of God's biblical character.

Despite that stereotype's Christian anti-Judaism, the suggestion got little traction in my church audiences. Because, of course, we had usually discussed Revelation by then, and my questioners knew that it imagined a terminal and cosmic violence greater than anything in the Old Testament. An Old Testament bad-cop God and a New Testament good-cop God were persuasive only to those who had never actually read the entire Christian Bible.

But in any case, it was quite clear that, one way or another, Christianity's Biblical Express Train, as I call it, thundered along on twin and *parallel* rails—one of divine violence and the other of divine nonviolence.

To discuss more deeply the character of the biblical God, I focused on one very important concept, namely, *justice*—especially with a biblical God of "justice and righteousness" (Jer. 9:24) who demands "justice and righteousness" of others (22:3). But that required some preliminary linguistic therapy.

In ordinary everyday language the unqualified term "justice" usually refers exclusively or at least primarily to *retributive* justice, with an emphasis on penalties and punishments. Think, as examples, of the U.S. Department of Justice or the Uniform Code of Military Justice. Each crime is met with a corresponding punishment. That is retributive justice. There are, however, two forms of justice—the justice of *distribution* and the justice of *retribution*—a distinction of supreme importance for both the Bible and this book. In fact, I will go a step farther and argue that distributive justice is the primary meaning of the word "justice" and that retributive justice is secondary and derivative.

For example, a judge is accused of racial prejudice in court proceedings. The prosecutors select one hundred cases of identical crime and similar circumstances involving white and black defendants. They find that the judge set bail and inflicted sentences two to three times as severe in black as in white cases. The conclusion is that the judge did not *distribute* retributive justice fairly, equitably, and justly.

In other words, for me—and for the Bible—distributive justice is primary; retributive justice is secondary and derivative. Put another way: justice is about the fair distribution of the subject involved. In the Bible, it is primarily about a fair distribution of God's world for all of God's people. For example, when the Bible cries out for justice, can one really think it is demanding retribution?

Give justice to the weak and the orphan;
maintain the right of the lowly and the destitute.
Rescue the weak and the needy;
deliver them from the hand of the wicked. (Ps. 82:3–4)

The heart of God's justice is to make sure that the "weak and the orphan" have received their share of God's resources for them to live and thrive. Retributive justice comes in only when that ideal is violated.

In summary, therefore, the disjunction between God as violent and nonviolent can be rephrased for the rest of this book like this: the biblical God is, on one hand, a God of nonviolent distributive justice and, on the other hand, a God of violent retributive justice. How do we make sense of this dual focus? How do we reconcile these two visions? This is what we will explore in the rest of the book.

Where Are We Now and What Comes Next?

I BEGIN WITH A *Where Now* and *What Next* that extends across this entire book, a word about two terms of crucial importance not only in this chapter but hereafter as well.

First, "Christian Bible." This term is neither apologetical nor polemical but simply descriptive for that set of sacred scriptures extending from Genesis through Revelation. I accept fully that the Christian Bible took the idea itself, most of its content, and much of its sequence from the Hebrew Bible, which preceded it. Indeed, if the first Christians had not been Christian (that is, Messianic) Jews that usage would have been conceptual theft, textual plagiarism, and cultural looting.

As it was, Rabbinic Judaism and Early Christianity arose with equal validity and complete integrity from the common matrix of Second Tempe Judaism's biblical tradition. They were twin daughters of the same mother and both were born in the terrible birthpangs of that first century CE. (Matrix and mother, by the way, come from the same Greek and Latin roots.)

Second, "distributive justice." How did that rather counterintuitive vision of God's distributive justice arise among Israelites and Jews within the biblical tradition? It was hardly overtly obvious in the ancient world then or the modern world now. It did not come from any imagined possibility or abstract theory of *civil* rights or *democratic* rights or *human* rights. It came instead from the experienced actuality and concrete reality of *household* rights. The well-run peasant household, with dues and duties, entitlements and responsibilities, was the biblical tradition's metaphor for both a well-run World at large and a well-run Country at home.

That is why God acts with "justice and righteousness in the *earth*" (Jeremiah 9:24) and the King with "justice and righteousness in the *land*" (Jeremiah 23:5; 33:15). From House through Land to Earth it should always be a matter of *distributive justice and restorative righteousness.* Hence the biblical tradition can accept extreme poverty as sometimes necessary (for example, during the Exodus from Egypt) but not extreme inequality. Imagine, it thinks, of entering a peasant household and finding some of the children starving while others are overfed. That is the obscenity haunting the biblical imagination, causing its God to demand adequacy for all and enough for each.

(If you operate within standard patriarchy, you might call the householder "Father" but, since one in three first-century children was fatherless by fifteen, that might be as much nostalgia as patriarchy. In any case, note how Christianity's official prayer begins with "Our Father [Householder]" before it gets to "Your Kingdom.")

I turn now to *Where Now* and *What Next* for this present chapter. I have argued in this chapter that the Christian Bible presents us with a God of nonviolent distributive justice but also one of violent retributive justice. It also proclaims Jesus the Christ as both the Christ of the nonviolent Sermon on the Mount and the Christ of the violent book of Revelation. But humans are made in "the image and likeness" of God (Gen. 1:26a, 27), and Christians are called to be "joint heirs" with Christ (Rom. 8:17) for the care and preservation of creation (Gen. 1:28; Rom. 8:19). How, then, are we to act against injustice and violence—nonviolently or violently?

This is the essential question behind my title *How to Read the Bible and Still Be a Christian*. Do we choose and follow one or the other option since *both* are presented as the character of the biblical God? But if one Christian chooses God as nonviolent, another may—with equal validity—choose God as violent. Is the answer to my titular "How?" simply, "It's your choice"? Or, alternatively, should we mix a transcendental cocktail of so many parts violence and so many parts nonviolence depending on personal taste or according to denominational tradition?

It is my task in the next chapter to suggest another and different option for *How to Read the Bible and Still Be a Christian*. Furthermore, and even more importantly, my proposed solution will not come externally from me but internally from the Christian Bible itself.

It comes from proposing a Christian theology of the Christian Bible by imagining the Bible as a whole—as a completed volume, as an organized unity, and as an integrated totality. Even though scholars may see the Bible as a collection of diverse works from authors with diverse backgrounds, theologies, and purposes, the church must deal with the Bible as a whole, as revelation, as guidance for our lives today. I plan to read that Christian Bible as if nobody ever told me about two discrete sections called an Old Testament and a New Testament. I will think about it as if our copies lacked any such divisions and we could read straight through, book after book, from Genesis to Revelation.

In Chapter 2 I explore the question "What does the Christian Bible reveal about its own imagination of God's character when we read it through as a complete unit and as an integrated whole?" Is there more there than a simple parallel bipolarity of violence and nonviolence?

CHAPTER 2

Centering

The Meaning in the Middle?

[I]t is with civilization that human "savagery" becomes
an agonizing part of the human condition. As
civilization dawns, the ground of human existence
turns an unearthly shade of red.
ANDREW BARD SCHMOOKLER, *The Parable of the Tribes*

DOES THE END OF a book determine the meaning of the story?
In other words, does the end define the beginning and middle of a
narrative? If the Christian Bible were a random collection of books,
I could possibly play one against another or prefer this one to that
one. But since I think of those books as organized sequentially with
a driving narrative thrust, must not the final book—John of Patmos's
Apocalypse—provide the full purpose and final meaning of it all?
What is at stake is whether the vision of Jesus and God portrayed
in the final book of Revelation trumps the other perspectives found
earlier in the Bible.

We usually assume that the meaning of a narrative is fully dis-
closed only at its conclusion. Think of how you might react if, deeply
engrossed in a movie, the screen went suddenly blank about six min-

utes before the finale; or you found your engrossing page-turner lacking the last fifty pages. We might be able to figure out every-thing important in a story if an earlier portion were left out, but we are at a loss if the ending is gone.

Perhaps Aristotle might help us here. In 350 BCE, he wrote that a plotted tale had to be a "whole" and "a whole is that which has a beginning, a middle, and an end" (*Poetics* 7). In other words, a story's ending is not more important than its beginning or middle; all the essential elements must be present for the story to be "whole." So could the meaning of a story be fully revealed at the start or in the middle or only and always at the end? Is the importance of the end to meaning some cosmic law or transcendental decree?

The simple answer is no, as the Bible itself will attest. I will make two exploratory probes into biblical stories to show why this is not the most important question. There is another movement within the Bible that sheds further light on the matter. My purpose in all this is not simply to solve the problem posed in my title *How to Read the Bible and Still Be a Christian*, but also to broach the possibility that there is an internal solution within the Christian Bible itself.

Two Exploratory Probes

MY FIRST EXPLORATORY PROBE starts in the book of Leviticus, which includes this rather stunning announcement from God: "The land shall not be sold in perpetuity, for the land is mine; with me you are but aliens and tenants" (25:23). In other words, since the land is life itself, householders are but agents and stewards of God as owner, and they are only tenant farmers on another's land and resident aliens in another's country. (It is as if God announced today: Capital belongs to me; you are all doubtful creditors and bad debtors.)

It is easy enough to imagine the purpose of taking one's ancestral land off permanent sale. The theory is that originally God distrib-uted the land fairly and equitably among the tribes, clans, and families of Israel. That distributive justice must never be annulled, and the rest of Leviticus 25 spells out in some detail what must happen if land needs to be sold temporarily, but never permanently.

Every fiftieth year was to be the Jubilee Year of liberation, redemption, and restoration. During that Jubilee Year, all rural property sold temporarily through necessity was to be returned to its original ancestral owners:

> And you shall hallow the fiftieth year and you shall proclaim liberty throughout the land to all its inhabitants. It shall be a jubilee for you: you shall return, every one of you, to your property and every one of you to your family. . . . In this year of jubilee you shall return, every one of you, to your property." (25:10, 13)

In fact, the buyer of such alienated rural property did not actually own the land but only its produce, pending the land's return in the next Jubilee Year. The buyer is instructed, "If the years are more [to the next Jubilee], you shall increase the price, and if the years are fewer, you shall diminish the price; for it is a certain number of harvests that are being sold to you" (25:16).

It is interesting, by the way, that the Jubilee Year started "on the day of atonement" (25:9). It is almost as if the very necessity of having a Jubilee Year pointed to something sinful that required forgiveness. In any case, all of this is quite clear in theory: land may be sold temporarily but never permanently. So how did that beautiful distributive justice work out in practice? Think of one rather extreme example of its annulment—but possibly a paradigmatic one for very many less extreme instances.

King Ahab of northern Israel made the following offer to Naboth: "Give me your vineyard, so that I may have it for a vegetable garden, because it is near my house; I will give you a better vineyard for it; or, if it seems good to you, I will give you its value in money" (1 Kings 21:2). That certainly sounds fair enough. We might have instead expected from a king to a commoner: you have it, I want it, do you have a problem with that?

But Naboth knows his Torah and responds: "The Lord forbid that I should give you my ancestral inheritance" (21:3). Thereupon, Ahab's wife has Naboth executed on trumped-up charges and gives his vineyard to her husband (21:4–16). It is not necessary, by the way, to demonize Queen Jezebel. She is simply a Canaanite princess who believes in an economic theology of open markets and free trade and, concluding that Naboth needlessly insulted her husband, acted accordingly (21:15).

I repeat that Naboth's vineyard is an extreme case and not an ordinary example of how to negate Leviticus 25. But we know that another's land was permanently acquired, if not by buying and selling, then at least by mortgaging and foreclosing. Otherwise, Isaiah would not have needed to lament, "Ah, you who join house to house, / who add field to field, / until there is room for no one but you, / and you are left to live alone / in the midst of the land!" (5:8).

Furthermore, scholars have often wondered, if the Jubilee Year was actually observed regularly every fiftieth year, why do we have so little mention of it across our later texts? If, as is likely, it was not observed, then the core of the Priestly tradition––to which Leviticus belongs—is reduced from divine decree to mere suggestion.

Be that as it may, I want you to think for a moment about the sequence of yes-and-no, affirmation-and-negation, acceptance-and-rejection, assertion-and-subversion in that just-seen attempt to maintain distributive justice in landownership under God. Put another way, there is a struggle between God's radical ideal for us (Lev. 25:23), which I call the *radicality of God*, and the standard coercive ways that cultures in fact operate (Isa. 5:8), which I call the *normalcy of civilization*.

Hold on to that tensive dialectic as I turn from Old to New Testament and from one end of the Christian Bible to the other for my second exploratory probe.

Of the New Testament's twenty-seven books, thirteen are attributed to the Apostle Paul. But scholars have agreed that those thirteen letters should be divided into three groups. First, seven letters were *certainly* written by Paul: 1 Thessalonians, Galatians, 1 and 2 Corinthians, Philippians, Philemon, and Romans. A further three were *probably not* written by him: 2 Thessalonians, Colossians, and Ephesians. And a final three were *certainly not* written by him: 1 and 2 Timothy and Titus. (Those italicized words represent common scholarly judgments, not dogmatic postulates or doctrinal principles.)

For this second exploratory probe I compare an example from those first two groups of letters, with a focus on the letters to Philemon and to the Colossians. Watch carefully what happens along that "Pauline" trajectory on the subject of slavery.

First, with regard to Philemon: The actual, historical Paul wrote to Philemon in the early 50s, most likely from the governor's prison at Ephesus. He was chained to a guard in the barracks but allowed help and support from other Christians. The one-chapter letter arose from a very particular situation and was not at all an abstract treatise on slavery.

Philemon's slave Onesimus (Greek for "useful") was in serious trouble with his master and fled to Paul for intercession; flight to an owner's *amicus* (friend) was permitted in such situations under Roman law. But while they were together, Paul converted Onesimus to Christianity: "I am appealing to you [Philemon] for my child, Onesimus, whose father I have become during my imprisonment" (v. 10).

Paul, however, is not just requesting that Philemon forgive Onesimus, but demanding that Philemon free him. Onesimus is to be treated "no longer as a slave but more than a slave, a beloved brother—especially to me but how much more to you, both in the flesh and in the Lord" (v. 16). That manumission, or official liberation, is in fact Philemon's Christian duty: Paul is "bold enough in Christ to command you to do your duty" and "confident of your obedience" (vv. 8, 21). But how, within the slave economy of the Roman Empire, can Paul make such a stunning demand and claim it as Philemon's *duty*?

For Paul, Christ had died *by* Rome to live *with* God. So, by baptism—imagined as a metaphor of burying in the grave rather than a metaphor of washing in the baptismal font (see Chapter 13)—Christians had died *to* Rome to live *for* God: "all of us who have been baptized into Christ Jesus were baptized into his death . . . we have been buried with him by baptism into death . . . we have been united with him in a death like his" (Rom. 6:3–5).

Those repeated past tenses ("have been"), addressed to living Christians, mean that in baptism they have died *to* Rome and live *for* God. That is, they have died to the core Roman values of victory and hierarchy and their derivative values of patriarchy and slavery. You will recall, for example, that it is precisely that taken-for-granted Roman value of the hierarchy of free over slave that is expressly negated by "baptism into Christ" in both Galatians 3:28 ("slave or free") and 1 Corinthians 12:13 ("slaves or free").

For Paul, in plainest language, a Christian householder cannot own a Christian slave—one cannot be equal and unequal in Christ at the same time—and the supreme Roman hierarchy of free over slave is abrogated in and by Christian baptism. How did this magnificent theory work out in practice? What happened to the radical vision of the historical Paul in those letters written in his name but after his death?

Next, then, with regard to Colossians: on one hand, this letter speaks directly to both slaves and masters, mentioning reciprocal responsibilities that a Roman householder might find offensive. On the other hand, it is now taken for granted in this letter that Christian householders will have Christian slaves:

> Slaves, obey your earthly masters in everything, not only while being watched and in order to please them, but wholeheartedly, fearing the Lord. Whatever your task, put yourselves into it, as done for the Lord and not for your masters, since you know that from the Lord you will receive the inheritance as

your reward; you serve the Lord Christ. For the wrongdoer will be paid back for whatever wrong has been done, and there is no partiality. Masters, treat your slaves justly and fairly, for you know that you also have a Master in heaven. (3:22–4:1; see Eph. 6:5–9)

What has happened is that a post-Pauline, pseudo-Pauline, and even or especially an *anti*-Pauline vision has quietly contradicted the vision of the historical Paul. But notice, of course, that all this is done in the name of Paul himself. In other words, Paul's vision of the *radicality of God* has been co-opted by the Roman *normalcy of civilization*.

In summary, then, from these two experimental probes (explored more fully later in the book), we see that as in the Old Testament so in the New, as with Torah so with Paul, a rhythm of assertion-and-subversion is emphatically present. A vision of the radicality of God is put forth, and then later, we see that vision domesticated and integrated into the normalcy of civilization so that the established order of life is maintained. Furthermore, *both* elements are cited from, in one case, the mouth of God and, in the other, the pen of Paul.

These two probes are admittedly limited to two traditions—the Priestly tradition in the Old Testament and the Pauline tradition in the New Testament. But they are scarcely unimportant ones. What they have in common is a pattern of yes-and-no, declaration-and-invalidation, pronouncement-and-annulment, assertion-and-subversion. Hold on, for the rest of this book, to that pattern of assertion-and-subversion.

A Rhythm of Assertion-and-Subversion

ALREADY IN CHAPTER 1 I specified the disjunction between non-violence and violence—be it for God or Jesus—as being between two different visions or ideals, one about nonviolent distributive justice and the other about violent retributive justice. My next step is to combine that with the two other just-seen disjunctions: both radicality and normalcy with assertion and subversion.

As we have already seen, even a superficial reading of the Christian Bible reveals God and Christ to be both violent and nonviolent in a somewhat bipolar if not schizophrenic fashion. It is as if the Biblical Express Train runs on twin parallel but very dissimilar rails.

But as seen in the two exploratory probes, I propose that a deeper and more thoughtful study of the Christian Bible demands a different metaphor. There is, on that deeper level, a fascinating and interactive pattern between those parallel train tracks. There is a recurrent rhythm between the biblical vision of God's nonviolent distributive justice and God's violent retributive justice. The more accurate metaphor is not the Biblical Express Train but the Biblical Heartbeat.

Throughout the biblical story, from Genesis to Revelation, every radical challenge from the biblical God is both asserted and then subverted by its receiving communities—be they earliest Israelites or latest Christians. That pattern of assertion-and-subversion, that rhythm of expansion-and-contraction, is like the systole-and-diastole cycle of the human heart.

In other words, the heartbeat of the Christian Bible is a recurrent cardiac cycle in which the *asserted radicality of God's nonviolent distributive justice is subverted by the normalcy of civilization's violent retributive justice.* And, of course, the most profound annulment is that both assertion and subversion are attributed to the same God or the same Christ.

Think of this example. In the Bible, prophets are those who speak for God. On one hand, the prophets Isaiah and Micah agree on this as God's vision: "they shall beat their swords into plowshares, / and their spears into pruning hooks; / nation shall not lift up sword against nation, / neither shall they learn war any more" (Isa. 2:4 = Mic. 4:3). On the other hand, the prophet Joel suggests the opposite vision: "Beat your plowshares into swords, / and your pruning hooks into spears; / let the weakling say, 'I am a warrior'" (3:10). Is this simply an example of assertion-and-subversion between prophets, or between God's radicality and civilization's normalcy?

That proposal might also answer how, as noted in Chapter 1, Jesus the Christ of the Sermon on the Mount preferred loving enemies and praying for persecutors while Jesus the Christ of the book of Revelation preferred killing enemies and slaughtering persecutors. It is not that Jesus the Christ changed his mind, but that in standard biblical assertion-and-subversion strategy, Christianity changed its Jesus.

This means, however, that the revelation of the radicality of God speaks through the *historical* Jesus in the former preference (loving enemies), since scholars agree that these core sayings collected in the Gospels are among the earliest collections of his sayings and are probably the most closely tied to the historical figure; but the normalcy of civilization (killing enemies) speaks through the *apocalyptic* Jesus, a Jesus envisioned many decades after the Christian community had become more established.

Or, think of this similar dichotomy: In the late 330s BCE, Alexander the Great lunged down the Levantine coast of the eastern Mediterranean and, after savage sieges, rode through the shattered gates of Tyre and Gaza on his famous warhorse, the battle charger Bucephalus. In direct and deliberate contrast, this is how the prophet Zechariah described the Messiah entering the gates of Jerusalem:

> Rejoice greatly, O daughter Zion!
> Shout aloud, O daughter Jerusalem!
> Lo, your king comes to you;
> triumphant and victorious is he,
> humble and riding on a donkey,
> on a colt, the foal of a donkey.
> He will cut off the chariot from Ephraim
> and the war-horse from Jerusalem;
> and the battle bow shall be cut off,

and he shall command peace to the nations;

his dominion shall be from sea to sea,

and from the River to the ends of the earth. (9:9–10)

You will notice the explicit contrast between the peace donkey and the warhorse. Furthermore, the Messiah's donkey is described very carefully as a full-bred donkey and not that half-horse, half-donkey known as a mule, making it clear that the animal he was riding was nothing like a (war)horse.

When Jesus enters Jerusalem during that Palm Sunday demonstration in fulfillment of Zechariah, Mark simply mentions the single peace donkey. (Imagine Jesus coming into Jerusalem on a donkey from Bethany in the east and Pilate coming in on a warhorse from Caesarea in the west.) Matthew, however, intensifies the demonstration—and the lampoon—by having Jesus ride a nursing female donkey, a jenny, with her little colt trotting along beside her: "Jesus sent two disciples, saying to them, 'Go into the village ahead of you, and immediately you will find a donkey tied, and a colt with her; untie them and bring them to me.' . . . they brought the donkey and the colt, and put their cloaks on them, and he sat on them" (21:1–2, 7).

That is the *assertion* of the historical Jesus on the biblical peace donkey. But we have already seen its *subversion* in the book of Revelation. Remember Christ as the rider on the white horse from Chapter 1 and recall that great feast he prepared for the vultures from the bodies of those "killed by the sword of the rider on the horse, the sword that came from his mouth; and all the birds were gorged with their flesh" (19:21). In summary:

Radicality of God:	Historical Jesus on the nonviolent peace donkey	(Matt. 21:1–11)
Normalcy of Civilization:	Apocalyptic Christ on the violent warhorse	(Rev. 19:11–21)

This biblical patterning of yes-and-no justifies my choice of the nonviolent Jesus of the Incarnation over the violent Jesus of the

Apocalypse as the true Jesus. Put simply, the nonviolent Jesus is the Christian Bible's assertion, acceptance, and affirmation of the radicality of God while the violent Jesus is its corresponding subversion, rejection, and negation in favor of the normalcy of civilization.

The interest and value, the honesty and integrity, of the Christian Bible resides triumphantly in the dialectic of yes *and* no, assertion *and* subversion. This dialectic means that both Judaism and Christianity took the radical challenges of God seriously. (If, for example, we Americans took our vision of liberty and justice for all under God seriously, imagine the qualifications and reservations that would surround our Pledge of Allegiance.)

If the Bible were all good-cop enthusiasm from God, we would have to treat it like textual unreality or utopian fantasy. If it were all about bad-cop vengeance from God, we would not need to justify, say, our last century. But it contains *both* the assertion of God's radical dream for our world and our world's very successful attempt to replace the divine dream with a human nightmare.

The biblical problem is not, I emphasize, that the recipients of those divine challenges were evil, but that they were normal. The struggle is not between divine good and human evil but between, on one hand, God's radical dream for an Earth distributed fairly and nonviolently among all its peoples and, on the other hand, civilization's normal dream for me keeping mine, getting yours, and having more and more, forever. The tension is not between the Good Book and the bad world that is outside the book. It is between the Good Book and the bad world that are both *within* the book.

"An Unearthly Shade of Red"

YOU CAN EASILY UNDERSTAND my phrase "the radicality of God" when you think of those biblical manifestos against land greed in Leviticus, violence in the Gospels, and slavery in Paul that I just discussed. But why cite "the normalcy of civilization" in opposition to it? Do we not use the word "civilization" for all that is good, positive, and promising in the world around us? Is it not an insult to call individuals, groups, or countries "uncivilized"? How, then, can this chapter's epigraph speak so negatively of civilization, and, especially, why does it suggest that human culture in general preceded human civilization in particular?

One hint about this specific meaning of civilization is to remember that Mesopotamia—Greek for the land "between the rivers" Euphrates and Tigris—is called the "cradle of civilization." So there, in what is modern Iraq, civilization was conceived and born, created and developed at a certain point in time. Why then, why there, and how did it happen? Welcome to the Fertile Crescent, both for this and the next chapters.

Snow-capped mountains surround deserts in an arch from Israel to Iran. Between mountains and deserts, from Levantine coast to Persian Gulf, there is an intermediate layer of foothills and plains called evocatively and accurately the Fertile Crescent. There, originally but not uniquely, humans first invented that specific form of culture known as civilization in a process now called the Neolithic or New Stone Age Revolution or, better, Evolution. In what is usually called the "dawn of civilization," that R/Evolution developed from about 12,000 BCE to a first consummation between the Euphrates and the Tigris Rivers along the eastern reaches of that Fertile Crescent by 4000 BCE.

The stunning change in human living conditions during the Neolithic Age involved the evolutionary transition from gathering, hunting, and moving on to herding, farming, and staying put. Its climactic accomplishment was, however, the invention and perfection of irrigated agriculture on the floodplains of those twin rivers as snowmelt from the Taurus Mountains flooded southward with a fertile alluvium of silt and mud.

That Neolithic R/Evolution entailed the domestication, control, and command of grains, animals, and even people. Think of the organized labor necessary to prepare, conserve, and maintain the dikes, canals, and levees needed for irrigated farming on alluvial floodplains. Think of silt as both initial gift and final curse. The control of people's labor began as a matter of willing cooperation for the greater good of the many but eventually evolved into unwilling coercion for the greatest good of the few. Do not, therefore, ever, ever confuse the normalcy of civilization with the inevitability of human nature, for human nature had already got on without human civilization for millions of years.

Here is a freeze-frame moment from civilization's development around 2350 BCE in southern Mesopotamia. Urukagina, ruler of the Sumerian city of Lagash under its patronal deity Ningirsu, drew up a code of divinely mandated distributive justice.[1] He first recounts a long list of social injustices "from days of yore, from the day the seed of man came forth." For example: "The man in charge of the boat-men seized the boats. The head shepherd seized the donkeys. The man in charge of the fisheries seized the fisheries," and on, and on, and on. He then records how he reformed them all, including this one: "Urukagina made a covenant with Ningirsu that a man of power must not commit an injustice against an orphan or widow." (Please note that word "covenant" for Part III of this book.)

The state of affairs that necessitated Urukagina's reforms indicate the "progress" of civilization in Sumer by the middle of the third millennium BCE. The reforms indicate a struggle for power and justice between, on one hand, temple and commoners and, on the other, palace and aristocrats. The latter had obtained ascendancy because, after 2500 BCE, the dynasty of Ur-Nanshe in Lagash had launched wars that conquered all of Sumer. War gave the palace coercive power and so, "From the borders of Ningirsu to the sea, there was the tax collector." But the reforms in the Code of Urukagina gave collaborative power back to the temple, and so, "From the borders of Ningirsu to the sea, there was no tax collector."

Twin nurses, therefore, hovered around civilization's rocking cradle: one was violence, and the other was empire. Farmers cannot move their fields as nomads can their herds. Increased fertility pushed farmers to expand, and easy conquest tempted nomads to invade. Farmers needed to defend themselves and, already organized for irrigation, could easily be organized for defense—or better still, for that ever-expanding defense known as empire, invented by Sargon and his Akkadians in Mesopotamia by the late 2000s BCE.

It is not that civilization invented either constraint or violence. It is just that, as people got better and better at everything, so also they got better with escalatory constraint of others and escalatory violence against others. The eternal mantra started its dismal chant: *we will protect you from force outside by establishing force inside.*

Although my dialectic of God's radicality versus civilization's normalcy is created especially for this book, you already know that distinction from within the Christian Bible itself. Think of this: on one hand, "God so loved the world" (John 3:16), but on the other hand, "all that is in the world—the desire of the flesh, the desire of the eyes, the pride in riches—comes not from the Father but from the world" (1 John 2:16). This ambiguity in the term "world" is between the *world as creation* (what I call the radicality of God) and the *world as civilization* (what I call the normalcy of civilization).

The Norm of the Christian Bible

WE SOMETIMES SAY, IN hyperbolic shorthand, that the Bible *is* the word of God. Actually, of course, we should say more accurately that the Bible *contains* the word of God. But even that correction is not enough. It is not adequate simply to think of the Christian Bible as a divine message received and transmitted in human response. Why? Because that response both accepts the divine challenge explicitly and yet often rejects it. And, moreover, both assertion and then subversion are often attributed to God himself.

The first and fundamental question of this book is this: How do we Christians know which is our true God—our Bible's violent God, or our Bible's nonviolent God? The answer is actually obvious.

The norm and criterion of the Christian Bible is the biblical Christ. Christ is the standard by which we measure everything else in the Bible. Since Christianity claims Christ as the image and revelation of God, then God is violent if Christ is violent, and God is nonviolent if Christ is nonviolent.

This is even given in what we are called. We are called *Christ*-ians not *Bible*-ians, so our very name asserts the ascendancy of Christ over the Bible. But this only raises a second question. Which Christ do we mean? The nonviolent Christ riding on the peace donkey in the Gospel, or the violent Christ riding on the white warhorse in Revelation? In other words, a second normative criterion and decisive standard must be established.

If, for Christians, the biblical Christ is the criterion of the biblical God, then, for Christians, the historical Jesus is the criterion of the biblical Christ. This is, once again, rather obvious. Christianity counts time down to the birth of the historical Jesus and up from that nativity. His historical birth is the hinge of time, breaking Christian history into a before and after rather than running it all toward its apocalyptic consummation. And that, of course, is why certain Christians ask "WWJD," that is, "What would Jesus do?" rather than "WWBS," or "What would the Bible say?"

My proposal in this book is that *the same individual* studied as the Jesus of history by academic research and accepted as the Christ of faith by confessional belief is the norm and criterion of the Christian Bible. In other words, the meaning of that Bible's story is in its *middle*, in the story of Jesus in the Gospels and the early writings of Paul; the climax of its narrative is in the *center*; and the sense of its nonviolent center judges the (non)sense of its violent ending.

Therefore, and with all due respect to Islamic tradition, we are not "the People of the Book." We are "the People *with* the Book," but even more importantly, we are "the People *of* the Person." This is why a favorite Christian quotation from John's Gospel does not say that "God so loved the world that he gave his only Book," but "God so loved the world that he gave his only Son" (3:16).

Christianity's godsend is not a book but a person, and that person is the historical Jesus. It is precisely that historical Jesus whom Christians proclaim as "the glory of Christ, who is the image of God" (2 Cor. 4:4). Succinctly put, for Christians, Incarnation trumps Apocalypse.

Where Are We Now and What Comes Next?

ALTHOUGH THIS BOOK'S TITLE is *How to Read the Bible and Still Be a Christian*, my plan is not just to propose my own personal solution to the problem. My hope is to probe a problem in the Christian Bible so that we discover a solution that is internally revealed from the very depths of the problem itself.

The surface problem is the bipolar or even schizophrenic portrayal of the biblical God as both nonviolent and violent, as nonviolent in distribution and violent in retribution. The same dichotomy envelops the biblical figure of Christ—on peace donkey and on warhorse. I use the metaphor of a Biblical Express Train with its twin and parallel rails for that dialectic.

Beneath this surface problem, however, a deeper one appears. Those twin aspects—be they of God or of Christ—form a repeated pattern of assertion-and-subversion. Nonviolence and violence are not just parallel but interactive biblical processes. They present a *"yes"* from the radicality of God's nonviolent distributive justice that is then followed by a *"no"* from the normalcy of civilization's violent retributive justice. The metaphor of the Biblical Express Train with parallel tracks cedes place to that of the Biblical Heartbeat with interactive rhythms.

It is here that we begin to glimpse a solution to the book's titular *How to Read the Bible and Still Be a Christian*. Here is what I propose:

> *The norm and criterion of the Christian Bible is the biblical Christ*
> *but*
> *the norm and criterion of the biblical Christ is the historical Jesus.*

By "norm" or "criterion" I mean that we must not put on only Christ-glasses to read the Christian Bible; we must also put on Jesus-glasses to see the biblical Christ. For example, the peace donkey of the historical Jesus in the Gospels trumps the warhorse of the apocalyptic Jesus in Revelation. Surely we must at least *claim* to side with God's radicality over civilization's normalcy.

This, by the way, is emphatically not the old challenge of the "Jesus of history" versus the "Christ of faith." The new challenge is whether we consider the "Jesus of history" and/or "the Christ of faith" to have been nonviolent or violent. This is a new and different challenge, not just another dreary repetition of an outdated one.

The Christian Bible is actually a small library disguised as a book but presented as a story. If that story's meaning were at the end, with the apocalyptic Jesus Christ, we might not bother to read the entire story; but if it is in the middle, with the historical Jesus Christ, we have to explore our way very carefully to and from that midpoint. What comes before it, and what comes after? We are starting, then, on a journey through the deepest structures and not just the surface facets of the Christian Bible in order to let it answer our titular challenge of *How to Read the Bible and Still Be a Christian*.

These first two chapters are an overture to the rest of this book, and as such, they took a preliminary sweep across the entire Bible. Now, with the "Challenge" of Part I defined, I start to test that just-proposed solution across the entire Christian Bible, one major tradition after another. We start where that biblical story opens among the trees of a beautiful garden in Genesis 2–3 and end along the streets of a great city in Revelation 22.

In preparation for the next chapter, I remind you of the word "matrix" from Chapter 1. We Christians are accustomed to interpreting Genesis 2–3 within the matrix of Christian tradition, doctrine, and imagery. Within that standard interpretation, the God of Eden's garden certainly begins Genesis 2 as a God of sweeping nonviolent distributive justice but certainly ends Genesis 3 as a God of equally sweeping violent retributive justice.

For in our tradition isn't Eden about the inaugural *act* of human disobedience begetting a *state* of divine punishment? We have been told about that story as the "fall" not just of Adam and Eve, but of all their descendants. Surely, therefore, Eden certifies inaugurally that the biblical God is about the violence of threat and punishment, sanction and penalty, about retributive justice above all else. But what if we see Genesis 2–3 not with later Christian eyes, but with earlier Hebrew ones, or even, and especially, with ancient Mesopotamian eyes?

What will happen if we read Genesis 2–3 and revisit Eden within its original Fertile Crescent matrix? What ancient ghosts and spectral images from the second or even the third millennium haunt this story from the first millennium? Attention to the original matrix of a story and respect for the story's purpose within its world allow ancient voices to speak fully and clearly before we hasten to affirm or deny what we have not yet even heard, let alone understood.

Our answer to *How to Read the Bible and Still Be a Christian* takes us on a journey that begins in the garden of Eden, and as we enter it, we should remove our Christian shoes and put on Mesopotamian sandals.

PART II

Civilization

CHAPTER 3

Conscience

O Adam what have you done? For though it was you who sinned,
the fall was not yours alone, but ours also who are your descendants.
4 EZRA 7:48 (LATE FIRST CENTURY CE)

Adam is, therefore, not the cause, except only for himself,
but each of us has become our own Adam.
2 BARUCH 54:19 (EARLY SECOND CENTURY CE)

THE TRUE AGE OF the world has long been a matter of debate. William Shakespeare finished his romantic and pastoral comedy *As You Like It* between 1598 and 1600. In Act 4, Scene 1, Rosalind tells Orlando that individuals have died from many causes in the past but never from love. No, not even though "the poor world is almost six thousand years old." That throwaway line simply followed the general Western consensus that creation took place around 4000 BCE, a date calculated by adding up chronological details and genealogical tables given in the Christian Bible.

During 1642–1644, after Parliament had beheaded Charles I and discovered that regicide did not solve everything, John Lightfoot, Anglican priest, master of St. Catharine's College, Cambridge, and later vice chancellor of the university, published a book with this magnificently ornate title: *A Few and New Observations upon the Book of Genesis: the Most of Them Certain; the Rest, Probable; All, Harmless, Strange and Rarely Heard of Before.* Lightfoot calculated creation's start at nightfall on Saturday evening, September 12, 3929 BCE.

A few years later, during 1650–1654, James Ussher, Church of Ireland priest, vice chancellor of Dublin's Trinity College, Archbishop of Armagh, and Primate of All Ireland, published a book with this even more all-encompassing title: *Annals of the Old Testament, Deduced from the First Origins of the World, the Chronicle of Asiatic and Egyptian Matter, Produced Together from the Start of Historical Time to the Beginnings of the Maccabees.* Ussher calculated creation's start at nightfall on Saturday evening, October 23, 4004 BCE.

Today we think that our universe began with that Big Bang around 14 billion years ago, that Earth began about 4.5 billion years ago, and that our own particular species began about 200,000 years ago. In our contemporary context, therefore, it is rather easy to mock those seventeenth-century divines and/or those biblical chronologies and genealogies. At this point, however, two alternative attitudes and questions are possible.

One question asks, gleefully, why the Bible got it so wrong that it imagined the age of the universe to be in the low thousands while we recognize it to be in the low billions. The other question asks, thoughtfully, why, while inventing their genealogies and chronologies, did the biblical authors invent them so as to establish creation around 4000 BCE? Why such feeble antiquity? In the late 2000s BCE, by contrast, a Sumerian scribe listed eight kings who had ruled "before the flood" for a total of 241,000 years. If you are imagining the distant past, why settle for 4,000 years when you could make it, say, 400,000?

Hold that question about time in mind as we turn to the question about place and notice how place is much more direct and explicit than time: "And the Lord God planted a garden in Eden, in the east. . . . A river flows out of Eden to water the garden, and from there it divides and becomes four branches . . . Pishon . . . Gihon . . . Tigris . . . Euphrates" (Gen. 2:8, 10–14).

Creation began with a garden "in the east" (2:8), that is, east from the viewpoint of ancient biblical scholars in Israel (2:8b). The garden is superbly or even transcendentally well-watered by an unnamed super-river that flows through it on the inside and then forms four huge rivers on the outside.

The Euphrates and Tigris Rivers are well-known, and indeed, as we already noted, Mesopotamia is a Greek name that refers to the land "between the rivers," which we know today as Iraq. Those twin rivers rise fewer than twenty miles from one another in eastern Turkey's Taurus Mountains and then flow southward to the Persian Gulf.

The modern identity of the Pishon and Gihon Rivers is still subject to educated guesswork. But, of course, no super-river divides into the Euphrates, Tigris, Pishon, and Gihon—no matter how those latter two are identified. The author of Genesis seems to be imagining some mythical location in northern Mesopotamia as the source of four great rivers—certainly the Euphrates and Tigris, and possibly also the Halys and Aras.

In any case, that garden in Eden is imagined as a super-garden well-watered by a super-river and presumably located in northern Mesopotamia. (That location for the garden may also explain why "the mountains of Ararat" were chosen for the ark's landfall in Gen. 8:4. Re-creation in Gen. 8–9 started again where it began in Gen. 2–3.)

Where do we find ourselves when we combine 4000 BCE as time and Mesopotamia as place? After Chapter 2, we already know the answer. We find ourselves amid the climax of the Neolithic Revolution, amid the dawn of civilization, on the mighty plain of Mesopotamia.

Civilization's dawn for Sumer was creation's date for Israel. The date was totally inaccurate chronologically but fully accurate metaphorically. In any case, for Genesis 2–3, our world was gifted from divinity to humanity around 4000 BCE in Mesopotamia as a garden made by God. It is time, therefore, to enter that garden. But we do so through the matrix-gateway of Sumerian imagination, far, far back in the 2000s BCE.

Try to bracket for now the much later Christian matrix and interpretation, doctrine and dogma, catechism and convention about "original sin." You might even prepare yourself for a new way of seeing the story of Eden by noticing that such words as "sin," "disobedience," and "punishment," let alone "fall," never occur anywhere in Genesis 2–3. Instead, approach the biblical story about Adam and Eve by thinking about a Mesopotamian story about an earlier and equally primordial couple named Gilgamesh and Enkidu.

"Must I Lie Down Too, Never to Rise, Ever Again?"

GILGAMESH WAS AN ACTUAL, historical figure from around 2700 BCE, a priest-king of Uruk—Erech in Genesis 10:10 and Warka in modern Iraq. Uruk in southern Sumer was the first great city in recorded human history. Gilgamesh rebuilt its six-mile-long walls, led its warriors in battle, and liberated it from submission to Kish in northern Sumer. Then, as transcendental fiction enveloped historical fact, Gilgamesh became the divine superhero of Mesopotamian tradition and the protagonist of the first great epic of world literature.

Here the alluvial soil of Sumer became the seedbed from which the Gilgamesh tradition spread around the Fertile Crescent from oral versions to written variants, from the Mesopotamian plain through the Anatolian plateau to the Mediterranean Sea, from Sumer and Akkad, through Babylonia and Assyria, to Ugarit and Israel. (A fragment of the Epic of Gilgamesh was found at Megiddo dated to the 1300s BCE.)

I begin, therefore, in Sumer with one of its five extant stories about Gilgamesh. The story concerns the "Death of Gilgamesh" (ETCSL 1.8.1.3),[2] and I focus here on two motifs in it, namely, dream and lament.

In the dream section, Gilgamesh's night vision is interpreted to mean that the supreme God "Enlil, the Great Mountain, the Father of Gods, has made kingship your destiny, but not eternal life." Then follows the chant of Gilgamesh's impending death with emphasis on its human inevitability:

> You must have been told that this is what the bane of being human involves.
> You must have been told that this is what the cutting of your umbilical cord involved.

The darkest day of humans	awaits you now.
The solitary place of humans	awaits you now.
The unstoppable flood-wave	awaits you now.
The unavoidable battle	awaits you now.
The unequal struggle	awaits you now.
The skirmish from which there	
is no escape	awaits you now.

Even though the Gods consult together about him, review his heroic exploits, and ponder making him an exception, nothing can save Gilgamesh. The only human granted immortality is the flood hero, Ziudsura (Sumer's Noah), because he had saved life on Earth in his great boat. There can be no other exceptions—not even for Gilgamesh.

In the lament section, all of that is repeated but with emphasis on the contrast between even the most absolutely extraordinary life and an absolutely ordinary death:

The great wild bull has lain down	and is never to rise again.
Lord Gilgamesh has lain down	and is never to rise again.
He who was unique in . . .	
has lain down	and is never to rise again.
The hero fitted out with a	
shoulder-belt has lain down	and is never to rise again.
He who was unique in strength	
has lain down	and is never to rise again.

He who diminished wickedness
   has lain down   and is never to rise again.
He who spoke most wisely
   has lain down   and is never to rise again.
The plunderer (?) of many
   countries has lain down   and is never to rise again.
He who knew how to climb
   the mountains has lain down and is never to rise again.
The lord of Kulaba has lain down and is never to rise again.
He has lain down on his death-bed and is never to rise again.
He has lain down on a couch
   of sighs   and is never to rise again.

These motifs of dream and lament already contain the core problem of the later Epic of Gilgamesh: the challenge of human mortality, especially as personified in the hero who lives an extraordinary life but dies an ordinary death—just like everyone else.

It is probable, by the way, that those various Sumerian stories were integrated into an overarching epic only as the non-Semitic Sumerian language gave way to the Semitic Akkadian language and its twin dialects of Babylonian and Assyrian.

Be that as it may, and granted at least its Sumerian bases, I turn now to look at the Epic of Gilgamesh or, to name it more accurately, the Epic of Gilgamesh and Enkidu. That great epic, that base narrative for entertainment and education from the Persian Gulf to the Levantine coast, is my matrix in this chapter for correctly understanding Genesis 2–3.

The epic is extant today in two major versions. The earlier Babylonian version dates to around 2000 BCE and derives from four tablets preserved in separate museums around the world. The later Babylonian version dates to around 700 BCE and derives from the palace and temple libraries of Ashurbanipal, "King of the World, King of Assyria." It is preserved today on twelve tablets in the British Library.[3]

In both of these Babylonian versions, Gilgamesh is the archetypal model for the tragic fact of human mortality—just as in those Sumerian laments that I have just discussed—but now he is also the paradigmatic example for the fruitless search for human immortality. For present convenience and focus, I summarize the epic's content in three acts but I will emphasize the major difference between earlier and later Babylonian versions in Act III.

In Act I, the protagonists are a heroic couple of male and male—the literary archetype for a hero and his sidekick. Gilgamesh is a human being created downward from the divine world, and Enkidu is a human being created upward from the animal world. The twinned twosome decide to obtain immortality by achieving eternal fame through heroic exploits in distant places.

At first, all goes well, but then in Act II, tragedy strikes when Enkidu dies. Worse still than his death is the fact that he does not die exhausted by great endeavor or wounded in triumphant battle. He simply becomes sick, lingers in illness for days, and then dies—an ordinary, everyday, common death.

Gilgamesh mourns inconsolably for his beloved friend, but even more, he mourns for himself: "Shall I die too? Am I not like Enkidu? Grief has entered my innermost being." His mourning continues in that same dual fashion—for Enkidu and for himself:

My friend whom I love so much, who experienced every hardship with me, Enkidu, . . . the fate of mortals conquered him. Six days and seven nights I wept over him. I did not allow him to be buried until a worm fell out of his nose. I was frightened and I am afraid of death, and so I roam open country. . . . Am I not like him? Must I lie down too, never to rise, ever again?

This lament is repeated verbatim three times in the same tablet. The Epic of Gilgamesh and Enkidu has the honesty and integrity to face the truth: What does immortal reputation matter to a mortal human being? What Gilgamesh wants is eternal life, not just eternal fame.

In Act III, Gilgamesh has reverted to Enkidu's original state of roaming the wilderness as he laments his inconsolable grief across its trackless wastes. But maybe somewhere he can find the secret of eternal life for himself before it is too late. Here occurs a very significant divergence between earlier and later Babylonian versions of the epic. It is important for us to look at both, as the former clarifies the message of the latter.

I begin with the earlier version and two admonitions lacking in the later one. Gilgamesh is first accosted by the Sun-God Shamash with this negative comment: "Gilgamesh, where do you roam? You will not find the eternal life that you seek."

Next, he meets Siduri, or Sabatum, a divine tavern keeper who is also the Goddess of wine and wisdom. His first hope is to settle down with her and obtain vicarious immortality through that relationship: "Now that I have found you, alewife, may I not find the death I dread."

But the Goddess disabuses him of that hope immediately: "Gilgamesh, where do you roam? You will not find the eternal life you seek. When the Gods created mankind they appointed death for mankind, kept eternal life in their own hands." That, however, is only her negative response. She continues with this even longer and very positive one: "So, Gilgamesh, let your stomach be full. Day and night enjoy yourself in every way, every day arrange for pleasures. Day and night dance and play. Wear fresh clothes. Keep your head washed, bathe in water. Appreciate the child who holds your hand. Let your wife enjoy herself in your lap."

Notice two points about this injunction. First, the last two lines are deliberately reversed so that "child" precedes "wife," progeny precedes marriage. And it is not marriage with an immortal Goddess, but with a mortal woman who produces the child who crowns the joy of life and is the only immortality possible to mortals.

The second point conforms to this emphasis. This biblical parallel to that most humane advice is often cited: "Go, eat your bread with enjoyment, and drink your wine with a merry heart; for God has long ago approved what you do. Let your garments always be white; do not let oil be lacking on your head. Enjoy life with the wife whom you love" (Eccles. 9:7–9a). It is a very good parallel, but no child is mentioned, and that draws further attention to the child's presence in the older Babylonian version of the Epic of Gilgamesh. If human immortality is impossible, progeny at least may be a kind of mortality with benefits.

It is very possible that this interchange ended some other version of the epic before it was absorbed into the later and longer one. As such, it would have formed an elegant diptych. It began with the originally wild man Enkidu lured into civilized life by sex with a prostitute. It would have ended with the newly wild man Gilgamesh lured back into civilized life by sex with a wife—and the birth of a child. (Would some Mesopotamians or only some moderns think of that as describing two steps into male maturity and masculine humanity?)

I turn next to the later Babylonian version in which Siduri is of only minor and passing importance. In that version, Gilgamesh decides to go in search of Ziudsura, also named Utnapishtim, "the far-distant one," the hero who had preserved animal and human life from extinction during the great flood. He had fulfilled his divine mandate: "Dismantle your house. Build a boat. Leave possessions, search out living things. Reject chattels and save lives." Because of that salvific obedience, the Gods had granted Utnapishtim and his wife immortality. Surely, therefore, muses Gilgamesh, Utnapishtim could reveal to him the secret of eternal life since only Utnapishtim and his wife had attained it.

Prodded by his wife, Utnapishtim finally tells Gilgamesh "the secret of the gods." He must acquire "a plant whose root is like camel-thorn, whose thorn, like a rose's will spike your hands. If you yourself can win that plant, you will find rejuvenation." But to obtain it, Gilgamesh has to attach heavy stones to his feet and dive down deep into the Apsu, the vast aquifer of fresh water beneath the earth.

Gilgamesh follows the instructions, and with the plant safely in his possession, he sets out for home to "Uruk the Sheepfold" intending to "give it to an elder to eat, and so try out the plant whose name would then be 'an old man grows into a young man.'" And then, of course, he too would eat it and "turn into the young man that I once was."

The obvious question is why, with the plant of eternal life in his grasp, does not Gilgamesh immediately eat it? Because, of course, it is the plant of eternal life *as eternal rejuvenation*. What use is eternal life if one is crippled, disabled, or feebly aged? Instead, the plant of life is the plant whereby "an old man grows into a young man" again and again forever.

But then disaster strikes. On his homeward journey, "Gilgamesh saw a pool whose water was cool, and went down into the water and washed. A snake smelt the fragrance of the plant. It came up silently and carried off the plant. As it took it away, it shed its scaly skin." As the only animal that is immortal by rejuvenation, the snake had jealously guarded its privileged status. Gilgamesh returned to Uruk to record his story, and as we saw in that funeral lament, he eventually died, the mortal hero of an immortal story.

I conclude this section on the Epic of Gilgamesh and Enkidu by emphasizing how the later version that included Utnapishtim's secret must be read in the light of the earlier one that included Siduri's advice. The searing message of the epic was quite clear around the Fertile Crescent. It was not an "if-only" but a "never-could" tale. Hearers did not think, *if only* Gilgamesh had not taken that cool swim, he would have been immortal; or *if only* that serpent had not stolen the plant, Gilgamesh would have succeeded in his quest for eternal rejuvenation.

What Siduri said and what the serpent did are but different ways of revealing the same truth: it is useless for mortals to seek immortality; to have immortality and lose it immediately is a parabolic way of saying that one never had it at all. Hearers or readers around the Fertile Crescent knew full well that the point of these stories was that in the animal world, only the jealous serpent, and in the human world, only the flood heroes had been granted immortality by the Gods. The message of Gilgamesh was clear and emphatic: you are mortal people, accept it; you are not immortal people, get over it.

I turn next from Gilgamesh and Enkidu in the epic of Adam and Eve in Genesis 2–3. I repeat my earlier question. When we begin with the former as matrix, do we see the latter differently—that is to say, correctly? As introduction, notice these fundamental parallels as clues to the matrix.

First, in the earlier Mesopotamian tradition of an inaugural human couple, the tale's protagonists were male-and-male as a heroic couple; for the later Bible, that couple is male-and-female as a married couple. (Those are the archetypal models across the world's literary classics—when was the first female-and-female dyad?)

Next, as with Gilgamesh-and-Enkidu, so with Adam-and-Eve, the two individuals seem necessary to constitute one complete whole. In the Epic of Gilgamesh and Enkidu, as we already noted, Gilgamesh is a human being created from the divine world downward, and Enkidu is a human being created from the animal world upward. They are both better together than either one is alone. Similarly, in Genesis, Eve comes *from* Adam, but then Adam returns *to* Eve in Genesis 2:23–24. (Notice that originally, the husband was to enter the wife's home and not vice versa. Which would you prefer if you were the bride?)

Furthermore, the Mesopotamian story has a plant of life-as-rejuvenation while the biblical story has a tree of life-as-rejuvenation. Finally, of course, in both cases, a serpent steals from humanity the gift of immortality.

The Tree of Life

GENESIS 2–3 IS A tale of two trees in a primordial garden. The first is the tree of eternal life, and, as seen already, that meant eternal rejuvenation. The second is the tree of the knowledge of good and evil. Both trees together are the domain of divinity; either tree alone is that of humanity. In the story, humanity is given the first tree, reaches for the second, and then loses the first one: "See, the man has become like one of us, knowing good and evil," says the Lord God; "and now, he might reach out his hand and take also from the tree of life, and eat, and live forever" (3:22).

Think about this story as if hearing it for the first time. In other words, hear it with ears attuned to the accents and emphases of the earliest Fertile Crescent and not to those of the latest Christian catechism. Notice, for example, how those twin trees are described rather awkwardly and unevenly when first introduced in Genesis 2:9:

> Out of the ground the Lord God made to grow every tree that is pleasant to the sight and good for food, the tree of life also in the midst [in the middle] of the garden, and the tree of the knowledge of good and evil.

Those two trees are presented with unusual syntactical awkwardness in Hebrew—as in English—although the difficulty is often smoothed over by using the vaguer "in the midst" rather than "in the middle" of the garden.

The problem of one or two trees "in the middle" of the garden reappears again when Eve tells the serpent, "God said, 'You shall not eat of the fruit of the tree that is in the middle of the garden, nor shall you touch it, or you shall die'" (3:3). The second tree gets the middle now, and there is no mention of the first tree.

Why not simply say, if such were intended, that the tree of life and the tree of the knowledge of good and evil were both in the middle of the garden? It is almost as if that second tree was an add-on to a first tree that was already securely planted "in the middle of the garden." That "almost as if" is exactly how I think this biblical story was creatively adapted in Genesis 2–3 by Israelite scholars working within the general intellectual matrix of the Fertile Crescent.

Ever since Sumer, Mesopotamian tradition held that divinity was immortal and humanity was not—a nice, clear, permanent distinction. Only the human hero of the flood (and his wife) had been raised to divine status and thereby granted eternal life. But that was a unique privilege for his unique salvific action of preserving life on Earth. He was, however, the exception that proved the rule. After-life was merely after-death in Kur—Mesopotamian Sheol, or Hades—a place of spectral ghosts and shadowy figures. As its doorman asks in "Inana's Descent to the Nether World": "Why have you travelled to the land of no return? How did you set your heart on the road whose traveler never returns?" (ETCSL 1.4.1).

As I focus, first, on that tree of eternal life in Genesis 2–3, I see spectral images from Mesopotamia hovering all around it. Behind the primordial domestic pair of Adam and Eve is the primordial heroic pair of Gilgamesh and Enkidu; behind the serpent-spoiler in the garden is the serpent-spoiler by the pool; and behind the tree of eternal life is the plant of eternal life.

Israel knew, as did the entire Fertile Crescent, that the Epic of Gilgamesh and Enkidu was not a tragic tale of "if only" Gilgamesh had not taken that cool swim, he would have been immortal. They also knew that Genesis 2–3 was not a tragic tale of "if only" Adam had not taken that first bite, humanity would have been immortal. Both these stories were metaphorical warnings against transcendental delusions of human immortality. They were parables proclaiming that death is our common human destiny.

It is a profound misreading to consider the Epic of Gilgamesh and Enkidu or the story of Adam and Eve as narratives of an eternal life that was once obtained but then swiftly and tragically lost by human beings. Their common narrative of immortality as something humanity once had but quickly lost carries the message that humankind never could have had it at all. If a human grasps eternal life, some transcendental trickery by those who have it as unique privilege—be they divine, human, or animal—will take it away one way or another. In summary: not keeping it for long meant never having it at all.

On questions of eternal life, Israel espoused that stern and honest realism. It was geographically close to Egyptian territory but intellectually much closer to Mesopotamian theology. And so, for most of its history (up to the last two centuries BCE), Israel could create the majesty of Torah, the glory of prophecy, the beauty of psalmody, and the challenge of wisdom without affirming an eternal afterlife for itself. Israel may have left Egypt, but it never left Mesopotamia.

The Tree of the Knowledge of Good and Evil

I TURN FINALLY FROM that tree of eternal life to the tree of the knowledge of good and evil. I emphasize that it is not the former but the latter tree that displays most clearly Israel's powerful transformation of its Near Eastern heritage. You could, for example, easily imagine a close tracking between Mesopotamia and Israel on that former tree—along these lines: The Lord God gives Adam and Eve a plentiful garden with all of its trees for food, except the tree of eternal life "in the middle" of the garden. To touch it was to die. The serpent denies that will be their fate, they eat, and they are sent from the garden into the normalcy of human life.

That would have been a minimal Israelite adaptation of Mesopotamian options. But instead, Genesis introduces that second tree:

> Out of the ground the Lord God made to grow every tree that is pleasant to the sight and good for food, the tree of life also in the midst of the garden, and the *tree of the knowledge of good and evil*.
>
> " . . . but of the *tree of the knowledge of good and evil* you shall not eat, for in the day that you eat of it you shall die."

" . . . for God knows that when you eat of it your eyes will be opened, and you will be like God, *knowing good and evil*."

. . . Then the Lord God said, "See, the man has become like one of us, *knowing good and evil*; and now, he might reach out his hand and take also from the tree of life, and eat, and live forever." (Gen. 2:9, 17; 3:5, 22; italics mine)

These are the only places in the entire Bible where the knowledge of good and evil or knowing about good and evil is mentioned. These are not simple opposites intended to mean all knowledge or knowledge about everything. If that were intended, it would have been very easy to balance the tree of life with the tree of knowledge.

In other words, I take very seriously that it is not just the tree of knowledge but precisely and explicitly the tree of the knowledge *of good and evil* from which Adam and Eve have eaten—that is, the tree of ethical awareness, or the tree of moral integrity, or most simply, the *tree of conscience*. Our humanity, Genesis concludes, is not distinguished by being immortal, for that is an impossibility, but by being *moral*—and that is a responsibility. Alone among all the animals, we do not just have instinct to control us but also conscience to guide us. That is all we know on Earth, and all we need to know.

Finally, it is instructive to read what God says, in poetry, to each of the three protagonists as that garden is closed to them forever. The serpent is no longer the uniquely immortal animal but simply the uniquely dust-eating animal (3:14–15). Eve will endure birth-labor and husbandly control (3:16). Adam will endure work-labor and a resistant earth (3:17–19). That divine poetry allots one verse for Eve, two for the serpent, and three for Adam.

It is traditional to think of Genesis 2–3 as concerned with obedience and disobedience, human sin and divine punishment, and in a word, the "fall" of humanity. But of course, none of these words or concepts is ever mentioned in the text. Humankind had chosen to live within the challenge of conscience rather than within the delusion of immortality. In other words, realities are not penalties, and human consequences are not divine punishments.

The story of Eden's tree of eternal life or Gilgamesh's plant of eternal youth were *not* tragedies of paradise lost. They were simply and serenely parables of impossibility. Human destiny did not offer eternal youth, and neither did it offer a happy afterlife. Put another way, Mesopotamia was not Egypt. But why, by the way, was Mesopotamia so different from Egypt with regard to belief in an after-death life?

Maybe it was a sense of fragility against solidity—mud-brick ziggurats against huge-stone temples. Maybe it was a matter of uncertainty against certainty—living between two unpredictable annual floods from the Tigris and Euphrates Rivers against living beside a single predictable one from the Nile. Maybe it was a problem of insecurity against security—the open and continuous landmass of Asia and Europe against the almost entirely cut off and separated northeast corner of Africa. For whatever reasons, Mesopotamia—and then Israel—never succumbed to Egypt's grand delusion of eternal life for humanity after death.

Think of Genesis 2–3 as a divine challenge or an evolutionary wager. There exists one single species protected from destroying itself and/or its world *only* by deliberate conscience rather than by automatic instinct. What do you think is going to happen and how will the story end?

Where Are We Now and What Comes Next?

THIS BOOK ATTEMPTS TO explain how we are to reconcile a God of both nonviolent distribution and violent retribution since both appear side by side throughout the Christian Bible. Or, again, how we reconcile the Gospel's nonviolent rider on that donkey of peace with Revelation's violent rider on that horse of war. Here in Chapter 3, we started our journey into the biblical story with the garden of Eden, and there, it would seem, we met a God who certainly began Genesis 2 with non-

violent distributive goodness but ended Genesis 3 with violent retributive sanction—not only for Adam and Eve, but for the whole human
race. Are we not facing the dilemma of *How to Read the Bible and Still
Be a Christian* by the very first pages of our Bible?

In this chapter, however, we have read the Bible's primordial story
of Adam and Eve, the serpent-spoiler, and the tree of eternal life
within the matrix of Mesopotamia's earlier story of Gilgamesh and
Enkidu, the serpent-spoiler, and the plant of eternal life. We have not
read it within the later matrix of Christian interpretation as narrat-
ing an inaugural fall and an original sin.

When those twin stories are read together, within that Fertile
Crescent matrix, their common message is that mortality is our
human destiny, and a story of having immortality but immediately
losing it is simply a metaphor for never being able to have it at all.
Gilgamesh's cool swim and lost plant or Adam's first bite and lost tree
were not tragedy, but inevitability.

We also saw in this chapter something far more significant for
the Christian Bible and this book. Humanity chose—yes, that word
is quite deliberate—to eat from and live by that second tree, the tree
of the knowledge of good and evil—that is, the tree of conscience.
That was Israel's magnificent adaptation and creative expansion of its
Mesopotamian heritage in composing Genesis 2–3.

In Chapter 4, we move into Genesis 4 and some rather obvious
questions. If Genesis 2–3 are not about divine retribution, does retribution at least appear in Genesis 4? What happens as humanity
moves out of the garden of Eden with only conscience as its guide? Is
it stalked by a God of violent retribution?

Also a crucial question is when the word "sin" is first mentioned
in the Bible—by whom and in what context? Is our Bible's first mention of "sin" preceded by threats from God against it and/or succeeded by punishments from God because of it? If "original sin" did
not happen in Genesis 2–3 with creation, does it happen in Genesis
4 with civilization? What is the precise content of original sin in
Genesis 4 of the Christian Bible?

CHAPTER 4

Violence

From the first chipped stone to the first smelted iron took
nearly 3 million years; from the first iron to the
hydrogen bomb took only 3,000.
RONALD WRIGHT, *A Short History of Progress*

As we saw earlier, the late Samuel Noah Kramer, professor in the Oriental Studies Department of the University of Pennsylvania, gave his book *History Begins at Sumer* the subtitle *Thirty-Nine Firsts in Recorded History.* Among those "firsts" is one called "*Logomachy: The First Literary Debates.*" The Greek term *logomachy* means "word war" or "trash talk." Except, of course, that our trash talk seldom reaches the level of those Sumerian word wars, which were composed in poetry as experiments in thought. But thought about what?

Consider first the personified protagonists who dispute for primacy in each of these still-extant Sumerian debate poems. They are "Hoe Against Plow," "Grain Against Sheep," "Winter Against Summer," "Bird Against Fish," "Copper Against Silver," and "Date Palm Against Tamarisk Shrub." The general pattern is very consistent in the first five of these debate poems, and probably also in the now too-fragmentary sixth one. The sequence is Inaugural Situation, Interactive Debate, and Victory Decision. In all of them, victory is divinely decreed in favor of, respectively, Hoe, Grain, Winter, Bird, Copper, and, presumably, Date Palm.

Above all else, however, the Sumerians *thought* about the components of the Neolithic Revolution and its ultimate "gift" of civilization in southern Mesopotamia. They not only went through that process as others would do after them, but, since they had invented writing, they left us the records of their thinking about it. With these debate poems, Sumer's intellectuals were conducting probes into civilization's cultural gifts and constraints, benefits and liabilities, priorities and preferences.

"In What Is the Farmer Superior to Me?"

THERE IS, HOWEVER, ONE other extant example of this Sumerian dispute genre, but it has a more complicated format involving a debate within a story and can therefore be called either a story or a debate.

Kramer calls this story "The Wooing of Inanna" (or Inana) and notes that "in formal structure it actually differs from the others of this [debate] genre. It is built up more like a playlet with a number of characters." It has also been titled "Dumuzid and Enkimdu," or, more fully, "Dumuzid and Enkimdu: The Dispute Between the Shepherd-God and the Farmer-God."[4]

For my present purpose, I emphasize that final title because it is the Sumerian dispute between the divine brothers Shepherd God and Farmer God that I consider in this chapter as the matrix for the biblical conflict between the human brothers Shepherd Abel and Farmer Cain in Genesis 4. Both cases involve conflict—benign or malignant—and both cases involve a major external deity—Goddess or God.

There are four characters in the Sumerian drama: Utu, God of the Sun and (distributive!) Justice; his sister, Inana, Goddess of Fertility and Warfare; the Shepherd God Dumuzid; and his brother, the

Farmer God Enkimdu (ETCSL 4.08.33). The story begins with Utu
advising Inana to marry Dumuzid. But she refuses: "The shepherd
shall not marry me. . . . Let the farmer marry me." That leads into
the *debate* between her two possible spouses.

First, Shepherd Dumuzid demands to know "in what is the farmer
superior to me?," and he goes on to compare his products with those
of Enkimdu, "the man of dikes and canals." This is actually not the
expected debate format with the shepherd extolling his own products
and denigrating the farmer's, and then the farmer doing the same
back. In this case, Shepherd Dumuzid simply insists that his products are every bit as good as Farmer Enkimdu's, so why should Inana
reject him and choose the other? His speech ends, as it began, with,
"In what is the farmer superior to me?"

Next, Shepherd Dumuzid tries to escalate the conflict: "The
Shepherd Dumuzid from the plain where he was provoked a quar-
rel" with Farmer Enkimdu. But the latter refuses to accept the challenge, saying: "Why should I compete against you, shepherd? . . . Let
your sheep eat the grass of the riverbank, let your sheep graze on my
stubble."

Finally, "the dispute between the shepherd and the farmer" ends
as Inana decides to marry Shepherd Dumuzid and he returns Farmer
Enkimdu's peaceful gesture by inviting him to their wedding feast:
"As for me, I am a shepherd: when I am married . . . Farmer Enkimdu, you are going to be counted as my friend."

Sumer's divine brothers, Shepherd Dumuzid and Farmer Enkimdu, become the Bible's human brothers, Shepherd Abel and
Farmer Cain: Eve "conceived and bore Cain. . . . Next she bore his
brother Abel . . . a keeper of sheep, and Cain [was] a tiller of the
ground" (Gen. 4:1–2). But, when each offers God gifts from their
twin Neolithic domestications of, respectively, grain and sheep, God
prefers the later-born Abel to the earlier-born Cain (4:3–5).

This is, of course, the typical preference of the biblical God in
countercultural challenge to a patriarchal world where, by male primogeniture, the firstborn son is always the heir. God chooses, for

example, the younger Isaac (17:19) over the older Ishmael (16:11) and the younger Jacob (25:26) over the older Esau (25:25). God's socio-subversive decision is that "the elder shall serve the younger" (25:23). We have, in Genesis 4:4b–5a, preliminary warning of that cultural challenge as God prefers Abel over Cain. That divine preference sets up the movement of the drama. What will Cain do to Abel in revenge for God's snub?

What follows throughout Genesis 4 is the briefest bare-bones summary of the Sumerian evolutionary achievement—namely, the development of irrigated farming on the alluvial floodplain of southern Mesopotamia; the invention of urban living in cities like Eridu and Larsa, Kish and Uruk, Nippur and Ur; and the creation of stories and debates, poems and proverbs that pondered the implications and results of these stunning achievements. But Genesis adds one very significant extra element in its summary of civilization's Mesopotamian dawn. The mark of Cain becomes the mark of civilization.

"Sin Crouches but You Will Rule over It"

WITHIN THE STORY OF Cain and Abel, there are two similarly structured poems, one in 4:6–7 at the start of the chapter and the other in 4:23 at its end. The former comes as a warning from divinity as God speaks to Cain, and the latter comes as a boast from humanity as Lamech speaks to his wives. Read as a pair, these twin poems emphasize the biblical challenge as Genesis 4 expands and transforms the Neolithic's ancient dispute of Sumer's Farmer God against Shepherd God.

To honor that paired emphasis, the translations I use for both poems are those of Robert Alter, the Class of 1937 Professor of Hebrew and Comparative Literature at the University of California at Berkeley.[5] In the former poem God says to Cain:

Why are you incensed,
and why is your face fallen?
For whether you offer well,
or whether you do not,
at the tent flap sin crouches,
and for you is its longing
but you will rule over it. (4:6–7)

This is a startling comment and has important implications for the Bible—and for this book. Notice, for example, that God does not say you could or might, should or must rule over it, but "you *will* rule over it" (NRSV uses the word "must" rather than "will").

First, Genesis 4:6–7 contains the earliest mention of sin in the Bible, and the word is in the singular—not "sins" as of many but "sin" as of one.

Next, sin is not imagined as some internal and irresistible force either common to the human race in general or to Cain alone in particular. Instead, it is likened by God to an external feral feline that crouches to attack you at your tent flap in the desert camp.

Finally and climactically, Cain can and should be able to conquer sin just like any other wild beast that might assault him. Notice, for example, how that final line changes the twin line into a dramatic three-line climax. The poem's most important line is "you will rule over it." But unfortunately, we must read that line—for Cain then and for all of humanity now—not as "you will" but as "you can [*but will not*] rule over it."

Instead, sin rules over Cain. He murders his brother Abel "in the field" (4:8), that is, in his own domain as farmer, and then

the Lord said to Cain, "Where is your brother Abel?" He said, "I do not know; am I my brother's keeper?" And the Lord said, "What have you done? Listen; your brother's blood is crying out to me from the ground! And now you are cursed from the ground, which has opened its mouth to receive your brother's blood from your hand. When you till the ground, it will no longer yield to you its strength; you will be a fugitive and a wanderer on the earth." (4:9–12)

The "ground" (*adamah* in Hebrew) has condemned Farmer Cain because he has sullied it with fratricidal blood. It is extremely significant that God does not act to punish Cain. He is, as it were, ostracized by the ground itself, exiled from the gains of the Neolithic Revolution. He has become, in our terms, an evolutionary throwback from farmer to, at best, hunter-gatherer. Notice that human consequences are not misinterpreted as divine punishments.

Cain, however, responds as if God rather than the Earth were the punisher: "Today you [God] have driven me away from the soil, and I shall be hidden from your face; I shall be a fugitive and a wanderer on the earth, and anyone who meets me may kill me"(4:14). God's response is, "Not so! Whoever kills Cain will suffer a sevenfold vengeance" (4:15a), and this statement requires very careful consideration.

Who is imagined as administering this "sevenfold vengeance"— God? Has human violence begotten the threat of even greater divine violence? Since Cain killed one, does God threaten to kill seven? Has Cain trapped God into escalating counterviolence?

Before you answer these questions, notice what happens next: "Cain knew his wife, and she conceived and bore Enoch; and he [Cain] built a city, and named it Enoch after his son Enoch" (4:17). Here is, in Genesis 4, a first succinct summary of the dawn of civilization as it consummates the Neolithic Revolution: *Farmer Kills Shepherd, Builds First City.*

Now go back to those questions about the "sevenfold vengeance" in 4:13–15. The fact that God is not threatening escalatory divine violence against anyone who murders Cain in 4:15 becomes clear with the second poem in 4:23, which, as Robert Alter says, "follows the parallelistic pattern of biblical verse with exemplary rigor."⁶ (Biblical poetic parallelism also came from Sumer.) Read it slowly:

> Adah and Zillah, O hearken my wives,
> You wives of Lamech, give ear to my speech.
> For a man have I slain for my wound,
> a boy for my bruising.
> For sevenfold Cain is avenged,
> and Lamech seventy and seven. (4:23)

The first and second two-line verses contain synonymous parallelism within each one. "Adah and Zillah" and "hearken" in the first line are repeated by "You wives of Lamech" and "give ear" in the second one. Similarly, "man" and "wound" in the third line are repeated by "boy" and "bruising" in the fourth one. But what about that third two-line verse?

On the one hand, with regard to format, those last two lines also contain typical biblical poetry. "Sevenfold" and "Cain" in the fifth line are repeated—but in *reversed* parallelism—as "Lamech" and "seventy and seven" in the last one. And, of course, the sequence of "seven" becoming "seventy and seven" is among the standard poetic types of numerical escalation in biblical tradition. For example, it appears, but for forgiveness rather than for vengeance, when Jesus tells Peter, "Not seven times, but, I tell you, seventy-seven times" (Matt. 18:22).

On the other hand, with regard to content, that escalation to "seventy and seven" presumes God's marking of Cain to prevent his murder and also its potential sevenfold revenge just seen in 4:15. In other words, while those first two verses represent an ancient boast-poem from Lamech, the addition of that third one connects Lamech across five generations back to Cain, which is significant—backwards—for understanding Genesis 4:15 and, indeed, all of Genesis 4.

Biblical "Sin" as Escalatory Violence

GENESIS 4 IS NOT simply about an original fratricide. It is about escalatory violence almost as a seductive inevitability. But, of course, it is also about a God who asserted that it *was not* inevitable and proclaimed that it could be overcome: "You will rule over it." In other words, *the normalcy of human civilization is not the inevitability of human nature.* (That, by the way, is my mantra for this book.)

We humans are not natural-born killers (if we were, would we suffer posttraumatic stress after battle?). The mark of Cain is on human civilization, not on human nature. Escalatory violence is our nemesis, not our nature; our avoidable decision, not our unavoidable destiny. It is our "original sin" but could then—and can still—be overcome.

The escalatory violence in Genesis 4 is depicted between desert tribes and not between nation-states—which did not yet exist at the time. Genesis 4 depicts the escalatory violence not of warfare, but of blood feud, of honor and shame relationships when small groups confront one another without overarching legal and juridical precedent or competent and adequate communal governance. (Are nation-states without a world government any different?)

Genesis 4 is not just about the original instance of fratricidal violence but about the primordial origins of escalatory violence—as sin or, better, as Sin. Abel is murdered—that is one victim. If Cain is murdered, his family will exact a sevenfold vengeance. But five generations later, if Lamech is killed, his family will exact a seventy-seven-fold vengeance.

It was, by the way, precisely to offset such escalation that Leviticus decreed, "fracture for fracture, eye for eye, tooth for tooth; the injury inflicted is the injury to be suffered" (24:20). Vengeance was to be one for one and not seven for one, let alone seventy-seven for one.

In other words, Genesis 4 is the biblical version of the Neolithic R/Evolution's climax in the dawn of civilization across the Fertile Crescent but especially in Mesopotamia some six thousand years ago. It is also, and unfortunately, a more historically accurate version than that happy-ending Sumerian story about Shepherd Dumuzid and Farmer Enkimdu. The second and fuller biblical summary in Genesis 4 reads like this: *Farmer Kills Shepherd, Builds First City, Violence Escalates Exponentially.*

Willed violence is, presumably, just like all our other human activities. We tend to get better and better at what we do—from, say, the Paleolithic caves of western France to the Neolithic houses of eastern Turkey, from herding with sheep and goats to farming with cattle and horses, and from stylus on clay, through pen on papyrus, to touch on screen.

We humans are not getting more evil or sinful but are simply getting more competent and efficient at whatever we want to do—including sin as willed violence. And so, we have become, as Genesis 4 warned us inaugurally, steadily or even exponentially better and better at violence. And now, at last, that capacity threatens not just the family or the tribe, but the world and the Earth.

From all of this, I take these four conclusions about "original sin" in the Bible. First, according to the explicit text of the Bible, "sin" occurred originally not in the divine garden of Genesis 2–3 but in the human field of Genesis 4. Second, "sin" in Genesis 4 is not a flaw in creation but in civilization, a fault not in nature but in culture. Third, original sin is not about individuals and sex but about communities and violence. It is about humanity's penchant for escalatory violence as its drug of choice. Fourth, sin is not inescapable or irresistible: "you will rule over it," says God in Genesis 4:7, as a divine wager on the human conscience.

My next step is to link Cain and Abel in Genesis 4 to Noah and the flood in Genesis 6–9 along that escalating trajectory of human, and now divine, violence. Notice, however, that the violence of divine retributive justice has not been present up to this point in the first half dozen chapters of our Bible. But, as you brace yourself now for the flood story, always remember that Israel adopted and adapted that story from Mesopotamian tradition. It did not imagine it or create it from its own soul.

"The Earth Was Filled with Violence"

YOU WILL RECALL FROM passing mentions in Chapter 3 that when divinity decided to destroy humanity, it exempted from annihilation the hero-savior named Ziudsura in Sumerian, Atrahasis or Utnapishtim in Akkadian, and Noah in the twin versions combined in Genesis 6–9. Nowhere, by the way, is the cultural continuity from Sumer to Genesis more evident than in the flood story of Genesis 6–9. But, as usual, my focus is on how that cultural inheritance was adopted and adapted, translated and transformed within the biblical tradition.

The too-fragmentary Sumerian *Flood Story* has the divine decree of annihilation by "a flood," but no reason is given. It says simply: "A decision that the seed of mankind is to be destroyed has been made. The verdict, the word of the divine assembly, cannot be revoked. The order announced by [the Gods] An and Enlil cannot be overturned" (ETCSL 1.7.4, Segment C).

On the other hand, *Atrahasis*, the Akkadian version of the flood saga,[7] gives a very specific reason for it and repeats it several times. The background is a conflict between the Sumerian Gods Enlil and Enki (called Ellil and Ea in Akkadian). They are, respectively, the older and younger sons of the supreme Gods, An of heaven and Ki of Earth. Here is the reason why humanity must be destroyed:

> The country became too wide, the people too numerous. The country was as noisy as a bellowing bull. The God grew restless at their clamor. Ellil had to listen to their noise. He addressed the great Gods: "The noise of mankind has become too much. I am losing sleep over their racket."

Because of "noise" from overpopulation, the Gods agree to annihilate humanity by flood. But Enki/Ea objects to the general divine agreement: "Why should I use my power against my people? The flood that you mention to me . . . that is Enlil's kind of work!" So Enki tells "the thoughtful man, Atrahasis . . . dismantle the house, build a boat, reject possessions, and save living things." And so humanity's future is assured.

I return now from that Mesopotamian flood tradition to the biblical version in Genesis 6–9, and my focus is still on the divine reason for that universal destruction.

But before considering it, I need an introductory comment. I follow the general scholarly consensus on the four major traditions interwoven as laminated layers in the Pentateuch (the first five books of the Bible: Genesis, Exodus, Numbers, Leviticus, and Deuteronomy). The four are known as the Yahwist tradition, from around 950 BCE; the Elohist tradition, from around 850 BCE; the Deuteronomic tradition, also from around 850 BCE; and the Priestly tradition, from around 500 BCE. But do not let those tentative dates obscure the fact that earlier parts were taken up into later ones as the whole was edited and reedited to its final form.

Two of those four sources or layers are intertwined in the biblical flood narrative—hence, for instance, the different numbers of animals given in Genesis 7:2–3 from the Yahwist tradition and 7:8–9 from the Priestly tradition. But my interest here is in how each tradition described the reason for God's action (note the differing names for God):

Yahwist Tradition	Priestly Tradition
The Lord (Yahweh) saw that the wickedness of humanity was great in the earth, and that every inclination of the thoughts of their hearts was only evil continually. (6:5)	The earth was corrupt in the sight of God (Elohim), and the earth was filled with violence. God saw that the earth was corrupt; for all flesh had corrupted its ways upon the the earth. God said to Noah, "I have determined to make an end of all flesh, for the earth is filled with violence because of them." (6:11–13)

In the Yahwist tradition the reason for God's cosmic destruction is humanity's "continual evil." But in the Priestly tradition a similar general indictment of "corruption" is twice specified as "violence."

Furthermore, in that latter source the problem is not that "all flesh" has become violent, but that Earth itself has become contaminated—like the ground by Abel's murdered blood in Genesis 4:10–11. In summary, therefore, the problem with Earth for the biblical God is not too much human "noise," but too much human "violence."

"I Will Never Again Curse the Ground Because of Humankind"

IT IS CLEAR THAT human violence has escalated exponentially from Cain to Lamech in Genesis 4 and thence to "the earth" in Genesis 6:11, 13. This is already bad enough, but one other factor renders the violence all the more devastating.

In Genesis 6, as distinct from Genesis 2–3 or 4, God has been sucked completely into humanity's escalatory violence. The transcendental solution for human violence is massive divine counter-violence: "I will blot out from the earth the human beings I have created—people together with animals and creeping things and birds of the air, for I am sorry that I have made them" (6:7). And this decision is repeated several times thereafter (6:17; 7:4, 21–23).

It is not just humanity but all of creation—except, perhaps, marine species—that are to be exterminated so Earth can start all over again from those saved within the ark. What began with Cain killing Abel escalated from humanity to divinity with God killing Earth. There is, however, one reason for hope—if not for us, then at least for the biblical God as this matrix of Genesis 1–11 concludes.

In *Atrahasis*, the Epic of Gilgamesh and Enkidu, and Genesis 8:20, sacrifice is offered outside the great boat as the flood subsides, and in all three cases the "pleasing odor" was acceptable to divinity. But only the biblical God

> said in his heart, "I will never again curse the ground because
> of humankind, for the inclination of the human heart is evil
> from youth; nor will I ever again destroy every living creature
> as I have done.

As long as the earth endures,
seedtime and harvest, cold and heat,
summer and winter, day and night,
shall not cease." (8:21–22)

Later, this divine decision is made into a solemn "covenant" between God and "every living creature"—that "never again" would God destroy life on Earth, and the rainbow would be the "sign" of that covenant between God and "all flesh that is on the earth" (9:9–17, note repetitions). There is no divine repentance for the flood's violence, but at least there is a divine promise of "never again."

Where Are We Now and What Comes Next?

WE HAVE JUST FINISHED this book's Part II on that peculiar human cultural development called civilization that appeared primordially on the Mesopotamian plains as the climax and consummation of the Neolithic R/Evolution. I interpreted those magnificent parables about Adam and Eve, Cain and Abel, Noah and flood within the interactive matrix of Mesopotamia's invention of civilization.

What have we learned from these chapters on *How to Read the Bible and Still Be a Christian*? The message of Genesis 2–3 is not about God's retributive justice and universal punishment for the whole human race but about humanity abandoning the delusion of immortality and accepting instead the responsibility of conscience. Again, and even more obviously, Genesis 4 is not about God punishing Cain but about the desecrated ground rejecting Cain and about escalatory violence as civilization's drug of choice. But all that changed in Genesis 6–9.

Granted that Israel accepted the flood story from its Mesopotamian matrix rather than creating it for itself; granted also that God promised "never again" to undertake such divine terrorism; nevertheless, we have found, before we reached a dozen chapters into our Christian Bible, a God whose retributive justice seems far more about general retribution than about specific justice. (What did the animals do wrong?) My book's challenge presses hard: How are we, as Christians, to read the Christian Bible?—a story that almost immediately presents us with a God who is far worse than our worst evil rather than far better than our best goodness.

My next step, and my major one toward a solution, is to back up from Genesis 9 to Genesis 1. This step is justified because both of these chapters are from the same Priestly tradition; and especially because Genesis 9 as God's re-creation looks explicitly, directly, and internally back to God's creation in Genesis 1.

After starting with Genesis 1, I look once again at Genesis 9 to compare them. Here are some constitutive questions as we proceed. Why in Genesis 1 is creation not described as a covenant but in Genesis 9 re-creation *is* described as a covenant (repeated seven times in 9:8–17)? Indeed, what is "covenant"?—a vision so important that it is the title for my book's Part III.

Why was "covenant" chosen to express the relationship not just between God and Israel at home, but also between God and the world at large? What mode or style of divine-human relationship does that word encompass? What are the benefits and liabilities of specifying that relationship precisely as covenant? What, for example, is imagined when a "new covenant" is proclaimed by Jeremiah (31:31), Paul (1 Cor. 11:25; 2 Cor. 3:6), or the epistle to the Hebrews (8:8, 13; 9:15; 12:24)?

When human beings imagine a *relationship* with divinity, they must work with metaphor, model, and matrix. This holds for everyone, everywhere, every time. But what metaphor is chosen, what model is preferred, and what matrix is available are crucial elements of identity and destiny. Our biblical journey continues onward from Genesis 6–9, therefore, but only after and through a return to Genesis 1.

PART III

Covenant

CHAPTER 5

Creation and Covenant

That sacred seventh day . . . a relief and relaxation
from labor . . . not to free men only,
but also to slaves, and even to beasts of burden . . .
even every species of plant and tree;
for there is no shoot, and no branch, and no leaf even which it is
allowed to cut or to pluck on that day . . . but everything is at liberty
and in safety on that day, and enjoys, as it were, perfect freedom.
PHILO, *Life of Moses* 2.4.21–22

GENESIS 1 OPENS THE Christian Bible, but its importance and significance go far beyond that. Why? Because it was composed and located by the Priestly tradition of Israel as the initial overture to and inaugural manifesto for the entire Pentateuch and even the entire Hebrew Bible. Read Genesis 1 very, very carefully, says the Priestly tradition, because this is what the biblical story is all about.

Furthermore, as you read—yes, actually read—Genesis 1, you will find it clear that the authors knew that they knew nothing about the details and logistics of creation but thought that they knew exactly what it meant and precisely what God intended in and by it. I say this is clear because it is proclaimed by the very *artistry* of the chapter's composition and thus the very *art*ificial nature of its description. Here is how I read the work with that emphasis on *art*istic structure as an indicator of authorial intention, literary purpose, and textual meaning.

"God Said, 'Let Us Make Humankind in Our Image'"

TWO COMPOSITIONAL ELEMENTS STAND out immediately. One is that God is imagined as a divine architect (unlike the divine potter of Gen. 2:7) who step by step balances the world's preparation in 1:3–13 with its completion in 1:14–31. Another element is those consistently repetitive expressions throughout both stages: "And God said . . . Let there be . . . And it was so . . . And God saw that it was good . . . And there was evening and there was morning." Above all else, however, that opening expression "And God said" is the major index of both art and intention in the Priestly tradition's creation story.

Those priestly authors looked around their Mesopotamian-inherited world and saw eight huge chunks of stuff to be identified and organized as God's creation. But they then crammed those eight chunks of stuff into not eight, but six days, like this:

Day 1 (1:3–5): And God said . . .
Day 2 (1:6–8): And God said . . .
Day 3 (1:9–13): And God said . . . And God said . . .
Day 4 (1:14–19): And God said . . .
Day 5 (1:20–23): And God said . . .
Day 6 (1:24–31): And God said . . . And God said . . .

It is hard to imagine a clearer indication of purpose or more evident index of intention. Even if eight chunks of stuff exist, they must all fit into six days because all of creation must climax with the Sabbath on the seventh day.

It is as if to say, crudely and rudely, that not even God at creation could ignore the Sabbath. Or, more politely and accurately, that all of creation was crowned with and by the Sabbath. (Humanity is not the crown of creation. We are the work of a late Friday afternoon, and best work is seldom done on a late Friday afternoon.)

Think, therefore, about the final message of Genesis 1 as *Image, Rule, and Sabbath*. First, humanity is created in the image and likeness of God (1:26a, 27). Next, that status is immediately identified as having dominion or rule over all else on Earth (1:26b, 28)—that is what our divine image means. Finally, that God whose image we bear is the God of Sabbath rest. We are to rule the Earth for, with, by, and in that Sabbath God. And that is, *internally*, our human destiny and identity, not just, *externally*, a divine decree or command.

I add three comments before turning to consider what is the character of a God whose climax of creation is Sabbath rest.

The first one is that God's first gift to humanity of God's own image and likeness is precisely what constitutes God as a God of distributive justice. What greater and more gracious act of divine justice is there than to distribute to all the human race an internal identity and destiny as God's own image and likeness?

The next comment is that not the slightest hint of threat or sanction, possible penalty, or potential punishment exists in this ecstatic vision of creation. Indeed, if one invokes internal identity and destiny rather than external decree or command, any rejection or default would beget internal consequences rather than external punishments.

As I use those two terms, by the way, *consequences* flow internally from an act, whereas *punishments* flow externally from it. For example, a drunk driver hits a tree and is killed by the impact—that is a consequence; a drunk driver hits a tree and is fined by the police— that is a punishment.

The final comment is that in the utopian perfection of God's creation-dream, no blood ever stains the ground. All alike, animals and humans, are vegan and eat only "every green plant" (1:29–30)— hence, that "peaceable Kingdom" of Isaiah 11:6.

I return to this understanding of Genesis 1 later in the chapter, but now I consider the character of that Sabbath God who created humankind in God's own image and likeness.

"So That Your Ox and Your Donkey May Have Relief"

I BEGIN WITH THE Sabbath Day. Within the section known as the Book of the Covenant in Exodus 20:22–23:19 is a decree about the Sabbath day that clearly spells out its purpose and intention:

> Six days you shall do your work, but on the seventh day you shall rest, so that your ox and your donkey may have relief, and your homeborn slave and the resident alien may be refreshed. (23:12)

This command and its "so that" purpose are later repeated and expanded to include "your son or your daughter . . . or any of your livestock, or the resident alien in your towns" (Deut. 5:12–14).

We might not think today of equal rest for all as a matter of basic distributive justice (unless, of course, you experience or think about certain jobs, shops, or factories where inadequate rest pushes some people beyond human endurance into violent reprisal). The purpose, reason, and intention of the Sabbath day was to give *all alike*—householders, children, slaves, animals, and immigrants—the same rest every week. It was not rest *for* worship of God, but rest *as* worship of God.

In other words, the Sabbath day as rest in Genesis 1 is both a *part* and a *sign* of something far deeper than itself—namely, that the crown of creation and the destiny of humanity is distributive justice in a world not our own. The Sabbath day placed distributive justice—where all God's people get a fair share of all God's earth—as the rhythm of time and the metronome of history. This follows, of course, from the distributive justice of God's own image and likeness as gracious divine gift to humanity—without even the possibility of any discrimination.

I emphasize that in the biblical tradition nonviolent distributive justice is not a command *by* God but is the character *of* God. This is why God's first and inaugural distribution to humankind is God's own image and likeness that thereby creates us as agents, stewards, and managers of God's world. To put it another way: the arc of the evolutionary universe is long, but it bends toward distributive justice.

Next, I continue with the Sabbath Year. Since the biblical tradition is the accurate and honest account of divine assertion and human subversion, every seventh year there was an attempt to negate that later subversion and regain the earlier assertion—on three major points:

1. *Slaves freed:* "When you buy a male Hebrew slave, he shall serve six years, but in the seventh he shall go out a free person, without debt" (Exod. 21:2).

2. *Debts liquidated:* "Every seventh year you shall grant a remission of debts . . . every creditor shall remit the claim that is held against a neighbor" (Deut. 15:1–2).

3. *Land rested:* "In the seventh year there shall be a sabbath of complete rest for the land . . . you shall not sow your field or prune your vineyard" (Lev. 25:4).

This last command is not simply the good agricultural policy (at least for the land) of crop rotation. The reason is redistributive justice or restorative righteousness: "You may eat what the land yields during its sabbath—you, your male and female slaves, your hired and your bound laborers who live with you; for your livestock also, and for the wild animals in your land all its yield shall be for food" (Lev. 25:6–7). Maybe, at least every seventh year, human subversion of Torah can be reversed toward its divine assertion.

Finally, there is the Sabbath Jubilee. If every Sabbath year cannot accomplish the divine dream of distributive justice, maybe if it could be accomplished every fiftieth year, every sevenfold set of Sabbath years, divine assertion could begin all over again:

You shall count off seven weeks of years, seven times seven years, so that the period of seven weeks of years gives forty-nine years. Then you shall have the trumpet sounded loud; on the

tenth day of the seventh month—on the day of atonement—
you shall have the trumpet sounded throughout all your land.
And you shall hallow the fiftieth year and you shall proclaim
liberty throughout the land to all its inhabitants. It shall be
a jubilee for you: you shall return, every one of you, to your
property and every one of you to your family. (Lev. 25:8–10)

Rural holdings could be lost through the foreclosure of a mort-
gage since outright sale was forbidden (recall Naboth's vineyard from
Chapter 2). Every fiftieth year all alienated lands were to be restored
to their original owners. The reason was, as discussed earlier, that
"the land shall not be sold in perpetuity, for the land is mine [God's];
with me you are but aliens and tenants" (Lev. 25:23).

The Priestly tradition in Leviticus 25 recapitulates that of Genesis 1. This is why the Sabbath Jubilee always started on the Day of
Atonement because needing a Sabbath Jubilee meant that the Sabbath day and Sabbath year had failed—therefore, atonement. Or, to
repeat the prophet Isaiah from Chapter 2,

Ah, you who join house to house,
who add field to field,
until there is room for no one but you,
and you are left to live alone
in the midst of the land! (5:8)

My next step is a return once more to the Priestly tradition's
ending of the flood story (remember God's "never again"?) but to
see it now through that explicitly connected earlier vision in Genesis 1. What does it mean that creation in Genesis 1 never mentions
covenant, while re-creation in Genesis 9 emphasizes it strongly but
interprets it strangely?

"The Everlasting Covenant Between God and Every Living Creature"

FIRST, THE PRIESTLY TRADITION of God's creation in Genesis 1 is renewed in Genesis 9:1–7. Here is the former version, and notice the four main elements of *divine image, human fertility, earthy rule,* and *food supply:*

> Then God said, "Let us make humankind in our image, according to our likeness; and let them have dominion over the fish of the sea, and over the birds of the air, and over the cattle, and over all the wild animals of the earth, and over every creeping thing that creeps upon the earth."
>
> So God created humankind in his image,
> in the image of God he created them;
> male and female he created them.
>
> God blessed them, and God said to them, "Be fruitful and multiply, and fill the earth and subdue it; and have dominion over the fish of the sea and over the birds of the air and over every living thing that moves upon the earth." God said, "See, I have given you every plant yielding seed that is upon the face of all the earth, and every tree with seed in its fruit; you shall have them for food. And to every beast of the earth, and to every bird of the air, and to everything that creeps on the earth, everything that has the breath of life, I have given every green plant for food." (1:26–30)

We have seen already that our divine image consists precisely in earthly rule as stewards, and managers of a world not our own. We are divine agents for, with, and under a God of distributive justice and restorative righteousness.

Those four major points of *divine image, human fertility, earthly rule,* and *food supply* are repeated in Genesis 9 but with very significant qualifications and additions on that fourth point (italicized below):

> God blessed Noah and his sons, and said to them, "Be fruitful and multiply, and fill the earth. The fear and dread of you shall rest on every animal of the earth, and on every bird of the air, on everything that creeps on the ground, and on all the fish of the sea; into your hand they are delivered. Every moving thing that lives shall be food for you; and just as I gave you the green plants [in Gen. 1:29–30], *I give you everything. Only, you shall not eat flesh with its life, that is, its blood. For your own lifeblood I will surely require a reckoning: from every animal I will require it and from human beings, each one for the blood of another, I will require a reckoning for human life.*
>
> > Whoever sheds the blood of a human,
> > by a human shall that person's blood be shed;
> > for in his own image
> > God made humankind.
>
> And you, be fruitful and multiply, abound on the earth and multiply in it." (9:1–7)

Humans are now permitted to eat animals but must signify that as divine permission rather than human right since life-as-blood belongs to God.

Furthermore, murder, as in Genesis 4, is explicitly mentioned but in words I deliberately repeat: "Whoever sheds the blood of a human, / by a human shall that person's blood be shed" (9:6). It is as if, in those lines of reversed poetic parallelism, God declines to establish divine punishment for human murder. Instead, God simply allows human consequence rather than asserting divine sanction.

Next, within the same Priestly tradition, Genesis 9:1–7 is the re-creation of human creation in Genesis 1:26–39, yet Genesis 9 emphasizes *covenant* while Genesis 1 never mentions it:

Then God said to Noah and to his sons with him, "As for me, I am establishing my *covenant* with you and your descendants after you, and with every living creature that is with you, the birds, the domestic animals, and every animal of the earth with you, as many as came out of the ark. I establish my *covenant* with you, that never again shall all flesh be cut off by the waters of a flood, and never again shall there be a flood to destroy the earth." God said, "This is the sign of the *covenant* that I make between me and you and every living creature that is with you, for all future generations: I have set my bow in the clouds, and it shall be a sign of the *covenant* between me and the earth. When I bring clouds over the earth and the bow is seen in the clouds, I will remember my *covenant* that is between me and you and every living creature of all flesh; and the waters shall never again become a flood to destroy all flesh. When the bow is in the clouds, I will see it and remember the everlasting *covenant* between God and every living creature of all flesh that is on the earth." God said to Noah, "This is the sign of the *covenant* that I have established between me and all flesh that is on the earth." (9:8–17)

You will have noticed that sevenfold drumbeat repetition of the word "covenant" (my italics). But notice as well that in this case, "covenant" means a unilateral promise given unconditionally by God to the whole world and all creation. There is not a hint of any sanction for human default or penalty for human rejection. God says "never again" rather than "never again unless . . . "

We might ask: In the biblical tradition, is that the meaning of covenant? Does it indicate a unilateral, unconditional, and unsanctioned divine promise? In other words, what are the metaphor, model, and matrix for the biblical concept of covenant within the ancient Near East? In answer, we turn for a moment from Mesopotamia to Anatolia, from the 2000s BCE to the 1000s BCE, and from Sumerians to Hittites.

"These Are the Words of the Great King"

THE HITTITE EMPIRE LASTED from the 1700s to the 1100s BCE but reached its height in the mid-1300s BCE when its sway extended from the capital at Hattusa in central Anatolia—now modern Boğazkale, 124 miles east of Ankara—to as far away as Mesopotamia.

As suzerain, the great king of Hatti bound subordinate vassal kings to him by sacred covenants sworn before multiple mutual Gods whereby those subordinates invoked on themselves divinely sanctioned curses for infidelity and blessings for fidelity. The formal components and sequential structures of those Hittite-style covenants became traditional across the ancient Near East during the succeeding centuries.

That type of alliance also became, in answer to the preceding question, the metaphor, model, and matrix whereby the biblical covenant became the dominant image for the relationship between the macrocosm of divinity and humanity as well as the microcosm of God and Israel in the biblical tradition. (Israel was "chosen" as God's experimental project because, if even one single people could not live by distributive justice, what chance was there for all peoples?) Think of divinity as suzerain with humanity as vassal, or God as suzerain with Israel as vassal.

A representative Hittite example is the sacred treaty between the suzerain Mursilis II, great king of Hatti, and his vassal Duppi-Tessub, king of the Amorites in the northern Levant.[8] It has five major elements: *Preamble, History, Law, Witness,* and *Sanction* (throughout this book I retain these terms as capitalized and italicized to indicate their technical covenantal meanings).

The *Preamble* (four lines) makes quite clear the superior-to-subordinate relationship involved: "These are the words of the Sun Mursilis, the great king, the king of the Hatti land, the valiant, the favorite of the Storm-god," with the vassal-recipient not even mentioned in that opening. Recall from Joshua 24:2a: "Thus says the Lord, the God of Israel."

The *History* (fifty-five lines) recalls past relations between suzerain and vassal. It especially emphasizes what the suzerain has done for the vassal in the past, maybe even making him constitutively what he is: "I sought after you . . . sick and ailing," says Mursilis to Duppi-Tessub. Recall what God did for Israel listed at length in Joshua 24:2b–13 before renewing the "covenant" in Joshua 24:25a. But also recall that *History* started at creation in the full biblical imagination.

The *Law* (ninety lines) lists the major stipulations and obligations, demands and commands, of the contractual alliance. This is, of course, the heart of the covenant as it defines the relationship of suzerain and vassal. Recall the "statutes and ordinances" in Joshua 24:25b or the laws in the "covenant code" in Exodus 20:19–23:33.

The *Witness* (thirty-six lines) cites a long list of divine beings and cosmic forces who are witnesses to and guarantors and enforcers of the sworn testimony of the vassal. Along with the multiple and named Gods of both parties, Mursilis cites "the mountains, the rivers, the Tigris and the Euphrates, heaven and earth, the winds and the clouds." Obviously, biblical covenant cites no such polytheistic witnesses, but it does mention those cosmic forces. In Deuteronomy, Moses says, in "covenant" contexts, that "I call heaven and earth to witness" (4:26; 30:19; 31:28).

The *Sanction* (eleven lines) records the curses and blessings, in that order, by which the multiple Gods would reward the vassal for fidelity or punish him for infidelity to that covenant sworn before them all.

Apart from these five major sections, other elements may also be present: *Erection* promises a standing stone or stele as copy and/or commemoration of the alliance (Josh. 24:26b–27); *Repetition* proposes renewal of the treaty at certain times by public ritual or reading (Deut. 27:9; 31:10–13); and *Deposition* requires placing the alliance text at the feet of the Gods in the temples of the respective participants. (Hence the core of Israel's covenantal law—the tablets of the Ten Commandments—was kept in the ark of the covenant at the feet of God imagined as invisibly enthroned upon it.)

The core of those suzerain-vassal covenants was, of course, the *Law* ordering or forbidding certain actions that were accepted as sworn commitments by the subject-kings. Before and after *Law* were the two main motivations—and watch this distinction hereafter—with past *History* before present *Law* and future *Sanction* after it. The Hittite-style model emphasized past *History* even more than future *Sanction* as a primary motivation, with reminders of what the suzerain had done *for* the vassal rather than threats of what he might do *against* him. (Notice the line count above.)

Furthermore, in this Hittite treaty, that *Sanction* is evenly balanced between curses and blessings, and they are given in that order. Still, although the Hittite suzerain had promised, of course, "to be loyal" to his vassal, no curses for infidelity nor blessings for fidelity are invoked against the suzerain himself. The *Sanction* simply states, concerning "the words of the treaty and the oath that are inscribed on this tablet," that

> *Should Duppi-Tessub not honor* these words of the treaty and the oath, may these gods of the oath destroy Duppi-Tessub together with his person, his wife, his son, his grandson, his house, his land, and together with everything that he owns.
> *But if Duppi-Tessub honors* these words of the treaty and the oath, may these gods of the oath protect him together with his person, his wife, his son, his grandson, his house, and his country.

I agree completely with the last half century's consensus of scholarship that the Hittite-style suzerain-vassal treaty was the metaphor, model, and matrix for the divine covenant in the biblical tradition. (I repeat that those treaties were never secular treaties but always sacred contracts.) Covenant in the biblical tradition is, therefore, a religio-political, religio-social, and religio-economic commitment between God and the world as macrocosm or God and Israel as an experimental microcosm.

Where Are We Now and What Comes Next?

THE ESSENTIAL PROBLEM OF *How to Read the Bible and Still Be a Christian* is rather obvious when, as early as Genesis 6–9, escalatory human violence in the world is solved by divine super-escalatory violence *against* the world. But, to be fair, that was the biblical tradition doing its best with a classic story, adopted from its Mesopotamian matrix and adapted to its own God at start and finish.

To start, the annihilation is not from too much human noise but from too much human violence. To finish, there is that unconditional divine promise of "never again." Furthermore, Genesis 9 deliberately sends us back to reread Genesis 1 and asks us to ponder the relationship between creation and covenant.

Think now about what we have just seen about creation in Genesis 1 and re-creation in Genesis 9 within that matrix of the ancient Near Eastern understanding of covenant. It is a sacred bilateral contract between a dominant and a subordinate party. It is the major mode of control between suzerain and vassal, empire and colony.

The structural core of those imperial covenants allowed emphasis on or movement in either of two directions. Using the technical covenantal terms I have just discussed, loyalty and obedience to covenantal *Law* could arise from gratitude for past *History* and/or from fear of future *Sanction:*

History	←	*Law*	→	*Sanction*
↓		↓		↓
gratitude for past benefits		*present loyalty because of gratitude and/or fear*		*fear of future punishments*

In this chapter the Priestly tradition in Genesis 1 and 9 gave not the slightest hint of *Sanction* with regard to creation and re-creation since covenant was not mentioned at all in the former case and used for a unilateral, unconditional, and unsanctioned promise in the latter. (A covenant is, by definition, a bilateral commitment.) That was a kinder, gentler adaptation of the Hittite-style covenant where *History* overshadowed *Sanction* and where, within *Sanction*, curses and blessings were brief and evenly balanced.

Recall from Chapter 4 those four traditions intricately combined in the Christian Bible's opening Pentateuch. We already saw the Priestly tradition at the start of those five books; we meet next the Deuteronomic tradition at their close. And with that tradition, the challenge of *How to Read the Bible and Still Be a Christian* starts to look truly impossible.

In Chapter 6, the covenantal pendulum swings powerfully from the Priestly to the Deuteronomic tradition, and swings strongly toward the *Sanction* end of the core trilogy of *History, Law,* and *Sanction*. It is not, of course, that past *History* is ever forgotten, but now future *Sanction* dominates. And within *Sanction*, curses and punishments dominate over blessings and rewards.

Our first point will be to see that Deuteronomic vision of covenant and then to ask why it shifted from a gratitude for past *History* to a fear of future *Sanction*. Why did *Sanction* start to dominate its covenantal vision? To put it another way: What changed in the Bible's ancient Near Eastern matrix that best explains that Deuteronomic emphasis?

The final question is whether that *Sanction*-heavy vision in the book of Deuteronomy actually works in practice as the Deuteronomic tradition seeks to interpret biblical history in terms of blessings and rewards for covenantal fidelity and curses and punishments for covenantal infidelity. Furthermore, does the Bible elsewhere always agree with that Deuteronomic vision of the relationship between God and the world or God and Israel?

CHAPTER 6

Blessing and Curse

You realize by now the part you played
To stultify the Deuteronomist
And change the tenor of religious thought.
ROBERT FROST, "God to Job," *A Masque of Reason* (1945)

IN 931 BCE THE united monarchy of David and Solomon split, over the issue of excessive taxation, into the divided monarchy that separated the northern Kingdom of Israel from the southern Kingdom of Judah. When that northern Kingdom was destroyed by the ascendant Assyrian Empire in 722–721 BCE, refugees, fleeing to relative safety in the more isolated south, took with them their own traditions, such as that of the Elohist and the Deuteronomist (recall them from Chapter 4).

About one hundred years later, in 621 BCE, the high priest Hilkiah informed King Josiah of Judah that he had found the book of Deuteronomy, which he called the "book of the law," in the Jerusalem Temple (2 Kings 22:8). Thus began what today is called the Deuteronomic Reform under the slogan "one God in one Temple—at Jerusalem" (note, for example, Deut. 12:13–14).

Sanction: Curses over Blessings

WHAT IS MOST STRIKING and even startling about the book of Deuteronomy is how it is dominated by covenant, with covenant dominated by *Sanction*, and with *Sanction* dominated by curses over blessings. To put it another way: this book's God of distributive justice is dominated by its God of retributive justice. Watch, for example, how the book climaxes with this multiple *Sanction* section in Deuteronomy 27–30.

First is a ritual and antiphonal renewal of the covenant to be performed with representatives invoking blessings for fidelity and curses for infidelity to which all the people must answer "Amen": "When you have crossed over the Jordan, these shall stand on Mount Gerizim for the blessing of the people: Simeon, Levi, Judah, Issachar, Joseph, and Benjamin. And these shall stand on Mount Ebal for the curse: Reuben, Gad, Asher, Zebulun, Dan, and Naphtali" (27:12–13).

Yet in what follows there is no sixfold invocation of both blessings and curses but only a twelvefold invocation of curses (27:14–36): "'Cursed be anyone who makes an idol or casts an image, anything abhorrent to the Lord, the work of an artisan, and sets it up in secret.' All the people shall respond, saying, 'Amen!'" (27:15); and, "'Cursed be anyone who deprives the alien, the orphan, and the widow of justice.' All the people shall say, 'Amen!'" (27:19). Curses predominate over blessings.

Next is a sequence of blessings, "if you will only obey the Lord your God" (28:1–14), which are overbalanced almost fourfold by curses, "if you will not obey the Lord your God" (28:15–68): "Blessed shall be the fruit of your womb, the fruit of your ground, and the fruit of your livestock, both the increase of your cattle and the issue of your flock" (28:4); and, conversely, "Cursed shall be the fruit of your womb, the fruit of your ground, the increase of your cattle, and the issue of your flock" (28:18). Read, if you can take it, all those very specific curses from 28:15 through 28:68.

Finally, as if that were not enough, there are more curses in 29:19–27, followed by a lesser number of blessings in 30:1–10. As an example, if you are cursed, you will see your land with "all its soil burned out by sulfur and salt, nothing planted, nothing sprouting, unable to support any vegetation, like the destruction of Sodom and Gomorrah" (29:23); but if you are blessed, "the Lord your God will bring you into the land that your ancestors possessed, and you will possess it; he will make you more prosperous and numerous than your ancestors" (30:5).

Why has covenant become, in this Deuteronomic tradition, so thoroughly *Sanction*-ridden? And even granted that it is *Sanction*-obsessed, why do curses and punishments so thoroughly outnumber blessings and rewards? What is the matrix for this excessively negative vision of covenant that passed from northern Israel in the late 700s to southern Judah in the late 600s BCE? My answer to this question comes, as always, from considerations of its matrix within the ancient Near East.

By the 700s BCE, the powerful Bronze Age Hittite Empire was long gone, and the even more powerful Iron Age (Neo)Assyrian Empire was in full ascendancy. On one hand, as you will recall, the Hittite-style covenants from the 1300s and 1200s BCE usually concluded with a summary statement of curses for infidelity and blessings for fidelity—recall that brief and evenly balanced example of such a *Sanction* from Chapter 5.

On the other hand, however, the Assyrian-style treaties from the 700s and 600s BCE multiply *Sanction* exponentially, usually containing curses without any blessings and invoking those curses with symbolic enactments and terrifyingly explicit rituals. From treaty texts to siege tactics, Assyria used imperial terror as deliberate military strategy and calculated foreign policy. I propose that the Deuteronomic tradition accepted, for better or for worse, the contemporary Assyrian-style sacred treaty as its ongoing understanding of God's covenant with Israel.

"Do Not Set over Yourselves Another King, Another Lord"

I GIVE YOU ONE paradigmatic example of those Assyrian-style suzerain-vassal treaties, and I draw special attention to its style and format, that is, to the violence and even terrorism of the *Sanction* sworn by vassals as self-curses for any future infidelity. You will notice how it differs from the Hittite style of *Preamble, History, Law, Witness,* and *Sanction* seen in Chapter 5.

In May of 672 BCE, Esarhaddon of Assyria held a solemn imperial convocation during which he established sworn covenants with nine small Kingdoms on his Iranian frontier. The best preserved, and therefore the exemplar, of the nine was with the Median king, Ramataia of Urukazabarna; and like all the other kings, Esarhaddon demanded sworn allegiance to his son Ashurbanipal as his designated successor. That and that alone is the single stipulation in the *Law* of this treaty, and it is pounded over and over again with numbing repetition.[9]

Preamble and Witness: The *Preamble* (lines 1–12 and 41–50) frames the divine *Witness* (lines 13–40) so that those divine beings and cosmic forces appear immediately with no *History* section present at all.

Law and Sanction: Then, a long list of *Law* in the style of "if you . . . " (lines 51–413) forms a dialectic with a long list of *Sanction* in the style of "may (you) . . . " (lines 423–529). For example: *"if you* remove it [the treaty text], consign it to fire, throw it into water, bury it in dust, or by some trick destroy, annihilate, or turn it face down . . . *may* tar and pitch be your food, donkey urine your drink, naphtha your ointment, river rushes your covers, and evil spirits, demons, and lurkers select your houses as their abodes" (lines 410–413, 492–493).

Next, as if those "if you . . . may you" curses were not enough, there is another long list of "just as . . . so may" curses. These are enacted rituals in which the vassals participate symbolically in their own destruction for any future infidelity (lines 560–668). For example: *"Just as* these yearlings and spring lambs, male and female, are cut open and their entrails are rolled around their feet, *so may* the entrails of your sons and daughters be rolled around your feet" (lines 551–554). This type of covenantal ritual, by the way, is also presumed behind the "cutting" of the covenant in Genesis 15:7–21 or Jeremiah 34:28.

Think, finally and especially, about two details in this treaty's *Law*. One is that love means loyalty: "if you do not love the crown-prince designate Ashurbanipal, son of your lord Esarhaddon, king of Assyria, as you do your own lives . . . " (lines 266–268). Another is that loyalty means exclusivity: "Do not set over yourselves another king, another lord" (line 301). Compare those two commands with these lines from Deuteronomy: "Hear, O Israel: The Lord is our God, the Lord alone. You shall love the Lord your God with all your heart, and with all your soul, and with all your might" (6:4–5).

Sanction as curses takes up about 254 of 674 lines (38 percent) from Esarhaddon's exercises in dynastic paranoia. In answer to this chapter's first question, those Assyrian-style suzerain-vassal treaties—with their heavy emphasis on *Sanction* rather than *History* and, within *Sanction*, on curses for infidelity rather than blessings for fidelity—are the contemporary metaphor, model, and matrix for the Deuteronomic vision of covenant. Indeed, it is even possible to show direct contacts between Assyrian and Deuteronomic covenantal curses. Here are two examples.

First, the Esarhaddon/Ramataia treaty gives these twin curses in sequence: "May Sin, the luminary of heaven and earth, clothe you in leprosy . . . My Shamash, the light of heaven and earth . . . take away your eyesight" (lines 419–422). That appropriately combines the Moon-God Sin as father of the Sun-God Shamash in the cursing *Sanction*. But Deuteronomy also places leprosy and blindness in similar conjunction: "The Lord will afflict you with the boils of Egypt, with ulcers, scurvy, and itch, of which you cannot be healed. The Lord will afflict you with madness, blindness, and confusion of mind" (28:27–28).

Second, Esarhaddon threatens drought when "all the gods . . . turn your soil into iron . . . and rain does not fall from a copper sky . . . but let it rain burning coals in your land instead of dew" (lines 528–531). Deuteronomy also threatens drought: "The sky over your head shall be bronze, and the earth under you iron. The Lord will change the rain of your land into powder, and only dust shall come down upon you from the sky until you are destroyed" (28:23–24).

I cite these parallels because their presence in Deuteronomy 28 reflects on the very character of Israel's covenantal God. If one opposes God-Yahweh of Israel to God-Ashur of Assyria, in that process God-Yahweh of Israel should not develop into God-Ashur of Assyria.

Finally, even the Priestly-style covenant became influenced by that Deuteronomic-style vision of *Sanction*. Leviticus 26, for example, was edited after the Babylonian exile in the 500s or 400s BCE, as you can see from 26:34–46 where the exile is interpreted as a remedial Sabbath for the land. Notice its division into blessings in the shorter 26:3–13 and curses in the longer 26:15–68.

In summary, therefore, I argue that the Deuteronomic tradition's vision of Israel's covenant with God was modeled on contemporary Assyrian-style treaties and thereby greatly enlarged the role of *Sanction* within covenant and curses and punishments within *Sanction*.

Rewrite History or Rethink Theology?

THE DEUTERONOMIC VISION OF covenantal *Sanction* worked in two directions. First, from present to future: if you obey, you will be blessed; if you disobey, you will be cursed. And second, from present to past: you are blessed, therefore you obeyed; you are cursed, therefore you disobeyed. Consider, for example, this Deuteronomic promise:

> If you will only obey the Lord your God . . . the Lord will cause your enemies who rise against you to be defeated before you; they shall come out against you one way, and flee before you seven ways. . . .

But if you will not obey the Lord your God . . . the Lord will cause you to be defeated before your enemies; you shall go out against them one way and flee before them seven ways. (Deut. 28:1, 7, 15, 25)

This example leads to an obvious question: Were such blessings and curses always empirically verifiable and consistently credible both inside and outside the Deuteronomic tradition?

That theology was applied, for example, to judge as good or bad the kings of Judah and Israel in the historical books that come after the book of Deuteronomy. Did theory work out in practice? Were good kings always awarded with blessings and bad kings always punished with curses? Here are two striking examples that contradict Deuteronomy's serene assurance. Watch how history is then corrected to conform with theology.

The cases concern a bad king who lived too long and a good king who died too young. This double discrepancy between monarchic history and Deuteronomic theology was recognized by the author known as the Chronicler who wrote a theologically "correct" version of 2 Samuel and 1–2 Kings during the Persian restoration around 400 BCE. His solution was not to rethink theology, but to change history—like this.

The Case of King Manasseh: Manasseh was a very bad king by Deuteronomic standards (2 Kings 21:2), yet he reigned from 697 to 642 BCE—longer even than David. How could that be? He *must* have done something good and was being blessed and rewarded, and the Chronicler rewrites the story accordingly:

History Written: "Manasseh misled them to do more evil than the nations had done that the Lord destroyed before the people of Israel. . . . Now the rest of the acts of Manasseh, all that he did, and the sin that he committed, are they not written in the Book of the Annals of the Kings of Judah?" (2 Kings 21:9, 17)

History Rewritten: "Manasseh misled Judah and the inhabitants of Jerusalem, so that they did more evil than the nations whom the Lord had destroyed before the people of Israel. . . . *The Lord brought against them the commanders of the army of the king of Assyria, who took Manasseh captive in manacles, bound him with fetters, and brought him to Babylon. While he was in distress he entreated the favor of the Lord his God and humbled himself greatly before the God of his ancestors. He prayed to him, and God received his entreaty, heard his plea, and restored him again to Jerusalem and to his Kingdom.* . . . Now the rest of the acts of Manasseh, his prayer to his God, and the words of the seers who spoke to him in the name of the Lord God of Israel, these are in the Annals of the Kings of Israel." (2 Chron. 33:9, 11–13, 18; italics mine)

Actually, Manasseh was one of Esarhaddon's subservient vassals according to the Assyrian annals, and furthermore, Esarhaddon ruled from Nineveh, not Babylon (681–669 BCE). The italics above show how the later Chronicler attempted to bring royal history into line with Deuteronomic theology.

The Case of King Josiah: Josiah was a very good king who had introduced that Deuteronomic Reform in 621 BCE, as we saw above. Furthermore, his birth had been prophesied a century and a half earlier: "A son shall be born to the house of David, Josiah by name," said the Lord in 1 Kings 13:2. Finally, as the book of Sirach said of the kings of Judah, "Except for David and Hezekiah and Josiah, / all of them were great sinners, / for they abandoned the law of the Most High" (49:4).

Yet, despite Deuteronomic theology, Josiah was killed in battle in 609 BCE. How is that possible? He must have done something wrong, and once again, the Chronicler invents a reason:

History Written: "Pharaoh Neco king of Egypt went up to the king of Assyria to the river Euphrates. King Josiah went to meet him; but when Pharaoh Neco met him at Megiddo, he killed him. His servants carried him dead in a chariot from Megiddo, brought him to Jerusalem, and buried him in his own tomb." (2 Kings 23:29–30)

History Rewritten: King Neco of Egypt went up to fight at Carchemish on the Euphrates, and Josiah went out against him. *But Neco sent envoys to him, saying, "What have I to do with you, king of Judah? I am not coming against you today, but against the house with which I am at war; and God has commanded me to hurry. Cease opposing God, who is with me, so that he will not destroy you." But Josiah would not turn away from him, but disguised himself in order to fight with him. He did not listen to the words of Neco from the mouth of God, but joined battle in the plain of Megiddo.* The archers shot King Josiah; and the king said to his servants, "Take me away, for I am badly wounded." So his servants took him out of the chariot and carried him in his second chariot and brought him to Jerusalem. There he died, and was buried in the tombs of his ancestors." (2 Chron. 35:20–24; italics mine)

Again, the italics show what the Chronicler has inserted to bring history into conformity with theology. But with neither of these kings—one a model of evil, the other of goodness—does the Deuteronomic tradition's *Sanction* work without history being rewritten.

In other words, Deuteronomic theology does not even work within the Deuteronomic tradition itself. Classic discrepancies such as Manasseh and Josiah required historical "correction" by the Chronicler to bring history into line with theology. Furthermore, the same happens even more strikingly outside the Deuteronomic tradition.

The Case of Job: In the 300s BCE, the book of Job laid bare the intransigence of Deuteronomic theology especially with regard to its bidirectionality. I mean that, as mentioned earlier, one could interpret and argue backward within covenant *Sanction* so that present sufferings were divine punishments for past sins. Hence, since Job was suffering terribly now, he must have sinned terribly then.

In Job 3–37 we listen to bad theology clothed in great poetry as Job's friends—all by-the-book Deuteronomists, or Deuteronomic fundamentalists—tell him that his sufferings are clearly divine punishments for sin and that if he repents, God will surely forgive him. It was not that Job had sinned and therefore suffering would happen; it was that suffering had happened and therefore Job had sinned. We—hearers or readers—know from the very start of the book that such a Deuteronomic interpretation of Job's situation is false, and indeed, God negates it at the start (1:8) and finish (42:7) of the book.

The book of Job should have served, as quoted from Robert Frost's playlet in this chapter's epigraph, "To stultify the Deuteronomist / And change the tenor of religious thought." But, sadly, the book of Job was but a speed bump on the Deuteronomic superhighway. The delusion of divine punishments still prevails inside and outside religion over the clear evidence of human consequences, random accidents, and natural disasters. This does not simply distort theology; it defames the very character of God.

Where Are We Now and What Comes Next?

WHEN I CONSIDER ONE final time the start and finish of the Pentateuch and contrast again the Priestly tradition in Genesis 1 with the Deuteronomic tradition in Deuteronomy 28, I glimpse again that biblical rhythm of expansion-and-contraction, assertion-and-subversion. As that rhythm becomes ever clearer as the very heartbeat of the biblical tradition, we will see the basic solution for *How to Read the Bible and Still Be a Christian*. Read it *all* carefully and thoughtfully, recognize radicality's *assertion*, expect normalcy's *subversion*, and respect the honesty of a story that tells the truth.

That insistent dialectic of assertion-and-subversion appears at the very core of covenant itself. That core is the threefold sequence from past *History* through present *Law* to future *Sanction*, and that allows theology to move backward and emphasize *History* or to move forward and emphasize *Sanction*. Both past *History* and future *Sanction* are always present in the biblical tradition, but sometimes direction or even emphasis is everything. The figure diagrams this movement:

History   ←   *Law*   →   *Sanction*
↓   ↓
Priestly Tradition   *Deuteronomic* Tradition

I call this model the *Covenantal Divide*, and I repeat that those directions are not absolutely exclusive options but are fatefully different emphases. It makes a profound difference whether from that central core of covenantal *Law* in the present, one moves mostly to past *History* in gratitude to God or mostly to future *Sanction* in fear of God. What is ultimately at stake across that *Covenantal Divide* is the character of the biblical God as one of distributive justice or of retributive justice, as graciously nonviolent or punitively violent.

Next, then, in Chapter 7, I turn from Torah to Prophecy, but I am still probing the fundamental question of divine punishments *for* evil or human consequences *from* evil. My problem is that the prophets advocated God's distributive justice insistently, courageously, and magnificently, but they also threatened God's retributive justice consistently, relentlessly, and concomitantly.

There must be, say the prophets, distributive justice on earth *or else* there will be retributive justice from heaven. Where did the certainty and courage of that vision come from? What came to it—for better and for worse—from the matrix within which it moved, and without which it could never have moved at all? For always and ever, for them and for us, matrix is destiny.

CHAPTER 7

Prophecy and Prayer

For who has stood in the council of the Lord
so as to see and to hear his word?
Who has given heed to his word so as to proclaim it?
JEREMIAH 23:18

IN THE BIBLICAL TRADITION, the *nabi*, translated rather weakly by our word "prophet," is an individual "called" or "sent" or "raised up" to proclaim a divine message—one that is often in conflict with the absolute force of royal power. For example, God "sent" Moses to confront Pharaoh in Exodus 3:10, "sent" Samuel to confront Saul in 1 Samuel 15:1, and "sent" Nathan to confront David in 2 Samuel 12:1.

With the space constraints of this single book in mind, I focus on a single paradigmatic case study for the entire prophetic tradition. My example is that of the eighth-century BCE prophet named Isaiah whose mission and message are now found in Isaiah 1–39 (the rest of the book was written by later prophets).

The fateful matrix of Isaiah 1–39 is Assyria's westward-expanding imperialism between approximately 750 and 700 BCE. As already seen in the preceding chapter, and to be seen again in this one, Assyria's Levantine onslaught cast lasting shadows over the land of Israel, over its understanding of covenant, and even over the very character of its God. That gives me guiding questions for this chapter that involve the source of prophetic identity, the model of prophetic matrix, and the challenge of prophetic content.

PROPHETIC IDENTITY
"I Said, 'Here Am I; Send Me!'"

THE FIRST STAGE IN prophetic identity and self-consciousness is, of course, the divine covenant, and that basis is always presumed even if not always mentioned. One example will suffice—and notice how it integrates both the world and Israel:

> The earth lies polluted
> under its inhabitants;
> for they have transgressed laws,
> violated the statutes,
> broken the everlasting covenant.
> . . . [But] the Lord of [heavenly] hosts will reign
> on Mount Zion and in Jerusalem. (Isa. 24:5, 23)

The next step in prophetic consciousness is the divine council, where God is enthroned in heaven surrounded by hosts of seraphim-courtiers—as in the ecstatic vision of Isaiah in 738 BCE:

> I saw the Lord sitting on a throne, high and lofty; and the hem of his robe filled the temple. Seraphs were in attendance above him; each had six wings: with two they covered their faces, and with two they covered their feet, and with two they flew. And one called to another and said:
>
> > "Holy, holy, holy is the Lord of hosts;
> > the whole earth is full of his glory."

. . . Then I heard the voice of the Lord saying, "Whom shall I send, and who will go for us?" And I said, "Here am I; send me!" (6:1–3, 8)

In that self-identity, the prophet is more than a mere herald who delivers, by speech and/or script, a message he has been given. He is a high official who stands, by ecstatic vision, in the heavenly court and divine council of God. Having heard and seen the entire proceedings, he is sent to deliver the result as empowered plenipotentiary.

The final step in prophetic self-awareness is the divine complaint, which the prophet is privileged both to see and to hear. (In this context, the word "complaint" means a juridical accusation and prosecution in a court of law.) The model is what happened in the Assyrian court-council at Nineveh when a vassal was accused of breaking covenant.

Invasion would follow, of course, but war was justified by invoking those cosmic powers and divine forces who were *Witness* of the sacred covenant in the first place. An example is the imperial lawsuit-complaint of Ashurbanipal of Assyria against Urtaku of Elam (676–664 BCE):

The Gods judged my lawsuit against Urtaku, king of Elam, whom I had not attacked (yet) he attacked me. . . . In my stead they brought about his defeat, smote his vanguard, and expelled him (back) to the borders of own land. . . . They overthrew his rule (kingship), removed his dynasty, and let another assume the rulership of Elam.

Imperial military vengeance was justified theologically before the Gods named as *Witness* of covenant and avengers of its breach.

Earthly and imperial complaint involved a legal indictment, juridical decision, and solemn condemnation in a suzerain's lawsuit with a rebellious vassal. Similarly, in the heavenly lawsuit and transcendental judgment of a divine complaint, the suzerain-God unleashes *Sanction* against vassal-Israel as covenantal rebel. Notice this drumbeat: "Hear, O heavens, and listen, O earth; / for the Lord has spoken: / I reared children and brought them up, / but they have rebelled against me . . . rebel . . . rebel . . . rebels . . . rebels" (1:2, 5, 20, 23, 28).

At this point a caution is in order because the internal certainty that accompanies ecstatic experience does not necessarily correlate with its external accuracy. Ecstasy is an altered state of normal awake-consciousness and as such is a hard-wired possibility of our human brain. It is not supernatural but natural; or better, it is a serene negation of that inept distinction. Ecstatic vision and ecstatic audition, ecstatic relocation and ecstatic transformation may be produced by fever or focus, medication or meditation, physical isolation or sensory deprivation.

Here, however, is the intractable challenge. The *event* of an ecstatic trance derives from the chemistry in the brain, but the *content* of an ecstatic trance derives from the theology in the mind. What entranced prophets saw in heaven validated and empowered what they brought with them from earth. The result combined both the very best understanding of the covenantal God of nonviolent distributive justice and the very worst understanding of the covenantal God of violent retributive justice. The basic message—clear, consistent, and courageous across three hundred years—demanded just distribution on earth or else stern retribution from heaven.

What are the metaphor, model, and matrix for that mode of prophetic consciousness—from divine covenant through heavenly council to transcendental complaint? The answer is brilliantly revealed in one single historical incident during the Assyrian Empire's southward attacks against Egypt in the late 700s BCE.

PROPHETIC MATRIX
"Thus Says the Great King"

ASSYRIA WAS THE MOST powerful and also the most ruthless empire of its time. It used atrocity as imperial policy so that, where terror preceded its army, the army might not need to follow. The curses in its vassal treaties and the actions in its military reprisals were not directed just against rebel rulers and their dynasties, but explicitly against their lands and populations as well.

Hezekiah of Judah, seduced by promises of Egyptian support, rebelled against King Sennacherib of Assyria. The biblical account of what happened next is quite extraordinary, with almost sixty verses verbatim across two chapters in both 2 Kings 18–19 and Isaiah 36–37. The date of Sennacherib's campaign was 701 BCE or, possibly, a second campaign in 688 BCE. I focus here on four major aspects of the opening scene in the drama of Jerusalem's deliverance from the Assyrian threat.

The first aspect concerns speech and text. Having devastated nearby Lachish, Sennacherib sent three of his highest officials, named by their titles, to meet three of Hezekiah's at the southeastern corner of the city walls to negotiate Jerusalem's surrender—or else.

Sennacherib's last-named official is identified as "the Rabshakeh," or vizier. It is he who delivers the imperial message. (Is he a northern Israelite elite-scribe deported to Assyria in 722–721 BCE?) The full story is related in 2 Kings 18:1–36 (= Isa. 37:1–21), and the Rabshakeh's address is historically quite accurate. Such diplomatic threats were normal Assyrian imperial protocol—before the military attacked. The Assyrian Rabshakeh carries a letter and reads it to Hezekiah's negotiators before delivering it to them.

That is a first element that enters the prophetic tradition from the imperial Assyrian matrix: the prophet will also say "hear the word of God" and then present the message as both speech and text. Isaiah is both a speaking and a writing prophet.

The second aspect concerns the king and the people. In the classical suzerain treaty the inferior party was usually a vassal king, and *Sanction* was almost exclusively directed at him and his dynasty—what happened to his people was simply collateral damage. But, as noted above, Assyrian imperial policy made the population at large a specific part of the vassal treaty. Colonial depopulation and imperial repopulation were Assyrian inventions, and thence the "lost tribes of Israel" after the Assyrian depopulated their northern homeland in 722–721 BCE.

In this case, the Rabshakeh speaks first to Hezekiah through his three representatives, warning him not to depend on Egypt (2 Kings 18:19–25 = Isa. 36:4–19) but then, despite objections from the king's representatives, he talks directly to the population, warning them not to depend on Hezekiah (2 Kings 18:28–35 = Isa. 36:13–20).

That is a second element that enters the prophetic tradition from the imperial Assyrian matrix: the prophet speaks not just to the king, but even more especially, to the people at large. After Isaiah's aforementioned vision, he is ordered, "Go and say to this people" (Isa. 6:9).

The third aspect concerns message and adaptation. The Rabshakeh is reading from the "letter" of Sennacherib, and he starts in standard messenger format using the first-person "I" of Sennacherib himself. But then he interjects a comment from himself by citing Sennacherib in the third person as "my master" (2 Kings 18:23–24 = Isa. 36:8–9).

That is a third element that enters the prophetic tradition from the imperial Assyrian matrix: neither the Rabshakeh nor the prophet is a simple message-bearer or letter-carrier. Both are high officials—one from an earthly and imperial court-council, and the other from a heavenly and divine court-council—and both can report, comment on, adapt, and expand the message as re/present/ative of the sender, that is, as making that sender creatively and persuasively present.

The fourth aspect concerns Sennacherib and God. This is the final element taken from the Assyrian matrix, and it is where prophetic adoption becomes radical adaption, as you can see in this comparison:

> *The Rabshakeh speaks as representative of Sennacherib:*
> "Thus says the great king, the king of Assyria" (2 Kings
>   18:19 = Isa. 36:4)
> "Hear the word of the great king, the king of Assyria!
> Thus says the king" (2 Kings 18:28 = Isa. 36:13)
> "Thus says the king of Assyria" (2 Kings 18:31 = Isa. 36:16)
> *The prophet speaks as representative of God:*
> "Thus says the Lord" (2 Kings 19:6 = Isa. 37:6)
> "Thus says the Lord, the God of Israel" (2 Kings 19:20 =
>   Isa. 37:21)
> "Thus says the Lord concerning the king of Assyria"
>   (2 Kings 19:32 = Isa. 37:33)

While the Rabshakeh speaks from the earthly court-council of Sennacherib, the prophet counterspeaks not from the earthly court-council of Hezekiah, but from the heavenly court-council of God.

PROPHETIC CONTENT
"Seek Justice, Rescue the Oppressed"

I RETURN NOW TO that covenantal lawsuit in Isaiah 1:1–9 discussed above under divine complaint. But the specific referent here is a devastated Judah and an isolated Jerusalem left behind as Sennacherib's army marched home to Nineveh, leaving Lachish destroyed but Jerusalem unconquered.

"Come now, let us argue it out," says God as judge to Israel as defendant.

> Your country lies desolate,
> your cities are burned with fire;

in your very presence
aliens devour your land;
it is desolate, as overthrown by foreigners.
And daughter Zion is left
like a booth in a vineyard,
like a shelter in a cucumber field,
like a besieged city. (Isa. 1:7–8)

This describes the *Sanction* imposed for Israel's breach of covenant, but what precisely was its specific default? What did Israel do wrong? The answer is composed of a negative followed by a positive element:

Negative Element, on Worship:

What to me is the multitude of your sacrifices?
says the Lord;
I have had enough of burnt offerings of rams
and the fat of fed beasts;
I do not delight in the blood of bulls,
or of lambs, or of goats.
When you come to appear before me,
who asked this from your hand?
Trample my courts no more;
bringing offerings is futile;
incense is an abomination to me.
New moon and sabbath and calling of convocation—
I cannot endure solemn assemblies with iniquity.
Your new moons and your appointed festivals
my soul hates;
they have become a burden to me,
I am weary of bearing them.
When you stretch out your hands,
I will hide my eyes from you;

even though you make many prayers,
I will not listen;
your hands are full of blood.

Positive Element, on Justice:

Wash yourselves; make yourselves clean;
remove the evil of your doings
from before my eyes;
cease to do evil,
learn to do good;
seek justice,
rescue the oppressed,
defend the orphan,
plead for the widow. (1:11–17)

I make two major points about that citation—deliberately taken as a paradigmatic case for prophetic content within the entire prophetic tradition.

First, that negative/positive dyad against the presence of worship amid the absence of justice is not simply a problem unique to Isaiah's time and place. Amos had that same dyad in 5:21–24, Hosea in 6:6, and Micah in 6:6–8. It almost cost Jeremiah his life in 7:7–5 and 26:1–24. You cannot, without acute hypocrisy, worship a God of justice in a state of injustice.

Second, notice the parallelism in the climactic conclusion where "doing good" is equated with "justice" and "justice" is equated with rescuing those politically, socially, and economically weaker. In other words, justice is not simply personal and individual, but more especially systemic and structural—especially for a society's vulnerable ones.[10]

Finally, what happens when divine covenant, divine council, and divine complaint decree that vassal-Israel has defaulted on the covenant of divine justice? "If you are willing and obedient, / you shall eat the good of the land; / but if you refuse and rebel, / you shall be devoured by the sword" (1:19–20a).

This is, however, about the only glimpse of a balance between blessing and curse. The rest is primarily curses and punishments:

> I will pour out my wrath on my enemies, and avenge myself
> on my foes!
> I will turn my hand against you;
> I will smelt away your dross as with lye
> and remove all your alloy. (1:24b–25)

This is, once again, the "or else" of the Deuteronomic tradition.

Looking across the entire prophetic tradition—with Isaiah 1–39 as a paradigmatic case study—I see and emphasize twin aspects, neither of which should ever be omitted. One aspect is the tradition's insistent divine demand for distributive justice for both Israel as microcosm and the world as macrocosm under God. The other aspect is an equally insistent threat of divine retributive justice as *Sanction* for maldistribution. In other words, the prophetic tradition grounded the best of covenantal *Law* in the worst of covenantal *Sanction*.

"Who Crowns You with Steadfast Love and Mercy"

AS JUST SEEN, THAT fateful duality of the Deuteronomic tradition's reading of covenantal *Sanction* forward from present sin to future suffering and backward from present suffering to past sin was also basic to the Prophetic tradition's demand for equitable distribution *or else* terrible retribution. How, then, did the Psalmic tradition, the Psalter as Israel's communal prayer book, respond to and within that theology?

First, and above all else, the God of the Psalter is the God of both creation for all the world and of covenant for all of Israel. Precisely as such, that God is one for whom "righteousness and justice are the foundation" of God's throne (Pss. 89:14; 97:2). You might think of creation as God's original act of distributive justice, as the gift of the world fairly and equitably given to all those in it:

> Happy are those whose help is the God of Jacob,
> whose hope is in the Lord their God,
> who made heaven and earth,
> the sea, and all that is in them;
> who keeps faith forever;
> who executes justice for the oppressed;
> who gives food to the hungry.
> The Lord sets the prisoners free;
> the Lord opens the eyes of the blind.
> The Lord lifts up those who are bowed down;
> the Lord loves the righteous.
> The Lord watches over the strangers;
> he upholds the orphan and the widow,
> but the way of the wicked he brings to ruin. (146:5–9)

And again: "Father of orphans and protector of widows / is God in his holy habitation" (68:5), for God "loves righteousness and justice" (33:5).

Among those and all the other creation hymns in the Psalter, one stands out as a celebration not just of creator or creation, but of our human status within that process. The opening and closing verse proclaim, "O Lord, our Sovereign, / how majestic is your name in all the earth!" (8:1 = 8:9). But between these frames comes this:

> When I look at your heavens, the work of your fingers,
> the moon and the stars that you have established;
> what are human beings that you are mindful of them,
> mortals that you care for them?
> Yet you have made them a little lower than God,
> and crowned them with glory and honor.

You have given them dominion over the works of your hands;
you have put all things under their feet,
all sheep and oxen,
and also the beasts of the field,
the birds of the air, and the fish of the sea,
whatever passes along the paths of the seas. (8:3–8)

This is Genesis 1:26–28 rephrased as a celebratory chant. Human *being* is not about an external command or a directive mandate, but about an internal destiny and constitutive identity. If we fail our identity and destiny, wouldn't the result be human consequence rather than divine punishment?

Second, with regard to covenant, one fear haunts the imagination of Israel at prayer—namely, the possibility of a dissolved covenant. Strictly speaking, a covenant is a bilateral contract. If either party defaults, the other is excused; the covenant is broken, dissolved, finished—for both parties. (A covenant is like an egg—you cannot break half of it.) The constant mention of God's "steadfast love" in the psalms expresses the hope that, even if Israel defaults, God will not. But Deuteronomic theology would not agree: *covenant is conditional* (Deut. 5:9b–10).

That dread fear arose especially with regard to the covenant concerning David's dynasty. Psalm 89, for example, has two layers. In the earlier preexilic one, God proclaims: "I have made a covenant with my chosen one, / I have sworn to my servant David. . . . Forever I will keep my steadfast love for him, / and my covenant with him will stand firm" (89:3, 28). But the later, postexilic layer concludes that God has "renounced the covenant with your servant" and "defiled his crown in the dust" (89:39) and finally pleads with God, "Lord, where is your steadfast love of old, / which by your faithfulness you swore to David?" (89:49).

Still, surely, God's "steadfast love" will maintain the covenant "forever." For example, the refrain "for his steadfast love endures forever" is repeated in every single one of the twenty-six verses of

Psalm 136. Also, the invocation of God's "steadfast love" is repeated again and again from Psalms 5:7 to 147:11, as if repeated assertion could assuage or annul the fear of covenantal dissolution. But how, granted covenant's intrinsic mutuality, could God be expected to maintain a broken covenant?

Notice two other words alongside "steadfast love" in this verse:

Bless the Lord, O my soul,
and do not forget all his benefits—
who *forgives* all your iniquity,
who heals all your diseases,
who redeems your life from the Pit,
who crowns you with steadfast love and *mercy*. (103:2–4)

If divinity's steadfast love preserves humanity's broken covenant, there must be forgiveness of *Sanction* or, failing that, at least mercy in *Sanction*.

Forgiveness is requested both individually (25:18) and collectively (79:9) and is granted both individually (32:5) and collectively (65:3): "For you, O Lord, are good and forgiving, / abounding in steadfast love to all who call on you" (86:5), but God is also "an avenger of their wrongdoings" (99:8).

Mercy, possible even with forgiveness refused, is also requested individually (40:11) and collectively (123:3) and is granted both individually (23:6) and collectively (116:5). That God is "merciful" is asserted regularly (86:15 = 145:8).

Just as the magnificent Prophetic tradition of divine distribution is marred relentlessly by the threat of divine retribution, so is the equally magnificent Psalmic tradition of celebratory praise marred relentlessly by pleading for forgiveness and crying out for mercy. But if you think not of divine punishments but of human consequences, you must also think not of divine forgiveness but of the possibility of human *change*, and not of divine mercy but of the *given time* within which that human change is possible, before it is too late.

Furthermore, if you imagine God with the metaphor of a person, prayer means speaking with that person. But if you imagine God with the metaphor of process, prayer means acting collaboratively with that process. Or, as Paul warned in Romans, "we do not know how to pray as we ought" (8:26).

"Ah, Assyria, the Rod of My Anger"

THINK WITH ME ONE final time about the 700s BCE and about the confrontation between Isaiah and Sennacherib, and even more so between Yahweh, God of Israel, and Ashur, God of Assyria.

We already saw, with the Deuteronomic tradition, that Assyria's covenantal emphasis on *Sanction* over *History* and, within *Sanction*, on curses over blessings had deeply influenced the biblical imagination of God in terms of external divine punishments rather than internal human consequences (Chapters 5 and 6).

But Assyria's divine mandate was an imperial expansion westward to Syria and then down the Levantine coast into Egypt. Thus, if Sennacherib was, as he claimed, "King of the World, King of Assyria," then Ashur was not just God of Assyria, but God of the World. Furthermore, Ashur was a very unusual Near Eastern deity, as he had neither divine consort nor divine family. He was not the personification of a natural force, but of Assyrian imperial power.

We also saw in this chapter that as Sennacherib marched home from unconquered Jerusalem, his contemporary Isaiah explained Judea's devastation as divine punishment for covenantal default on social justice (1:1–17). But two other prophecies from that same time insist that Yahweh, God of Israel—and not Ashur, God of Assyria—is God of the "whole earth" (10:14; 14:26).

Still, although Ashur as World-God facilitated Isaiah's contrary vision of Yahweh as World-God, matrix was, as always, an ambiguous gift for biblical tradition. With that model came Assyrian terrorism as ethnic identity, foreign policy, and military strategy. Here are three examples, almost at random:

> I covered the wide plain with the corpses of their fighting men. I dyed the mountains with their blood. (King Shalmanasar III, 859–824 BCE)
>
> I filled the plain with the bodies of their warriors, like grass. Their testicles I cut off, and tore out their privates like the seeds of summer cucumbers. (King Sennacherib, 704–681 BCE)
>
> I tore out the tongues of those whose slanderous mouths had uttered blasphemies against my God Ashur. . . . I fed their corpses, cut into small pieces, to dogs, pigs, vultures, eagles, the birds of the sky and the fish of the ocean. (King Ashurbanipal, 668–627 BCE)

Here, then, is the problem. Yahweh said, "Ah, Assyria, the rod of my anger— / the club in their hands is my fury!" (Isa. 10:5). Unfortunately, if Assyria is the agent of God's anger, it is also the norm of God's character. Far too much of the upper Tigris entered the lower Jordan; far too much of Assyrian imperial theology entered Israelite covenantal theology; far too much of the God Ashur entered into the God Yahweh in the biblical tradition.

"All the Foundations of the Earth Are Shaken"

I CLOSE THIS CHAPTER with a different vision of Yahweh as World-God. We stand once more amid the divine council in heaven but the Supreme God is surrounded this time by the subordinate Gods who rule the earth under a mandate from that High God: "God has taken his place in the divine council; in the midst of the gods he holds judgment" (Ps 82:1). This time, however, the divine complaint is not against Israel, but against those who rule the earth, against the powers that be:

> How long will you judge unjustly
> and show partiality to the wicked?
> Give justice to the weak and the orphan;
> maintain the right of the lowly and the destitute.
> Rescue the weak and the needy;
> deliver them from the hand of the wicked. (82:2–4)

This indictment begets neither apology nor excuse from the subordinate Gods but simply this response: "They have neither knowledge nor understanding, / they walk around in darkness" (82:5a). The powers that be do not even understand the accusation, do not recognize the problem, do not acknowledge their responsibility. They say, as it were: "We are about power. Who brought up this justice thing?"

Then comes this searing result: "all the foundations of the earth are shaken" (82:5b). There is nothing about external curses or punishments as *Sanction* from God. Instead there is the terrible consequence that injustice shakes the foundations of the earth.

But what about those sub-Gods who failed their divine mandate to maintain equity for all—especially those who are socially, politically, and economically vulnerable? What is the promised "judgment" (82:1)? Only this:

> I say, "You are gods,
> children of the Most High, all of you;
> nevertheless, you shall die like mortals,
> and fall like any prince." (82:6–7)

Once again, this is not an external punishment but an internal consequence. Gods of power die when their supporting power dies.

(What have you heard recently from Zeus or Jupiter?) But how could a God of distributive justice ever die unless the thirst for distributive justice were already dead in every human heart?

In summary, when you stand in ecstatic presence in the divine council and hear the divine complaint, it is very, very important to know what you brought with you and projected onto God, to know whether suffering is an external divine punishment or an internal human consequence, and to know whether God is violent or nonviolent.

Where Are We Now and What Comes Next?

THE PRICE OF THE Deuteronomic tradition's influence on the Prophetic and Psalmic traditions is that the character of the biblical God becomes more about covenant than creation in terms of the human-divine relationship, more about *Sanction* than *History* in terms of covenant, and more about curses than blessings in terms of *Sanction*.

For my titular problem, *How to Read the Bible and Still Be a Christian*, both the Prophetic and Psalmic traditions are extremely ambiguous on the character of God. Indeed, there is almost a rhythm of assertion-and-subversion within and across each tradition.

On the one hand, both traditions presume a God of nonviolent distributive justice and a world that should be managed in the image and likeness of that God. On the other hand, both traditions hold that vision in acute dialectic with a God of violent retributive justice. You will have heaven on earth, says their God, or I will give you hell here instead.

In other words, I can now extend that diagram for the *Covenantal Divide* I have already proposed:

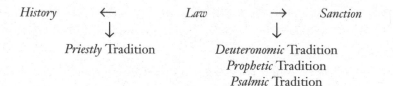

I think, once again, that we Christians must read both traditions, accept and follow their divine assertion, understand and not follow their human subversion, and appreciate the biblical honesty that retained that full dialectic of yes-and-no, expansion-and-contraction, vision-and-negation.

My next chapter considers two other traditions, the Wisdom or *Sapiential* tradition (*sapientia* is Latin for "wisdom") and the Kingdom or Eschatological tradition (*eschaton* is Greek for "last"). The former looks back to beginnings and the latter looks forward to endings. Each tradition sets out a way for people to read the Bible and think about how to remain in faithful covenant with God. This was a fidelity that was rendered extremely difficult within a matrix of international Greek culture that was already established and an international Roman power that was already developing.

I make one emphatic point as a conclusion from my preceding chapters and as a preparation for the following ones.

Imagine the upside-down triangle formed by the Anatolian plateau in the west, the Mesopotamian plain in the east, and the Egyptian valley in the south. Squeeze the sides of that triangle between the Mediterranean Sea and the Arabian desert, and there in the Levantine narrows is tiny Israel. It was the hinge of the three then-known continents of Europe, Asia, and Africa. It was the corridor, cockpit, and cauldron of imperial competition. With warring superpowers first to the north and south, then to the west and east, invasion for Israel was inescapable and defeat inevitable—despite Deuteronomy 28.

If Israel had spent all of its life on its knees praying, the only change in its history would have been to have died—on its knees praying. It is a crime against both humanity and divinity to tell a people so located that a military defeat is a punishment from God. This holds also, but for different reasons, on disease and drought, famine and even earthquake. No wonder, therefore, that Israel's Psalter is filled with cries for forgiveness and pleas for mercy.

External invasions, internal famines, and any other disasters were not divine punishments for *how* the people of Israel lived its covenantal life with God, but human consequences of *where* the nation of Israel lived it.

CHAPTER 8

Wisdom and Kingdom

Empire was accepted as the "maturity of the times" and the
unity of the entire known civilization, but it was challenged in its
totality by a completely different ethical and ontological
axis. . . . From the abyss of the social world always
arose the memory of what it tried to bury.
MICHAEL HARDT AND ANTONIO NEGRI, *Empire* (2000)

LUKE'S GOSPEL SPEAKS OF "the law of Moses, the prophets, and the psalms" (24:44). If you read that triad, you might think there is nothing else in the Bible, or at least nothing of any significance. But that is to ignore the Wisdom tradition, that latter-day Pentateuch of Job, Proverbs, Ecclesiastes or Qoheleth, the Book of Wisdom or Wisdom of Solomon, and Ecclesiasticus or Wisdom of Sirach. (Christians disagree, by the way, on whether those last three books are canonical, semicanonical, or noncanonical.)

The matrix for this tradition is not those imperial covenants of Anatolia or Mesopotamia but the scribal schools of Egypt that graduated skilled bureaucrats and learned retainers for the administration of palace and temple. Think, for example, of Israel under direct Egyptian control throughout the 200s BCE. I will discuss two very basic aspects of that Wisdom tradition. (Each continues this book's fundamental questions about the character of the biblical God.)

"She Is a Breath of the Power of God"

THE FIRST ASPECT IS by far the most important. This is the tradition's focus on Wisdom as God's divine medium for creation. Across the three books of Proverbs, Sirach, and Wisdom, Wisdom as personified process is splendidly described and gloriously exalted, especially as she speaks about herself in her own voice (Hebrew *hokhmah*, Greek *sophia*, and Latin *sapientia* are all feminine words for "wisdom").

First, in the book of Proverbs, Wisdom is both transcendent in heaven and immanent on earth. As transcendent,

> The Lord created me at the beginning of his work,
> the first of his acts of long ago.
> Ages ago I was set up,
> at the first, before the beginning of the earth. (8:22–23)

Then, Wisdom became God's agent for the rest of creation: "The Lord by wisdom founded the earth; / by understanding he established the heavens" (3:19). Finally, therefore, Wisdom was with God, was

> . . . beside him, like a master worker;
> and I was daily his delight,
> rejoicing before him always,
> rejoicing in his inhabited world
> and delighting in the human race. (8:30–31)

As immanent, Wisdom is personified as a philosopher walking the city streets in search of willing students. She "cries out" for followers: "in the street . . . in the squares . . . at the busiest corner . . . at the entrance of the city gates . . . on the heights . . . beside the way . . . at the crossroads . . . beside the gates . . . at the entrance" (1:20–21; 8:2–3). Wisdom is a very public, open, inclusive, nondiscriminatory seeker of students. Her only condition is a willingness to accept her as a gracious gift.

All of that is, as it were, a commentary on Genesis 1:26–28 and Psalm 8. Divine Wisdom has so infused all of creation with intelligibility that humanity can understand the meaning of creation (or of, if you prefer, evolution) by making observations about the created world, by summarizing those observations in proverbs and aphorisms, and by studying them with learned teachers.

Next, in the book of Sirach, the creation of humankind is deliberately reminiscent of Genesis 1: "The Lord created human beings out of earth . . . granted them authority over everything on the earth . . . endowed them with strength like his own, / and made them in his own image. / He put the fear of them in all living beings, / and gave them dominion over beasts and birds" (17:1–4). Furthermore, "Discretion and tongue and eyes, / ears and a mind for thinking he gave them. / He filled them with knowledge and understanding, / and showed them good and evil" (17:6–7). Notice that as in Genesis 2–3, knowledge of good and evil is a positive gift.

Furthermore, Wisdom as personified process glories in her cosmic and universal role at creation:

I came forth from the mouth of the Most High,
and covered the earth like a mist. . . .
Over waves of the sea, over all the earth,
and over every people and nation I have held sway. . . .
Before the ages, in the beginning, he created me,
and for all the ages I shall not cease to be. (24:3, 6, 9)

Finally, in the book of Wisdom, Wisdom is again personified magnificently as "the fashioner of all things . . . a spirit that is intelligent, holy . . . all-powerful, overseeing all / and penetrating through all spirits . . . more mobile than any motion; / because of her pureness she pervades and penetrates all things" (7:22–24). Again:

> For she is a breath of the power of God,
> and a pure emanation of the glory of the Almighty;
> therefore nothing defiled gains entrance into her.
> For she is a reflection of eternal light,
> a spotless mirror of the working of God,
> and an image of his goodness. (7:25–26)

And again:

> She is more beautiful than the sun,
> and excels every constellation of the stars.
> Compared with the light she is found to be superior,
> for it is succeeded by the night,
> but against wisdom evil does not prevail. (7:29–30)

As I read these verses over and over again, I have one very basic question: If Wisdom, as the immanent presence and external face of God, is not a person but a personified process, how do we know that the biblical God is not also a personified process rather than a person?

Restorative Charity or Distributive Justice?

THE SECOND ASPECT OF the Wisdom tradition raises a very delicate question. In our preceding chapters, from law through prophets to psalms, we have seen two correlative emphases: nonviolent distributive justice on earth *or else* violent retributive justice from heaven. I compare this now with the Wisdom tradition and then ask that question.

On one hand, the Wisdom tradition seems, at first glance, as focused on distributive justice as both the law and the prophets. Think of "righteousness, justice, and equity" (Prov. 1:3; 2:9) or this most prophet-style assertion: "To do righteousness and justice / is more acceptable to the Lord than sacrifice" (21:3). Or again, "The field of the poor may yield much food, / but it is swept away through injustice" (13:23).

Also, again and again, the tradition mentions the tandem pair of the poor and the needy: "there are those whose teeth are swords, / whose teeth are knives, / to devour the poor from off the earth, / the needy from among mortals" (30:14). Again: "They thrust the needy off the road; / the poor of the earth all hide themselves" (Job 24:4). And again: "My child, do not cheat the poor of their living, / and do not keep needy eyes waiting" for "the bread of the needy is the life of the poor; / whoever deprives them of it is a murderer" (Sir. 4:1; 34:25).

Furthermore, the tradition mentions those other vulnerable ones—the widows and orphans: "The Lord tears down the house of the proud, / but maintains the widow's boundaries. . . . Do not remove an ancient landmark / or encroach on the fields of orphans" (Prov. 15:25; 23:10). Again: "You have sent widows away empty-handed, / and the arms of the orphans you have crushed. . . . They drive away the donkey of the orphan; / they take the widow's ox for a pledge . . . for from my youth I reared the orphan like a father, / and from my mother's womb I guided the widow" (Job 22:9; 24:3; 31:18). And again: "Be a father to orphans, / and be like a husband to their mother; / you will then be like a son of the Most High, / and he will love you more than does your mother. . . . He will not ignore the supplication of the orphan, / or the widow when she pours out her complaint" (Sir. 4:10; 35:17).

Here, then, is that delicate question: Does the Wisdom tradition have the same passion for distributive justice as does the Prophetic tradition, or is it a passion for distributive charity? It is clearly against oppressing, ignoring, or refusing society's vulnerable ones. But is its focus on personal and individual justice rather than on systemic and structural economic justice on earth? Is the Wisdom tradition a radical vision of justice or a liberal vision of charity, and if it is the latter, what if the biblical God is a radical rather than a liberal?

On the other hand, with regard to retributive justice, the Wisdom tradition entails human consequences rather than divine punishments. Look at these divergent sequences:

Sequence 1: Covenant   →   Sanction   →   Divine Punishments
Sequence 2: Creation   →   Wisdom   →   Human Consequences

This is surely a profound breakthrough toward a nonviolent God, a cyclical return, as it were, to Genesis 1 or Psalm 8. Wisdom is so infused into the created fabric of cosmic existence and is offered so freely and openly to human conscience that any rejection of her begets internal consequences.

We have already glimpsed problems with Sequence 1, both from Israel's geopolitical position on the Levantine coast and from particular applications that did not work—Manasseh's too-long life, Josiah's too-early death, and Job's particular case.

But the Sequence 2—as a combination of the Priestly and the Wisdom traditions—offers an alternative vision. Wisdom reveals to us our created destiny, discloses for us our created identity with its rights and responsibilities. To reject Wisdom is not to break an external law and bring about divine punishments, but to destroy our internal character and bring about human consequences.

Finally, I repeat the suggestion from the end of the last chapter: if there is no such thing as divine punishments, but rather only human consequences, then there is no such thing as divine forgiveness, but rather only the possibility of human change; and there is no such thing as divine mercy, but rather only the time within which change is still possible before it is too late.

It is surely long overdue for us to rethink both the theory of divine punishment and the resultant practice of pleading for forgiveness and crying out for mercy throughout the Christian tradition. Instead, we could begin, aside from natural disasters and random accidents, to accept fully the human consequences for what we do, and especially to acknowledge the internal effects of denying our human identity and rejecting our human destiny—as proposed in, say, Genesis 1 and Psalm 8.

I turn next from beginnings to endings, from creation to re-creation, from the Wisdom or Sapiential tradition to the Kingdom or Eschatological tradition.

"Those Who Are Wise Shall Shine like the Brightness of the Sky"

MY PARADIGMATIC EXAMPLE HERE is the book of Daniel, a work fictionally and imaginatively located in the transition from the Babylonian (or Chaldean) Empire to the Median-Persian Empire in the 500s BCE, but factually and historically composed under the Syrian Empire in the 160s BCE. Its ruler, Antiochus IV Epiphanes, was always threatened by Egypt to the south and newly by Rome to the west. To protect at least his southern frontier, he attempted to force Israel into closer political, economic, and social subservience.

Finding resistance from the covenantal fidelity of the people, he desecrated the Temple and invoked a religious persecution. Or, as Daniel pseudo-foretold:

He shall speak words against the Most High
shall wear out the holy ones of the Most High,
and shall attempt to change the sacred seasons and the law;
and they shall be given into his power
for a time, two times, and half a time. (7:25; see also 8:9–12;
    9:27; 11:31–33)

That is, it took the Jewish Maccabean Revolt about three and a half years to defeat him (1–2 Macc.).

The editorial layering of the book is clearly indicated by the change of language from Aramaic in Daniel 2:4b–7:28 to Hebrew everywhere else. But much more significant is the change of genre from the stories in Daniel 1–6 to the visions in Daniel 7–12. Why such a striking difference in content, and why were stories and visions ever combined to form twin halves of the same book? There is an obvious continuity and an equally obvious discontinuity between these stories and visions, but the continuity is on the surfaces, and the discontinuity is in the depths.

Here are two surface continuities. First, the subject of both halves of Daniel is the interpretation of esoteric or secret data: dreams (chapters 2 and 4), visions (chapters 7, 8, and 10–12), mysterious texts (chapter 5), and prophetic scriptures (chapter 9). Second, the protagonists of both halves are "wise men" steeped in esoteric or mantic wisdom (*maskilim* in 1:4 and 11:33, 35; 12:3). They are certainly closer to the special knowledge in the Prophetic tradition than to the common knowledge in the Wisdom tradition, but still, they are esoteric interpreters rather than either prophetic witnesses or scribal teachers.

Here are two deeper discontinuities. First, interpretation is *by* Daniel in the stories but *to* Daniel in the visions—with, of course, divine assistance in both cases. Daniel can explain the mysteries of dreams and texts with indirect heavenly inspiration in chapters 2, 4, and 5. But he cannot explain the mysteries of his visions without direct heavenly interpretation from a divine intermediary, like the archangel Gabriel, in Daniel 8:16 and 9:21. Something new is here and will require a new name, which I explain below.

Second, in the pro-imperialist stories, even if royal rulers often start a tale arrogantly and cruelly, they usually end it by elevating Daniel at court, converting to the true God of heaven, and even singing God's praise across their dominions. Examples are Nebuchadnezzar (2:47; 3:29–4:3; 4:34–37) and "Darius the Mede" (6:25–27) but not Belshazzar—although he still exalts Daniel (5:29). Note especially those extreme accolades for Nebuchadnezzar *despite* his having devastated Jerusalem, destroyed the Temple, and depopulated Judah! (2:37–38; 5:18–19).

In the visions, however, pro-imperialist fantasy changes to anti-imperialist reality, as we see below in Daniel 7. Why? Because, even if those stories were credible under, say, the imperial Persian restoration during the 400s BCE, they were certainly no longer credible under the imperial Syrian persecution in the 160s BCE. That novel situation of religious persecution, as distinct from standard political oppression, created a sea change between earlier stories and later visions.

On the one hand, the *Sanction* of Deuteronomic theology is taken for granted and presumed to be normative throughout all of Daniel. In the stories, God rewards Daniel for his fidelity (1:9, 20), and, while he is protected by an angel in the lions' den (6:22), his accusers and their families are devoured (6:24). In the visions, Daniel summarizes past history as a Deuteronomic lament; for example: "All Israel has transgressed your law and turned aside, refusing to obey your voice. So the curse and the oath written in the law of Moses, the servant of God, have been poured out upon us, because we have sinned against you" (9:11).

On the other hand, in the stories, the *Sanction* of rewards or punishments is administered before death in this present life here below. Be it in the fiery furnace or the lions' den, the faithful ones are preserved from martyrdom. But in the visions, the *Sanction* is administered after death in the next life: "Many of those who sleep in the dust of the earth shall awake, some to everlasting life, and some to shame and everlasting contempt. Those who are wise shall shine like the brightness of the sky, and those who lead many to righteousness, like the stars forever and ever" (12:2–3).

In the light of those continuities and discontinuities between stories and visions, it is not plausible to suggest that the stories of Daniel 1–6 are there simply to introduce the character Daniel who will be the recipient of the visions of Daniel 7–12. Surely Daniel 1, or any single story about him in Daniel 2–6, would have sufficed for that purpose, and besides, why give Shadrach, Meshach, and Abednego a whole chapter to themselves (2:49–3:30) if it were all just to introduce Daniel?

My own explanation is, first, that there is a profound change from the basic theology of Daniel 1–6 to that of 7–12—at least with regard to God and imperialism; and, second, that their sequential combination in Daniel 1–12 proclaims the inadequacy of the theology of the stories and the ascendancy of the theology of the visions.

"The People of the Holy Ones of the Most High"

ONE PRELIMINARY POINT OF matrix is needed for what follows. Around the early seventh century BCE, Hesiod's *Works and Days* divided human history into five successive, and declining, eras: the Golden, Silver, Bronze, Heroic, and Iron Ages. But was it not possible to imagine a better world, even a perfect cosmos, in which that vision of inevitable decline was changed, reversed, transformed?

In the 170s BCE—that is, in the decade before Daniel was composed—the Roman historian Aemilius Sura, as recorded by Velleius Paterculus's *Compendium of Roman History*, said that "the Assyrians were the first of all races to hold world power, then the Medes, and after them the Persians, and then the Macedonians. Then . . . the world power passed to the Roman people" (1.6).

But, of course, Rome as the fifth Kingdom was not just one more of the same. The Roman Empire was the climax and consummation of the past. It was the final Kingdom. It was the last Kingdom. It was the eschatological Kingdom.

I turn now to Daniel 7 as my paradigmatic example of those visions in Daniel 7–12. But there the fifth or climactic, the last or eschatological Kingdom is not that of Rome but of God. I am moving, in other words, into another great biblical tradition—that of God's final transformation and ultimate transfiguration of an old earth ruled by imperial injustice to a renewed earth ruled by eschatological justice.

Daniel saw in his vision "by night the four winds of heaven stirring up the great sea, and four great beasts came up out of the sea, different from one another" (7:2–3). Here are those four beastlike empires with their representative rulers:

1. The first kingdom is Babylonia or Chaldea (7:4), represented by "Nebuchadnezzar" (2:1 through 5:18) and Belshazzar (6:1).

2. The second kingdom is Media (7:5), represented by the very fictional "Darius the Mede" (5:31; 11:1) or "Darius . . . a Mede" (9:1).

3. The third kingdom is Persia (7:6), represented by "Cyrus the Persian" (6:28) or "Cyrus of Persia" (10:1).

4. The fourth kingdom is Greece (7:7), represented by the never-named Alexander, "King of Greece" (8:5–21) or "Prince of Greece" (10:20) or "a warrior king" (11:3).

Those first three empires are all "like" feral beasts (lion, bear, leopard), but no such animal is deemed adequate to describe Alexander's Greece. It is simply "different" in its "devouring . . . breaking in pieces, and stamping" (7:7, 19, 23). But Alexander's early death in 323 BCE turned his victorious generals into competing warlords. Greek-Syria and Greek-Egypt, for example, fought one another seven times over a hundred years.

Next comes the final, climactic fifth kingdom. Daniel's night vision continues with God, the "Ancient One," surrounded by the angelic hosts of the divine council: "The court sat in judgment, / and the books were opened" (7:9–10). God's verdict condemns those four kingdoms—long gone at the time of Daniel's writing (7:12)—but especially the Greek-Syria subkingdom, not even counted among the four and very much present at the time of Daniel's writing (7:11, 26).

Daniel sees "one like a human being [RSV: "son of man"] coming with the clouds of heaven. / And he came to the Ancient One / and was presented before him" (7:13). (The NRSV is sensitive to change the term "son of man" to "human being" to avoid the Hebrew male chauvinism of the former.) The point is to say that imperial rule is "like a feral beast" (7:4–6), while divine rule is "like a human being" (7:13). We know, from elsewhere in Daniel, that this humanlike one is the archangel Michael, leader of the heavenly hosts (10:13, 21; 12:1).

History's climactic last kingdom is the "Kingdom of God," first described in the story (2:38b–44) and then mentioned thrice more (4:3, 34; 6:26) before the threefold sequence here in Daniel 7. First, God's Kingdom is "given" into the heavenly control of that archangel Michael (7:14), the "one like a human being." Next, it is to be "received" and protected by "the holy ones of the Most High," the heavenly hosts of angels (7:18, 22). Finally, it must be brought down to our earth and "given to the people of the holy ones of the Most High" (7:27).

We saw already that tiny Israel was poised precariously first between north and south, with Anatolia and Egypt or Mesopotamia and Egypt, and then between west and east, with Greece and Persia or Rome and Parthia. The people of Israel knew all too well about the great imperial kingdoms of their world. It was Israel's ancient hope—no, better, their ancient faith—that a God of justice in heaven would eventually establish a Kingdom of justice on this earth.

Daniel 7 decrees a fundamental conflict between two archetypal visions of life here on earth, between all past and present imperial kingdoms and a divine Kingdom, prepared already in heaven, protected there by angels, and promised for eventual arrival on earth. We are told that this earthly Kingdom of God, this last or eschatological Kingdom, will be both universal and everlasting, but we are not told when and how it will arrive on our earth, or what exactly it will look like in our world as a structure or a system, a project or a process. Here, however, is how the Kingdom of God is more fully described in other eschatological descriptions within the earlier biblical tradition.

"No One Shall Make Them Afraid"

THE EXPECTATION OF THE Kingdom of God was not original with Daniel 7. Israel had long believed in an eventual great Divine Cleanup of the World, an Extreme Makeover: World Edition, in which justice and peace would replace injustice and violence. The biblical tradition marched inevitably to this chanted mantra: God will overcome—someday.

Here are some earlier biblical equivalents to the Kingdom of God, and I insist that the vision, however it is named, is always about a renewed creation here below heaven in a radically changed world:

1. *The Harvest of God*
    The time is surely coming, says the Lord
    when the one who plows shall overtake the one who
        reaps,
    and the treader of grapes the one who sows the seed;
    the mountains shall drip sweet wine,
    and all the hills shall flow with it. (Amos 9:13)

2. *The Feast of God*
    On this mountain the Lord of hosts will make for all
        peoples
    a feast of rich food, a feast of well-aged wines,
    of rich food filled with marrow, of well-aged wines
        strained clear.
    And he will destroy on this mountain
    the shroud that is cast over all peoples,
    the sheet that is spread over all nations;
    he will swallow up death forever.
    Then the Lord God will wipe away the tears from all
        faces,

and the disgrace of his people he will take away from all
the earth,
for the Lord has spoken. (Isa. 25:6–8)

3. *The Community of God*
In days to come
the mountain of the Lord's house
shall be established as the highest of the mountains,
and shall be raised up above the hills.
Peoples shall stream to it,
and many nations shall come and say:
"Come, let us go up to the mountain of the Lord,
to the house of the God of Jacob;
that he may teach us his ways
and that we may walk in his paths."
For out of Zion shall go forth instruction,
and the word of the Lord from Jerusalem. (Mic. 4:1–2 =
Isa. 2:2–3; see also Zech. 8:20–23)

4. *The Peace of God*
i. *Between animals*
The wolf shall live with the lamb,
the leopard shall lie down with the kid,
the calf and the lion and the fatling together,
and a little child shall lead them.
The cow and the bear shall graze,
their young shall lie down together;
and the lion shall eat straw like the ox. (Isa. 11:6–7)

ii. *Between animals and humans*
The nursing child shall play over the hole of the asp,
and the weaned child shall put its hand on the
adder's den.

They will not hurt or destroy
on all my holy mountain;
for the earth will be full of the knowledge of the Lord
as the waters cover the sea. (Isa. 11:8–9)

iii. *Between humans*
[God] shall judge between many peoples,
and shall arbitrate between strong nations far away;
they shall beat their swords into plowshares,
and their spears into pruning hooks;
nation shall not lift up sword against nation,
neither shall they learn war anymore;
but they shall all sit under their own vines and under
    their own fig trees,
and no one shall make them afraid;
for the mouth of the Lord of hosts has spoken.
    (Mic. 4:3–4 = Isa. 2:4)

None of these visionary synonyms for the Kingdom of God is about the earth's destruction or abandonment; they are about its transformation and transfiguration. They are not about the end of the world's existence and our emigration elsewhere, but about the end of the world's evil, injustice, oppression, violence, and war. This vision was part of Israel's tradition for more than half a millennium before Daniel 7.

There is one codicil, however: if you find an expression like the "Kingdom of God" too antique and too male, my titles on those preceding texts give you some alternatives. But please, do not locate, say, the Peace of God elsewhere than on this earth. Also please, do not subvert its religio-political, ethico-moral, and socio-economic vision as other than a radical challenge to the normalcy of civilization.

"Where There Is No Vision, the People Perish"

DANIEL, IN THE JEWISH homeland of the 160s BCE, imagined the coming Kingdom of God without detailing its programmatic content. Others, in the Jewish Diaspora of the 150s BCE, gave content that echoed that just-seen Peace of God.

First, a preliminary word about matrix. The Sibyl was a female ecstatic and charismatic prophetess whose historical origins were as obscure as her raptured utterances. The Sibylline tradition was later maintained in texts that were recorded, redacted, and re-created from Greeks and Romans to Jews and Christians. Here, then, is how Egyptian Jews imagined God's "Kingdom for all ages" upon a transformed earth in the *Sibylline Oracles*:[11]

1. *The Transformed Physical World:* "For the all-bearing earth will give the most excellent unlimited fruit to mortals, of grain, wine, and oil and a delightful drink of sweet honey from heaven, trees, fruit of the top branches, and rich flocks and herds and lambs of sheep and kids of goats. And it will break forth sweet fountains of white milk" (3.744–749).

2. *The Transformed Animal World:* "Wolves and lambs will eat grass together in the mountains. Leopards will feed together with kids. Roving bears will spend the night with calves. The flesh-eating lion will eat husks at the manger like an ox, and mere infant children will lead them with ropes. For he will make the beasts on earth harmless. Serpents and asps will sleep with babies and will not harm them" (3.788–795).

3. *The Transformed Human World:* "There will be no sword on earth or din of battle, and the earth will no longer be shaken, groaning deeply. There will no longer be war or drought on earth, no famine or hail, damaging to fruits, but there will be great peace throughout the whole earth. King will be friend to king to the end of the age. The Immortal in the starry heaven will put in effect a common law for men throughout the whole

earth. . . . And then, indeed, he will raise up a Kingdom for all ages among men, he who once gave the holy Law to the pious, to all of whom he promised to open the earth and the world and the gates of the blessed and all joys and immortal intellect and eternal cheer. From every land they will bring incense and gifts to the house of the great God. . . . Prophets of the great God will take away the sword for they themselves are judges of men and righteous kings. There will also be just wealth among men for this is the judgment and dominion of the great God" (3.751–758, 767–773, 781–784).

It is quite easy—maybe with smile, smirk, or sneer—to dismiss such dreams of absolute physical fertility (no labor) or total animal benignity (no meat). It is quite easy to mock lions liking lettuce, panthers eating pasta, and jaguars choosing jam.

Maybe, in reading such eschatological imaginings, it is prudent to distinguish between a rhapsodic and impossible *utopia* (Greek for "not-place") and an ecstatic but possible *eutopia* (Greek for "good-place"). *Eutopia* imagines a social world of universal peace, a human world of nonviolent distributive justice where all get a fair and adequate share of God's world as God's Kingdom. If that is a silly fantasy or utopian delusion with no possible eventual advent, our human species may be as magnificent and doomed as was the saber-toothed tiger.

The book of Proverbs warns that "where there is no vision, the people perish" (29:18 KJV). But with the wrong vision, they perish even faster. *Eutopia* or eschatology may even be necessary if our species, protected by moral conscience rather than by animal instinct, is not ultimately to destroy itself—because escalatory human violence has never invented a weapon we did not use, never invented one less powerful than what it replaced, and never ceased to confuse lull with peace. Are those eschatological visions of distributive justice and universal peace nothing more than empty fantasies?

Finally, here is another example of those Jewish *Sibylline Oracles* to bring that eschatological faith up to the time of Jesus. It imagines that transformed human world like this: "The earth will belong equally to all, undivided by walls or fences. It will then bear more abundant fruits spontaneously. Lives will be in common and wealth will have no division. For there will be no poor man there, no rich, and no tyrant, no slave. Further, no one will be either great or small anymore. No kings, no leaders. All will be equal together" (2.319–324). This text is dated to the turn of the common era.

Where Are We Now and What Comes Next?

THE WISDOM OR SAPIENTIAL tradition and the Kingdom or Eschatological tradition both speak to the whole earth. Be it from start or finish, from beginning or end, from creation or re-creation, they speak to all of human history. But they do so with Israel as God's focal experiment and paradigmatic example for a just world (Sir. 24:23; Dan. 7:27). As God's "chosen people," biblical Israel is chosen to be the model for all people.

These two traditions present us once more with the Biblical Heartbeat of assertion-and-subversion that offers both problem and solution to my titular challenge of *How to Read the Bible and Still Be a Christian.* They do so within the matrix of Greek cultural power and Roman military might.

The magnificent assertion of Wisdom as the open intelligibility of creation—or, if you prefer, of evolution—is subverted, or at least mitigated, by a liberal emphasis on distributive charity rather than a radical demand for distributive justice. As always, in *How to Read the Bible and Still Be a Christian,* I urge you to accept assertion, resist subversion, and still acknowledge the honesty of a story that gives you both.

Similarly, the equally magnificent Eschatological tradition's assertion of God's dream for a transformed earth and a transfigured world of nonviolence—that is, for a Kingdom of justice and peace here below—is subverted by visions of divine violence in punishments and penalties for noncompliance.

One could imagine a combination of both of these assertions that proclaimed an eschatological wisdom that opposed the normal imperial wisdom of peace through victory with the radical divine wisdom of peace through justice. This is, by the way, exactly what the Apostle Paul proclaimed in 1 Corinthians 1:26–2:13: "We speak God's wisdom, secret and hidden, which God decreed before the ages for our glory" (2:7).

At this point, I return to the *Covenantal Divide* and enlarge it here once again:

Creation ← *History* ← *Law* → *Sanction* → *Eschaton*
↓ ↓ ↓
Priestly Tradition *Deuteronomic* *Kingdom*
Wisdom Tradition Tradition Tradition
Prophetic Tradition
Psalmic Tradition

In Part IV, I move into the first-century CE where the matrix involves huge paradigm shifts in both Roman politics and Jewish religion. At that century's start, Rome changed from a republic ruled by two elected aristocrats to an empire ruled by one dynastic autocrat. At its end, Judaism changed from a religion centered on the Temple and sacrifice to one centered on the Torah and study. Amid such seismic events, Jesus in the Jewish homeland or Paul in the Jewish Diaspora hardly seemed like earthquakes about to shake the foundations of their world. But they were, and how to read them and still be a Christian is by far the most difficult part of this book.

PART IV

Community

CHAPTER 9

Israel and the Challenge of Rome

The pendulum of history drips blood at every swing.
FREYA STARK, *Rome on the Euphrates* (1966)

DURING THE FIRST TWO hundred years of Roman presence in the Jewish homeland, four armed revolts occurred against that all-powerful imperial control. Josephus, in the *Jewish War* (*JW*) and *Jewish Antiquities* (*JA*); Philo, in *On the Embassy to Gaius* (*OEG*); and Cassius Dio, in *Roman History* (*RH*) all reported on these events, which happened more from Roman mismanagement than from Jewish intransigence:

1. Under Augustus (4 BCE): Separate revolts occurred all over the country, ending with two thousand people crucified in Jerusalem (*JW* 2:39–79 = *JA* 17.250–298).

2. Under Nero (66–74 CE): A centrally led revolt ended with Jerusalem devastated, the Temple destroyed, and Masada captured (*JW* 2.277–7.455).

3. Under Trajan (115–117): A revolt in Cyprus and North Africa was luridly rather than historically described at Rome (*RH* 68.32.1–3).

4. Under Hadrian (132–135): A massive guerrilla-style revolt was provoked by Hadrian's actions in Jerusalem (*RH* 69.12.1–14.4).

All of these rebellions are frequently mentioned and very well-known. But far less emphasized is the fact that, in Jewish response to Roman occupation, even more incidents of large-scale, organized, controlled, *nonviolent* resistance occurred, especially during the years between those first two violent revolts.

"We Will Die Sooner Than Violate Our Laws"

As you look at the following list of recorded nonviolent protests, notice two rather striking features. One is that they all happened in the lull between the armed revolts and legionary reprisals of 4 BCE and 66 CE. Another is that they were spread out under all the Julio-Claudian emperors from Augustus to Nero:

1. Under Augustus (6 CE): Against Quirinius's census for taxation, led by Judas the Galilean and Saddok the Pharisee (*JW* 2.118, 433; 7.253 = *JA* 18.1–10, 23–25; 20.102).
2. Under Tiberius (26–36): Against Pilate's iconic military standards in Jerusalem (*JW* 2.169–174 = *JA* 18.55–59; *OEG* 199–305).
3. Under Tiberius (26–36): Against Pilate's use of Temple funds for a Jerusalem aqueduct (*JW* 2.175–177 = *JA* 18.60–62).
4. Under Caligula (40): Against placing Caligula's divine statue in the Jerusalem Temple (*JW* 2.184–203 = *JA* 18.261–283; *OEG* 225–260; Tacitus, *Histories* 5.9.2).
5. Under Claudius (41–54): Against Fadus (44–46), the first Roman governor of the whole country, led by Theudas (*JW* 20.97–98; Acts 5:36).
6. Under Nero (54–68): Against Felix, the next governor (52–60), for "every kind of cruelty and lust," led by multiple

unnamed "prophets" (*JW* 2.258–260 = *JA* 20.167b–168). But also, and especially, one led by "the Egyptian" (*JW* 2.261–263 = *JA* 20.169–171; Acts 21:38).

The sequence of these actions seems a deliberate program to create a nonviolent alternative and prevent another violent revolt like the one in 4 BCE that left behind it a devastated homeland.

I give you warning when you read those sources—especially Josephus, for whom Roman rule was God's will, both politically and theologically. He accordingly excoriates alike both violent and non-violent resistance. But you can still notice that under Claudius and Nero, his texts always admit that the leaders were "prophets," and then he contents himself by calling them "imposters" or "deceivers" or "charlatans," or by saying that they had, compared with the violent rebels, "purer hands but more impious intentions."

Still, against that unqualified condemnation from a Jewish historian at the end of the first century CE; here is a much more qualified one from a Roman historian at the start of the second century: "Antonius Felix [52–60] practiced every kind of cruelty and lust, wielding the power of a king with all the instincts of a slave. . . . Still the Jews' patience lasted until Gessius Florus [64–66] became procurator: in his time war began" (Tacitus, *Histories* 5.9–10). Notice, by the way, that same accusation by both Josephus and Tacitus: "Felix practiced every kind of cruelty and lust."

Let us look for a moment at that program of nonviolent resistance started by Judas the Galilean and Saddok the Pharisee against the Roman census in 6 CE. It combined three elements creatively and powerfully—namely, eschatological vision, nonviolent resistance, and an acceptance of martyrdom, if necessary or inevitable. Josephus even admits that theology despite himself:

> They [the Jews] think little of submitting to death in unusual forms and permitting vengeance to fall on kinsmen and friends if only they may avoid calling any man master. Inasmuch as

most people have seen the steadfastness of their resolution amid such circumstances, I may forgo any further account. For I have no fear that anything reported of them will be considered incredible. The danger is, rather, that report may minimize the indifference with which they accept the grinding misery of pain. (*JW* 18:23–24)

Josephus invidiously combines all and any resistance to Rome into one *massa damnata*. It takes a very careful reading of his texts to distinguish clearly between, say, violent rural bandits and urban terrorists on the one hand and nonviolent prophetic martyrs on the other. Still, repeatedly, from Judas and Saddok in 6 CE until it was finally too late in 66 CE, certain Jews "with high devotion in their hearts, stood firm and did not shrink from the bloodshed [or hardship] that might be necessary" (*JA* 18:5) if nonviolent resistance resulted in martyrdom.

"We Are, As You See, Without Any Weapons"

I CHOOSE THE INCIDENT under Caligula regarding the placement of his divine statue in the Jerusalem Temple as a paradigmatic example of the ongoing program of massed nonviolent resistance between 4 BCE and 66 CE. I do so because we have reports about it from three separate sources: Josephus (twice), Philo, and Tacitus. Imagine it as a program involving these five component elements.

The first element is the *Roman situation*. During the winter of 39–40, Caligula ordered the Syrian governor Petronius to take two of his four legions south to Jerusalem and place a statue of Caligula's imperial divinity in the Temple. By April–May of 40 Petronius's army was encamped at Ptolemais on the Mediterranean coast, but by November he had gone eastward to Tiberias rather than southward to Jerusalem. He was prudently and wisely, but also deliberately and dangerously, delaying obeying the emperor's instructions. Caligula's insanity could have started the Great Roman War of 66–74 in 39–40 CE.

The second element is the *Jewish response*. Both Josephus and Philo emphasize the huge numbers of people who confronted Petronius at Ptolemais and Tiberias. Josephus writes that a "vast multitude" of Jews "assembled with their wives and children in the plain of Ptolemais" (*JW* 2.192). Philo says "a countless multitude like a cloud occupied the whole of Phoenicia" and "was divided into six companies, one of old men, one of young men, one of boys; and again in their turn one band of aged matrons, one of women in the prime of life, and one of virgins" (*OEG* 226, 227). And Josephus again: "many tens of thousands faced Petronius on his arrival at Tiberias . . . so many tens of thousands . . . in many tens of thousands" (*JA* 18.270, 277, 279).

The third element is *nonviolent resistance*. Both of these authors emphasize the nonviolent aspect of the Jewish reaction, one already evident in the calculated presence of women and children. At Ptolemais, Philo notes their comment, "'We are, as you see, without any weapons'" (*OEG* 229). At Tiberias, Josephus reports that the people said, "'On no account would we fight . . . but we will die sooner than violate our laws'" (*JA* 18.271).

The fourth element is an *agricultural strike*. Both authors also emphasize that this was active nonviolent resistance by agricultural strike. At Ptolemais in late April or early May of 40 CE, "it was just at that moment the very height of the wheat harvest and of all the other cereal crops" (*OEG* 249). At Tiberias, by late October or early November, "the country was in danger of remaining unsown—for it was seed-time and the people had spent fifty days idly waiting" on Petronius (*JW* 2.200). "They continued to make these supplications for forty days. Furthermore, they neglected their fields, and that, too, though it was time to sow the seed" (*JA* 18.272).

Herodian aristocrats appealed to Caligula, saying that "the people . . . had left their fields to sit protesting and . . . since the land was unsown, there would be a harvest of banditry" (*JA* 18.274). Petronius, in turn, promised an appeal to Rome on behalf of the protesters, encouraging them to "Go, therefore, each to your own occupation, and labor on the land . . . to attend to agricultural matters" (*JA* 18.283–284).

The fifth and final element is *collective martyrdom*. The active but nonviolent resistance by agricultural strike was explicitly backed by a readiness for collective martyrdom. The people told Petronius, "If we cannot prevail with you in this, then we offer up ourselves for destruction" (*OEG* 233), and "they presented themselves, their wives, and their children, ready for the slaughter" (*JW* 2.197). "Falling on their faces and baring their throats, they declared that they were ready to be slain" (*JA* 18.271). But, luckily for all concerned, that impasse was solved by the assassination of Caligula on January 24 of 41 CE. In the light of all that, I believe that Tacitus's description of the Jewish reaction to Caligula's statue is incorrect: "They chose rather to resort to arms, but the emperor's death put an end to their uprising" (*Histories* 5.9.2). Such an uprising would have been what was expected, but that is not what happened.

I turn next to see how the Romanization process of Israel began and to underline that those two very divergent options for resistance—nonviolent and violent—were both a reality from the very beginning under Herod the Great by 4 BCE.

"King of the Jews"

LATE IN THE YEAR 4 BCE, the Roman Senate voted unanimously for the Idumean-Jewish Herod to be their new "King of the Jews." That official decree replaced the century-old Judean-Jewish dynasty of the Hasmoneans with that of the Idumean-Jewish Herodians. Accompanied by his patron-sponsors, Octavian and Mark Antony, the "King of the Jews" ascended the Capitoline Hill to offer sacrifice to Jupiter Optimus Maximus, supreme God of the Romans. Herod then sailed home to take over his Kingdom and create a Roman Israel. Consider these actions:

For his Roman masters, he built a magnificent all-weather port on the open Mediterranean coast. It was a state-of-the-art facility using hydraulic cement that, mixed with volcanic tufa, solidified under water to form caissons for the great warehouse-topped breakwater piers. He called the port Sebastos (Greek for Augustus) and the city Caesarea.

Furthermore, he crowned city and port with the (very first?) Temple of Rome and Augustus, the divine couple at the center of the new world order. He carefully oriented it off the city's westward-facing grid so that its gleaming marble facade looked northwestward toward the harbor entrance and the faraway city of Rome. Romanization had begun hard—at least in the south of the country.

For his Jewish subjects, in another state-of-the-art construction, he enlarged the Temple's plaza to the size of fifteen football fields and called it the Court of the Gentiles. It is surely hard to imagine Herod as apostle of the Gentiles, but still, the Temple was now "a house of prayer for all peoples" (Isa. 56:7 = Mark 11:17).

Furthermore, to appease popular nostalgia by forming a Hasmonean-Herodian alliance, he married the Hasmonean princess Mariamme. (Later he executed her, and in protest, "Mary" became a favorite name for newborn females in the first-century Jewish homeland.)

Did all go well with Herod's twin-pronged project for creating Romanized Jews in a Roman Israel? Here is one particular and one general response from the people at his death in 4 BCE.

The particular one involved a demonstration of nonviolent resistance when it was falsely rumored that Herod had died. He had placed a giant golden eagle, the symbol of Roman power, atop the main gate of the Temple. Josephus describes "an insurrection of the populace" when two teachers, Judas and Matthias, persuaded their youthful students to tear it down and break it to pieces "at mid-day when numbers of people were walking about in the Temple." Herod forgave the general populace but burned alive the teachers and students involved in the destruction (*JW* 1.648–655).

Later, Josephus retells that activist demonstration much more fully and emphasizes that the unarmed protagonists knew beforehand that they were "doomed to death," waited to be arrested "courageously . . . while the rest of the multitude took to flight," and told Herod that they "would endure death or whatever punishment you will inflict on us . . . because of our devotion to piety" (*JA* 17.151–167).

Josephus interprets the event in the Hellenistic tradition of the noble death, but it is clear that in the Jewish tradition, it is a nonviolent act of protest, an activist demonstration backed by acceptance, if necessary, of martyrdom for God.

The general response occurred after Herod's actual death. It involved multiple and independent armed insurrections, violent revolts all over the country. Eventually three Syrian legions, along with large forces of Arab auxiliaries, moved inexorably southward to suppress all resistance.

The Syrian governor Varus "burned the city of Sepphoris [capital of Galilee] and reduced its inhabitants to slavery." Then he moved through Samaria to Judea, sacking all the fortified villages on his march. "The whole district became a scene of fire and blood, and nothing was safe against the ravages of the Arabs." Varus burned Emmaus to the ground and on finally reaching Jerusalem, "those who appeared to be the less turbulent individuals he imprisoned; the most culpable, in number about two thousand, he crucified" (*JW* 2.68–75 = *JA* 17.298).

From his multiple palace-fortresses to those two world-class construction projects, Herod's Romanization focused especially or even exclusively on the south of Israel—and in the generation *before* John and Jesus. But what about Galilee—and the generation *of* John and Jesus? And how was it that Herod's son Antipas had ruled there for more than a quarter-century in peace before resistance started against him in the 20s CE?

"The Sea of Galilee, Also Called the Sea of Tiberias"

FIRST, RECALL THAT THOSE acts of nonviolent resistance I have already mentioned usually had a specific occasion or a particular focus within the general Romanization of the country. Is that also true for John the Baptist and Jesus of Nazareth? Was there an individual flash point that sparked their resistance and ignited their movements against Herod Antipas, tetrarch of Galilee to the west and Perea to the east of the Jordan River?

Antipas's abiding dream was to become "King of the Jews." It was a dream he never abandoned—right to the end. After all, his father, Herod the Great, had been the Rome-appointed tetrarch of Galilee before advancing to become Rome-appointed "King of the Jews." Why could he not do the same? Antipas visited Rome on that mission, under Augustus in 4 BCE and again under Caligula in 37 CE. (He never made it, by the way, as it was Herod Agrippa who was appointed "King of the Jews" in 39 CE.)

Under Tiberius, emperor between Augustus and Caligula, Antipas made his second move to obtain his father's country and title. That, by the way, is my interpretation not of his thoughts, but of his actions—of two acts in particular, each of which demands interpretation since both elicited very serious opposition. Each is also modeled, in miniature, on what his father had done by building Caesarea Maritima for his Roman masters and by marrying a Hasmonean princess for his Jewish subjects.

For his Roman masters, Antipas attempted to increase his tax base by changing the capital city from Sepphoris in the Beth Netofa Valley to Tiberias on the Lake of Galilee. Ancients did not relocate their almost-sacred capital cities without serious reasons. Imagine the opposition to that relocation, both from aristocratic courtiers with elegant villas at Sepphoris and from artisans and scribes in its outlying villages. But Antipas did have a serious reason to make this move. He intended to impress Emperor Tiberius by commercializing the lake, monopolizing its fish—dried, salted, and sauced—for export, and thereby increasing revenue, tax, and tribute. And, of course, he called his new capital Tiberias in honor of the emperor.

For his Jewish subjects, the Herodian Antipas needed a Hasmonean bride. So he divorced Phasaelis, his Nabatean Arab wife, and married Herodias, granddaughter of the beloved Mariamme. Herodias divorced her husband to marry Antipas.

Then, with his lake newly commercialized and his marriage newly consummated, Antipas was all set, he hoped, to become—by Rome's appointment—"King of the Jews." But then John and Jesus entered the picture and focused precisely on that public-relations marriage—not just for moral reasons, but for religio-political resistance. (Faithful observance of Jewish law often quietly grounded and peacefully demonstrated resistance to Rome.)

John criticized Antipas's marriage because Herodias's divorced husband had been Antipas's own brother, but Jesus's criticism was more sweeping and severe against Antipas and Herodias:

> For Herod himself had sent men who arrested John, bound him, and put him in prison on account of Herodias, his brother Philip's wife, because Herod had married her. For John had been telling Herod, "It is not lawful for you to have your brother's wife." (Mark 6:17–18; also Matt. 14:3 and Luke 3:19)
>
> . . . [Jesus] said to them, "Whoever divorces his wife and marries another commits adultery against her; and if she divorces her husband and marries another, she commits adultery." (Mark 10:11–12)

I hold any further consideration of John and Jesus until the next chapter, but keep this instance in mind. You can already imagine how Antipas's relocated and renamed capital, along with its attendant commercialization of the Lake of Galilee, changed the economic situation for all those who had used the lake freely as communal property before the 20s CE. Hence this question: if "the earth is the Lord's and all that is in it" (Ps. 24:1), whose was the lake and all of its fishes?

"They Will Call Him Son of the Most High"

I CONCLUDE WITH A final element of the matrix in which both John and Jesus lived and died. It specifies the contemporary eschatological vision as messianic. But what does that mean?

In establishing God's Kingdom on Earth, would God use some agent, intermediary, ambassador, vice-regent, or plenipotentiary? If yes, would that agent be an earthly or a heavenly figure, or maybe even an earthly figure suffused with heavenly power? Would the agent be a priest, a prophet, or a king and be anointed not only with sacred oil, but also with transcendental power? (Hebrew's *Messiah* and Greek's *Christos* means "the Anointed One.") Here are two examples of the pre-Christian Jewish expectation of such a transcendental Messiah, both dating to the final half of the first century BCE.

The first example is from the *Psalms of Solomon*. Its matrix is the first direct experience of violent Roman power within the Jewish homeland. Pompey conquered Jerusalem and desecrated its Temple in 63 BCE: "a man alien to our race . . . a lawless one laid waste our land . . . he did in Jerusalem all the things that gentiles do for their gods in their cities" (17:7, 11, 14). But in 48 BCE Pompey was assassinated on an Egyptian beach: "his body was carried about on the waves in much shame, and there was no one to bury him" (2:27). So surely soon, surely now, God would

> raise up for them [the Jews] their king, the Son of David . . . to smash the arrogance of sinners like a potter's jar; to shatter all their substance with an iron rod; to destroy the unlawful nations with the word of his mouth . . . he will judge peoples and nations in the wisdom of his righteousness . . . all shall be holy, and their king shall be the Lord Messiah. [For] he will not rely on horse and rider and bow, nor will he collect gold and silver for war. Nor will he build up hope in a multitude for a day of war. (17:21, 23–24, 29, 32–33)

On the one hand, this coming Messiah is not exactly a pacifist, and the Romans seem destined for extermination rather than conversion. On the other hand, he is certainly not a military Messiah organizing a rebellion against Rome. Notice those repeated phrases about "the word of his mouth" (17:24, 35) or "the might of his word" (17:36). The ability to destroy one's enemies by "word" alone is a transcendental ability akin to the creative word of God in Genesis 1.

The other example is from a Dead Sea Scroll fragment found in Cave 4 at Qumran:

> He [the Messiah] will be called Son of God, and they will call him Son of the Most High. Like sparks of a vision, so will their Kingdom be; they will rule several years over the earth and crush everything; a people will crush another people, and a city another city. Until the people of God arises [or: until he raises up the people of God] and makes everyone rest from the sword. His Kingdom will be an eternal Kingdom, and all his paths in truth and uprightness. The earth will be in truth and all will make peace. The sword will cease in the earth, and all the cities will pay him homage. He is a great god among the gods [or: the great God will be his strength]. He will make war with him; he will place the peoples in his hand and cast away everyone before him. His Kingdom will be an eternal Kingdom.

Once again, if God "will make war" with this Messiah, he is hardly a pacifist. But with a transcendental figure, one could still wonder how exactly that "rest from the sword" would be accomplished.

Granted all that, one point, mentioned already in the preceding chapter, needs emphatic repetition. Israel against Rome was never simply the standard conflict of the conquered against the conqueror, a colony against an empire. Instead, it was a clash between eschatological visions as Israel proclaimed a still-future Golden Age and Rome an already-present Golden Age. A just, peaceful, and nonviolent world was the still-future eschaton for Israel but the already-present empire for Rome.

By the first century CE, it was for many in the Jewish homeland a time of choice between Roman and Jewish versions of that fifth and final Kingdom of Earth. It was, for many, a time for courageous decision between God and Rome, between fidelity and infidelity to covenantal law.

Finally, therefore, this question presses: How *precisely* was the ruling style of God different from that of Rome; how *exactly* were God's justice and peace different from those of Rome? If, as was certainly the case, the Pax Romana was established by war and conquest, violence and victory, was the Pax Divina to be established by similar but far, far superior force? Enter John and Jesus in the next chapter.

Where Are We Now and What Comes Next?

I THINK, AND NOT just with easy hindsight, that any Jewish teachers or thinkers, sages or prophets in early-first-century Roman Israel who did not wonder how to react to Roman imperialism failed their history, their tradition, their covenant, and their God. Reaction could be a withdrawal or a participation, an acceptance or a resistance, violence or nonviolence. But surely, between 4 BCE and 66 CE, it was clear that the Jewish homeland, and maybe even Judaism itself, was living through years that would be fateful for the future.

We have just seen that during those seventy years, there were so many instances of large-scale organized nonviolent resistance as to indicate a theoretical stance and a practical program for survival with dignity and integrity. Given that matrix, my next chapter on *How to Read the Bible and Still Be a Christian* focuses on the Baptism movement of John and the Kingdom movement of Jesus within it. By now you can probably guess my questions.

One is whether either or both of those protest movements included violent or nonviolent resistance to Rome. If the answer is negative, another question is even more difficult. Did either or both of them avoid present human violence since they expected divine violence in the future? If the answer, once again, is negative, will we find, as so we have often found across our biblical journey, that the assertion of divine nonviolence will be adapted into its subversion?

CHAPTER 10

Jesus and the Radicality of God

Not "Revelation"—'tis—that waits,
But our unfurnished eyes—
EMILY DICKINSON, "Poem 685" (c. 1863)

I COMPARE AND CONTRAST the programs of John and Jesus with no intention of exalting the latter over the former, or vice versa. I am convinced that Jesus learned tremendously from John and that he eventually changed his own vision because of what happened to his mentor. Later, when he came to disagree with John, he was still very careful not to disrespect him. Furthermore, it was probably the abiding popularity of John that protected Jesus from Antipas in Galilee. "That fox" (Luke 13:32) would have calculated carefully how long before he could execute another popular prophet.

"Wisdom Is Vindicated by All Her Children"

MY FIRST QUESTION ASKS whether, even within that common matrix of eschatology, nonviolence, and martyrdom, the visionary programs of John and Jesus involve continuity or discontinuity, agreement or disagreement.

On the one hand, Matthew gives them both the same announcement. First, "John the Baptist appeared in the wilderness of Judea, proclaiming, 'Repent, for the kingdom of heaven has come near'" (3:1–2); and, later, "Jesus began to proclaim, 'Repent, for the kingdom of heaven has come near'" (4:17). On the other hand, Luke makes their programs quite different as he has Jesus respond to John's question from prison (7:22). To repeat the question: Are the visionary programs of John and Jesus similar or different?

One rather fascinating indication of difference is in the Q Gospel—another source concerning Jesus that both Matthew and Luke used along with the book of Mark ("Q" is short for *Quelle*, German for "source"). It reports that opponents of John and Jesus, adversaries who disliked them both equally, described them like this:

> For John came neither eating nor drinking, and they say, "He has a demon"; the Son of Man [that is, Jesus, from Dan. 7:34] came eating and drinking, and they say, "Look, a glutton and a drunkard, a friend of tax collectors and sinners!" (Matt. 11:18–19 = Luke 7:33–34)

I leave aside those judgments about difference in character, but I accept those descriptions about difference in program. After all, people fast in preparation for the future, and they feast in celebration of the present (see also Mark 2:18–20).

Furthermore, Jesus began as a follower of John who accepted John's program. It is historically secure that John baptized Jesus in the Jordan, as underlined by a later evangelical diffidence in admitting that fact: Mark accepts it (1:9), Matthew debates it (3:13–15), Luke hurries it (3:21), and John omits it (1:36). But later, when Jesus finds his own voice, he announces, "Truly I tell you, among those born of women no one has arisen greater than John the Baptist; yet the least in the kingdom of heaven is greater than he" (Matt. 11:11 = Luke 7:28).

As far as I can see, therefore, their two programs are divergent, but I also emphasize that Jesus's movement involved a change from John's program to his own quite different one. The next step is to look first at John's Baptism movement and then comparatively at Jesus's Kingdom movement. Where exactly did they differ?

I make one preliminary warning: it is necessary to distinguish clearly between the historical John and the biblical John because in our present texts, John is focused primarily on Jesus. But John's program was fully operational before Jesus ever appeared on the public horizon. Josephus, for example, explains John's life and death without ever mentioning Jesus and calls John "the Baptist" without ever mentioning Jesus's baptism (*JA* 18.116–119).

Always remember, therefore, that the historical John, separate from our present biblical John, was not the forerunner of Jesus, but of God; not the preparer of Christ's advent, but of God's Kingdom. But that transformation from the historical to the biblical John is a preliminary example of the ongoing assertion-and-subversion process within the New Testament. It is a preliminary instance of what will happen to Jesus and to Paul in the rest of this Part IV on "Community."

"More Than a Prophet"

First, with regard to eschatology, I note that the historical John was an eschatologist, and indeed, an apocalyptic one—that is, a prophet who claimed a special divine revelation (*apocalypse* is Greek for "revelation") about God's Divine Cleanup of the World. In itself, such a revelation could be about any matter concerning God's Kingdom and not specifically about imminence or exclusively about violence. But in the heightened tension of Roman Israel, only one matter was of supreme importance: When would the Kingdom arrive? Soon? Now? And if not now, why not? In other words, apocalyptic eschatology is often taken, far too narrowly, to mean imminent or even violently imminent eschatology.

John had a very persuasive answer to "when?" and a very compelling program. The Kingdom was imminent, and its advent awaited only preliminary and preparatory endeavor. I summarize John's program in this imaginary conversation:

People: Empires are getting stronger, not weaker, so what holds up God's intervention, and what will God do about the Romans?

John: It is your sins that are the obstacle to God's advent. How can God come to an impure people?

People: So what can we do? How are we to become God's purified people ready for God's advent?

John: We will reenact God's last great liberation—in the Return from the Babylonian exile—and maybe also the even earlier one of the Exodus from Egypt. As in both those cases, we will come from the desert east of the Jordan. We will pass through the river with water cleansing our bodies and repentance cleansing our souls. We will then reenter the promised land in a purified state. Then, and it will be soon, God will come as promised from of old.

(Notice, by the way, that the Exodus was violent in both the exit from Egypt and the entrance into Canaan, while the Return was non-violent in both the exit from Babylon and the entrance into Israel.) In any case, whether right or wrong, John's program was tremendously persuasive and, faced with the military might of Rome, gave one at least some active hope for the imminent advent of God's Kingdom.

Also, of course, that imminent advent would require a transcendent divine intervention for which one should prepare but in which one could not participate. It was for God and God alone to transform the world, and Israel, and Galilee, and the Lake of Galilee. For John, God's Kingdom was a matter of imminent intervention.

Second, with regard to nonviolent resistance, note that it has two aspects—one concerning humans and the other concerning God. John's eschatological program was not humanly or physically violent. He was not, as it were, mustering desert marauders to wage guerrilla warfare with the troops of either Antipas or Pilate. How can I be sure of this? Because, although Antipas arrested John, he made no attempt to round up John's followers. That is how Rome dealt with nonviolent as opposed to violent sedition: execute the leader, and the followers will disperse and disappear.

The legal strategy of handling nonviolent dissent by executing the leader is codified by the most renowned of Rome's jurists in *The Opinions of Julius Paulus Addressed to His Son*: "The authors of sedition and tumult, or those who stir up the people, shall, according to their rank, either be crucified, thrown to wild beasts, or deported to an island" (Book V, Title XXII.1).

The other aspect of nonviolent resistance is even more important, as it involves the very character of God. Did John preclude human violence *now* to allow for overwhelming divine violence *soon*? The present biblical John gives us two contradictory responses on this question, as he is subjected to that biblical pattern of assertion-and-subversion. What was the answer of the *historical* John the Baptist?

Mark calls John "the beginning of the good news of Jesus Christ, the Son of God" and applies to him what "is written in the prophet Isaiah . . . the voice of one crying out in the wilderness: / 'Prepare the way of the Lord, / make his paths straight'" (1:1–3). That same quotation and application appears in Matthew 3:3, Luke 3:4, and John 1:23.

The quotation in Isaiah 40:3 was the rhapsodic and ecstatic proclamation of Second Isaiah (the prophet who came after the First Isaiah of Isa. 1–39 whom we met in Chapter 7) that the Babylonian exiles would be allowed to cross the desert wilderness and return home under the Persian restoration of the 500s–400s BCE.

In Mark's understanding of John, the advent of the eschatological Kingdom of God was like that great nonviolent liberation and celebration of half a millennium earlier. But when you turn to the Q Gospel, a very different picture of God's character and God's imminent advent emerges.

In the Q Gospel, John, although never physically violent, is rhetorically and brutally violent. He greeted "many Pharisees and Sadducees" or "the crowds" that came for baptism with the words, "You brood of vipers! Who warned you to flee from the wrath to come?" (Matt. 3:7 = Luke 3:7). He then specified that divine wrath with these twin and fiery metaphors:

> Even now the ax is lying at the root of the trees; every tree therefore that does not bear good fruit is cut down and thrown into the fire. . . . His [God's] winnowing fork is in his hand, and he will clear his threshing floor and will gather his wheat into the granary; but the chaff he will burn with unquenchable fire." (Matt. 3:10, 12 = Luke 3:9, 17)

In fact, Luke is so dismayed by that violent version of John's "good news" from the Q Gospel that he creates three rather more positive messages and places them in between his version of those twin metaphors:

> The crowds asked him, "What then should we do?" In reply he said to them, "Whoever has two coats must share with anyone who has none; and whoever has food must do likewise." Even tax collectors came to be baptized, and they asked him, "Teacher, what should we do?" He said to them, "Collect no more than the amount prescribed for you." Soldiers also asked him, "And we, what should we do?" He said to them, "Do not

extort money from anyone by threats or false accusation, and be satisfied with your wages." (3:10–14)

My conclusion is that for the historical John the Baptist, the Kingdom's advent involved not a violently avenging God, but a miraculously liberating God. I think, however, that the Q Gospel morphed John's God from nonviolent to violent. (In the next chapter we will see how it will do exactly the same to the historical Jesus.)

Third, with regard to potential martyrdom, Josephus wrote that "John, because of Herod [Antipas's] suspicions was brought in chains to Machaerus and there put to death" (*JA* 18.119). That martyrdom in a palace-fortress on a hilltop in the southernmost part of Antipas's Transjordanian territories is given as history in Josephus but as parable in Mark—he models it on the classic tale of a ruler's imprudent promise during a banquet feast.

From the Jewish matrix, Ahasuerus (imprudent), Haman (bad), and Esther (good) in the book of Esther morphed into Antipas (imprudent), Herodias (bad), and John (good) in Mark. Notice, for example, that open promise of "even half of my Kingdom" from Ahasuerus to Esther (5:3, 6; 7:2) and from Antipas to Salome (Mark 6:23).

From the Roman matrix, Mark models his story on the well-known Roman horror story about the consul Lucius Quinctius Flamininus in 184 BCE. He executed a condemned man during a banquet on the whim of his mistress Placentia. For Mark, Herodias is simply another Placentia and John's death another official obscenity.

I turn next from the Baptism movement of John to the Kingdom movement of Jesus but within that same contemporary triad of eschatological fervor, nonviolent resistance, and willingness for the possibility or inevitability of martyrdom.

"The Kingdom of God Is Among You"

FIRST, WITH REGARD TO eschatology: John claimed that God's Kingdom, the great Divine Cleanup of the World, was imminent. But eventually—and only eventually—Jesus said no, God's Kingdom was already present. For example: "If it is by the Spirit [or "finger," as in Luke] of God that I cast out demons, then the kingdom of God has come [*ephthasen*] to you" (Matt. 12:28 = Luke 11:20).

That "has come" is, by the way, an inexcusably weak translation of the Greek, because the verb *phthanein* does not mean simply "come" but rather "come before" or "anticipate" or "precede." A literal translation would be, "then already has come upon you the Kingdom of God." Here are some other examples of that already present Kingdom in the challenge of Jesus.

One is the title of this section: "Once Jesus was asked by the Pharisees when the kingdom of God was coming, and he answered, 'The kingdom of God is not coming with things that can be observed; nor will they say, "Look, here it is!" or "There it is!" For, in fact, the kingdom of God is among you'" (Luke 17:20–21). Saying that the Kingdom is "among you" indicates that it is an external, communal process, rather than simply "inside you" as an internal, private, and spiritual reality.

Another example of the present Kingdom is from the Q Gospel, which was heavily revised in Luke 16:16 but originally preserved in Matthew 11:12: "From the days of John the Baptist until now the kingdom of heaven has suffered violence, and the violent take it by force." What is attacked is already present.

Also, of course, are those startling beatitudes, not as promises about what will happen in the future but as statements about what is already present (Matt. 5:3–12 = Luke 6:20–23). Think, for example, of the first one, "Blessed are you who are poor, / for yours is the kingdom of God" (Luke 6:20). In that first clause, the Greek has no verb, "were" or "are" or "will be"—"Blessed the poor"—making it more of an absolute and unqualified assertion of blessedness. Something nonintuitive is happening here and now, because in God's kingdom the poor are no longer poor! The world's transformation has begun.

Finally, Mark sums up the message of Jesus with this: "The time is fulfilled, and the kingdom of God has come near; repent, and believe in the good news" (1:15). How do we know that "has come near" means not "is shortly imminent" but "is already present"? Recall from Chapter 8 that Daniel said "one like a son of man" (RSV) was to preserve the heavenly Kingdom of God until it descended to earth for "the people" (7:13, 18, 22, 27). But for Mark, that "one *like* a son of man" has become instead a title, with Jesus as "the Son of Man" already here on earth—in life (2:10, 28), in death and resurrection (8:31; 9:12, 31; 10:33, 45; 14:21, 41), and in majesty (8:38; 9:9; 13:26; 14:62). That the Kingdom of God was already present on earth for Jesus means that the Son of Man was already present on earth for Mark.

But what possible sense could such a claim make when the world was utterly unchanged—with Antipas in Tiberias, Pilate in Jerusalem, and Tiberius in Rome (or on Capri)? How was God's Kingdom already present when Rome's Kingdom was still clearly in charge? Jesus's assertion represented, and could only represent, a paradigm shift, a tradition swerve, a disruptive innovation within his contemporary Jewish eschatological expectation.

The paradigm shift from *imminent* to *present* necessarily entailed a shift from unilateral divine *intervention* to bilateral divine and human *cooperation*. (I remind you again that covenant was always a bilateral process.) Imagine Jesus saying: "You have been waiting for God while God has been waiting for you. No wonder God's Kingdom *has* never arrived. You have been awaiting intervention while God has been awaiting collaboration. No wonder God's Kingdom *will* never arrive."

Imagine also this question put to Jesus: "Do you mean that without our participation, the Kingdom will never, ever appear, will never, ever exist here below upon a transformed earth?" And Jesus says, "Yes!" The best commentary on this, besides Emily Dickinson's epigraph to this chapter, came from Archbishop Desmond Tutu, preaching at All Saints Episcopal Church in Pasadena, California, in 1999: "God, without us, will not; as we, without God, cannot."

Why did Jesus change from John's vision of imminent intervention to his own vision of present collaboration? I can think of only one reason: John expected God to come imminently, but what came imminently was Antipas. John died and God did nothing. Maybe, thought Jesus, there was no divine intervention, not now, not soon, not ever. There was, is, and will be only a divine and human covenant, collaboration, and participation.

I think that Antipas's execution of John changed Jesus's understanding of God's Kingdom from one of intervention to one of collaboration. *God's Kingdom comes only in so far as people take it upon themselves or enter into it.* It was a bilateral, participatory, collaborative, and covenantal program. For how can there be a kingdom without members, citizens, and communities?

But confusion started immediately. In the face of such a paradigm shift, some will reject it emphatically, some will accept it enthusiastically, and others, maybe the majority, will accept it but understand it within the older paradigm (as some have seen, for instance, a car as a horseless carriage, a radio as a wireless, and a computer as a visual typewriter).

The old paradigm imagined an imminent divine intervention; the new one envisioned a present divine and human collaboration. Those who accepted Jesus's vision of the already present but only-if-collaborative Kingdom almost immediately added on an imminent consummation to that process. The lure of "how soon?" returned to haunt forever the new Christian-Jewish vision.

Even those who, like Paul and Mark, insist on the Kingdom's here-and-now presence and the challenge of entering it promise an imminent consummation, and so, as we see in the next chapter, does the book of Revelation. That "over soon" was wrong, of course. Maybe even Jesus himself imagined a swift conclusion to the Kingdom's advent. But I myself am far from convinced on that point. My reason is not to claim that Jesus did not commit an error but because the strongest evidence of that belief seems to come not from the historical Jesus himself, but from what the earliest tradition placed on his lips.

Here are three examples that are *not* from the historical Jesus but from later tradition speaking through him: "Truly I tell you, there are some standing here who will not taste death until they see that the kingdom of God has come with power" (Mark 9:1); "Truly I tell you, this generation will not pass away until all these things have taken place" (Mark 13:30); "truly I tell you, you will not have gone through all the towns of Israel before the Son of Man comes" (Matt. 10:23). In any case, if Jesus said any of these things, he was flatly wrong—off by two thousand years, and still counting. His being right or wrong about the end of God's Kingdom did not damage his fundamental message, which was not about the *end* but about the *start* of God's Kingdom.

I also wonder whether discussing the Kingdom's end was, and still is, a refuge from facing the Kingdom's start; whether debating the Christian future was, and still is, a strategy for avoiding the Christian present. If we can postpone the entire eschatological challenge of God's Kingdom to a future, unilateral, divine intervention in heaven, we can avoid the challenge of a present, bilateral, divine and human collaboration on Earth.

Second, with regard to nonviolent resistance: For Jesus, as previously for John, I distinguish between human and divine violence. How do I know that the Kingdom movement was not at least planning physical human violence? I give the same answer as for John above. Pilate judged Jesus to be a revolutionary, and therefore he required an official, legal, and public execution of Jesus. But Jesus was nonviolent rather than violent, and therefore there was no need to round up any of his followers. Pilate got it exactly correct.

Josephus, in *Jewish Antiquities* from the end of the first century, and Tacitus, in *Annals* from the start of the second century, define "Christians" as followers of a "Christ." They agree that Jesus had been executed, but both immediately note that, despite that, his movement continued and spread:

When Pilate, upon hearing him [Jesus] accused by men of the highest standing amongst us, had condemned him to be crucified, those who had in the first place come to love him did not give up their affection for him. . . . And the tribe of the Christians, so called after him, has still to this day not disappeared. (*JA* 18.63–64)

Christus, the founder of the name, had undergone the death penalty in the reign of Tiberius, by sentence of the procurator Pontius Pilatus, and the pernicious superstition was checked for the moment, only to break out once more, not merely in Judaea, the home of the disease, but in the capital itself, where all things horrible or shameful in the world collect and find a vogue. (*Annals* 15:44)

In both of these texts, there is a certain implicit surprise that executing the leader failed to finish off the movement. That required some explanation—be it an unbroken love or a contagious pathogen. A leader killed *should* have meant a movement dead.

What about divine violence? Jesus's nonviolent resistance, and that of his followers, was explicitly based on the character of God, and our call to be members of God's Kingdom was seen as God's Family:

Love your enemies and pray for those who persecute you, so that you may be children of your Father in heaven; for he makes his sun rise on the evil and on the good, and sends rain. . . . Be perfect, therefore, as your heavenly Father is perfect. (Matt. 5:44–45, 48)

For Jesus, seeing humans as God's children derives from his fundamental vision of God as householder of the universal family in the world home. For example, in what some Christians call the Lord's Prayer, the term "Father" (Matt. 6:9 = Luke 11:2) is a patriarchal presumption, and a cultural misnomer, for "householder."

For Jesus, therefore, nonviolent resistance to evil is divine before it is human and should be human because it is divine. All, both friends and enemies, both defenders and attackers, must receive love and prayer. All must get their fair share in a world of God's single and universal family. That is how distributive justice works within a normal human family. It is not egalitarianism, but *enough-ism*.

Third, with regard to potential martyrdom: Jesus did not take his Kingdom movement to Jerusalem that Passover to get himself killed. For that, he need not have left Galilee. But after the death of John, he knew the possibility, but not the certainty, of death. Jesus did not plan martyrdom through suicide-by-official. The evidence is that he hoped to avoid it, probably because every martyr needs a murderer, and martyrdom should never be willed or wanted—only accepted and endured.

At the city gate and in the Temple plaza, his nonviolent demonstrations were protected by the "crowd" who followed him—despite and against their own authorities (Mark 10:46; 11:8–10, 18, 32; 12:12, 37). Furthermore, he left Jerusalem each night for the safety of Bethany (11:1, 11, 12, 19, 27; 14:3). By what we call Wednesday of Holy Week, the authorities had given up: "The chief priests and the scribes were looking for a way to arrest Jesus by stealth and kill him; for they said, 'Not during the festival, or there may be a riot among the people'" (14:1–2). In other words, Jesus had almost gotten away with his action; but "stealth" arrest at night on his way to Bethany and a swift crucifixion prevailed—facilitated by either Judas's treachery or Caiaphas's spies.

Finally, Jesus's vision of God's Kingdom is best seen in two parables—that is, stories that never happened as events in history but are profoundly true as symbols of vision and metaphors of content.

The first parable illustrates that choice between Barabbas and Jesus (15:6–8). Remember that Mark is writing after the Temple's destruction, Jerusalem's devastation, and Israel's desolation in the war of 66–74 CE. He imagines an earlier choice between two possible saviors.

One is the *violent* freedom fighter called "Barabbas [who] was in prison with the rebels who had committed murder during the insurrection." The other is the *nonviolent* Son-of-the-Father named Jesus. *Oh, Jerusalem*, mourns Mark, *you chose the wrong option.* As you can see, Barabbas's followers are arrested with Barabbas, but as mentioned above, Jesus's followers are not arrested with Jesus. The ultimate difference between Jesus and Barabbas is that between nonviolent resistance and violent rebellion.

The second parable creates a conversation between Pilate and Jesus (John 18:36). It is often only half cited, like this: "My kingdom is not from this world." If you stop there, it could mean that Jesus's Kingdom is not about this world, but about the next world, the next life, or heaven; not about anything political, but about purely religious matters; not about the external world, but about only the internal spiritual life. But here is Jesus's full parabolic statement:

> My kingdom is not from this world. If my kingdom were from this world, my followers would be fighting to keep me from being handed over. . . . But as it is, my Kingdom is not from here.

Notice that very deliberate framing structure: "not from this world" and "not from here" mean that Jesus's followers cannot use violence even to free Jesus from Pilate. The ultimate difference between Jesus and Pilate or between God's Kingdom and Rome's Empire is that between nonviolent resistance and violent oppression.

Where Are We Now and What Comes Next?

ONCE AGAIN, AS ALWAYS, so far on our biblical journey, that rhythm of assertion-and-subversion is very evident. In this chapter, we have seen it operative with regard to the Baptism movement of John. The assertion of the historical John about the imminent advent of God's

Kingdom as a nonviolent liberation akin to that of the return from Babylonian exile in Mark and John was subverted by the divine violence placed on John's lips in the Q Gospel. How to read John involves seeing that change, accepting his assertion, refusing its subversion, and appreciating the honesty and integrity of a biblical tradition that holds on to both affirmation and negation for our discrimination.

Having just seen what happened to John in this chapter, you can probably anticipate what will happen to Jesus in the next one. That will present the greatest challenge in *How to Read the Bible and Still Be a Christian*.

The problem is emphatically not that the historical Jesus was proclaimed as Christ or Son of God by those earliest Christian Jews, but that the nonviolent Jesus became the violent Christ and the violent Son of a violent God. As I have already emphasized, this is not a renewal of that defunct opposition between the "Jesus of history" and the "Christ of faith," but an opposition between the Jesus Christ of both history and faith as nonviolent or violent.

To put it another way: When the academy reconstructs the historical Jesus, is he nonviolent or violent? Also, when the church confesses the evangelical Christ, is he violent or nonviolent? Of course, the historical Jesus is profoundly and theologically significant for the biblical Christ, and Christianity, whether we like it or not, requires a theology founded and grounded on the historical Jesus. In other words, for Christians, God is revealed in Christ, but Christ is revealed in Jesus. If the norm of the Christian Bible is the biblical Christ, then the norm of the biblical Christ is the historical Jesus.

CHAPTER 11

Christ and the Normalcy
of Civilization

All who take the sword will perish by the sword.
MATTHEW 26:52

If you kill with the sword, / with the sword you must be killed.
REVELATION 13:10

ALL TOO OFTEN, IN my opinion, we humans escalate our violence from ideological through rhetorical to physical violence. *Ideological violence* judges certain others to be inhuman, subhuman, and lacking in one's own humanity. *Rhetorical violence* speaks on that presumption by debasing those others with rude names, crude caricatures, and derogatory stereotypes or by excluding them as political "traitors" or religious "heretics." *Physical violence,* and even lethal violence, acts on those presuppositions either by illegal attack or, if one has attained social power, by official, legal, political action.

In this chapter, I watch for any escalatory violence, ideological through rhetorical to physical, as the Kingdom movement of the historical Jesus is acculturated to the drag of Roman normalcy. In other

words, assertion bows to subversion and the radicality of God suc-
cumbs to the normalcy of civilization, as seen for the Christian Bible
so often throughout this book.

"You Snakes, You Brood of Vipers!"

HERE IS AN EXAMPLE of rhetorical violence, chosen almost at
random. In Luke, Jesus says: "Do not judge, and you will not be
judged; do not condemn, and you will not be condemned. Forgive,
and you will be forgiven" (6:37). But in John, he says to "the Jews,"
"You are from your father the devil, and you choose to do your father's
desires" (8:44). That is surely a statement of judgment, condemnation, and unforgiveness. That is surely rhetorical—but certainly not
physical—violence, and rhetorical violence is all that happens within
the Gospels themselves. Still, my question is this: *Did Jesus change his
mind, or did John change his Jesus?*

That case exemplifies, however, a far wider process. It exemplifies
the de-radicalization of the nonviolent Jesus and his acculturation
into the normal violence of civilization. Furthermore, that change is
already present in the earliest accounts about Jesus, and it proceeds
apace across the four canonical Gospels. But even granted the drag
of normalcy, why does that acculturating happen to Jesus so soon?

As Messianic or Christian Jews attempted to persuade their
fellow non-Messianic or non-Christian Jews of the Kingdom's collaborative or covenantal eschatology, they were met with both acceptance and rejection. Polemical interaction was probably bitter and
acrimonious on both sides, and indeed, rhetorical violence was standard in ancient—as in modern—political or religious, philosophical
or theological debate. Then as now, you argued with your opponent
by denigrating motive and intention or by destroying character and
integrity.

But when Messianic or Christian Jews and, eventually, Messianic or Christian Gentiles counterattacked *later*, they did not do

so by using rhetorical violence themselves but by placing it *earlier* on the lips of the historical Jesus. Here are four examples, and for them, recall that Q Gospel seen earlier as the other source—besides Mark—for both Matthew and Luke:

Example 1: Reaction to rejection. In Mark, Jesus tells his companions, "If any place will not welcome you and they refuse to hear you, as you leave, shake off the dust that is on your feet as a testimony against them" (6:11). In other words: "We're outta here!" But the Q Gospel escalated the rhetoric intensely, as you can see in Matthew and Luke. They both begin by following Mark's version (Matt. 10:14 = Luke 10:10–11a) but then continue with these condemnations from the Q Gospel:

> Truly I tell you, it will be more tolerable for the land of Sodom and Gomorrah on the day of judgment than for that town. . . . Woe to you, Chorazin! Woe to you, Bethsaida! . . . I tell you, on the day of judgment it will be more tolerable for Tyre and Sidon than for you. And you, Capernaum,
>
> > will you be exalted to heaven?
> > No, you will be brought down to Hades.
>
> . . . I tell you that on the day of judgment it will be more tolerable for the land of Sodom than for you." (Matt. 10:15; 11:21–24 = Luke 10:12–15)

It is not that Mark erased rhetorical violence from Jesus, but that the Q Gospel created it (recall from the last chapter how the Q Gospel did the same to the historical John the Baptist).

Example 2: Request for proof. People ask Jesus for a miraculous sign to validate his claims. In Mark, Jesus replies with this unqualified and emphatic refusal: "And he sighed deeply in his spirit and said, 'Why does this generation ask for a sign? Truly I tell you, no sign will be given to this generation'" (8:12). Once again, the Q Gospel escalates the saying by adding a threatening sign. Mark's simple "this generation" becomes "an evil and adulterous generation" that "asks for a sign, but no sign will be given to it except the sign of the prophet Jonah" (Matt. 12:39 = Luke 11:29–30; again in Matt. 16:4). Then the "sign of Jonah" becomes a double threat:

> The people of Nineveh will rise up at the judgment with this generation and condemn it, because they repented at the proclamation of Jonah, and see, something greater than Jonah is here! The queen of the South will rise up at the judgment with this generation and condemn it, because she came from the ends of the earth to listen to the wisdom of Solomon, and see, something greater than Solomon is here! (Matt. 12:41–42 = Luke 11:31–32)

Refusing a sign in Mark appears as giving a sign that becomes a condemnation in the Q Gospel.

How can we explain such differences? I locate the Q Gospel's tradition about Jesus in predominantly *Jewish* territory, around the lake in lower Galilee, that is, in the lands originally under Herod Antipas (note mention of Chorazin, Bethsaida, and Capernaum). But I locate Mark's tradition about Jesus in predominantly *Gentile* territory, to the far north and east of the lake, that is, in the lands originally under Herod Philip (note the mention of "the villages of Caesarea Philippi" in Mark 8:27).

I think that the Kingdom movement and Jesus traditions received much more opposition in predominantly Jewish rather than predominantly Gentile territory. Hence, the Q Gospel rather than Mark's Gospel attributes far more rhetorical counterviolence to Jesus. It is not that the Messianic Jews of the Q Gospel were nastier people than those of Mark's Gospel; it is simply that the opposition to them was far greater, and unfortunately, "their" Jesus responded accordingly. This interpretation is confirmed by these next two examples from Matthew's Gospel.

Example 3: Weeping and gnashing of teeth. This phrase usually describes the response of those rejected or condemned. It is used, but only once, in the Q Gospel: "I tell you, many will come from east and west and will eat with Abraham and Isaac and Jacob in the kingdom of heaven, while the heirs of the kingdom will be thrown into the outer darkness, where there will be weeping and gnashing of teeth" (Matt. 8:11–12 = Luke 13:28).

This is, as just discussed, a typical counterrejection placed on the lips of Jesus by the embattled Q Gospel's Christian Jews. But Matthew uses it five more times, and precisely at the end of parables by Jesus:

1. *Parable of wheat and weeds:* "The Son of Man will send his angels, and they will collect out of his kingdom all causes of sin and all evildoers, and they will throw them into the furnace of fire, where there will be weeping and gnashing of teeth" (13:41–42).

2. *Parable of good and bad fish:* "So it will be at the end of the age. The angels will come out and separate the evil from the righteous and throw them into the furnace of fire, where there will be weeping and gnashing of teeth" (13:49–50).

3. *Parable of having and not having a wedding garment:* "He said to him, 'Friend, how did you get in here without a wedding robe?' And he was speechless. Then the king said to the attendants, 'Bind him hand and foot, and throw him into the outer darkness, where there will be weeping and gnashing of teeth'" (22:12–13).

4. *Parable of the good and bad slave:* "The master of that slave will come on a day when he does not expect him and at an hour that he does not know. He will cut him in pieces and put him with the hypocrites, where there will be weeping and gnashing of teeth" (24:50–51).

5. *Parable of the good and bad agent:* "As for this worthless slave, throw him into the outer darkness, where there will be weeping and gnashing of teeth" (25:30).

Matthew is, I think, in an even more confrontational situation than was the writer (or writers) of the Q Gospel—and he is losing the struggle. I locate him after the great war against Rome in 66–74 CE and, whether he represents Messianic/Christian Jews versus non-Messianic/Christian Jews or, quite possibly, Messianic/Christian Pharisees versus non-Messianic/Christian Pharisees, clearly there is bitterness on both sides. This is even more evident in the next example.

Example 4: Hypocrites and snakes. The bitterness of Matthew against his opponents escalates and boils over in chapter 23. "Woe to you, scribes and Pharisees, hypocrites!" Jesus repeats six times (23:13, 15, 23, 25, 27, 28), calling them "blind guides" (23:16, 24), "blind fools" (23:17), and "blind" (23:19, 26) until the final climax of vituperation: "You snakes, you brood of vipers! How can you escape being sentenced to hell?" (23:33).

My point is not simply that Matthew uses rhetorical violence against (his fellow?) Pharisees because, no doubt, he had received or would receive the same name-calling in return. Indeed, then as now, rhetorical violence was the mainstay of heavy debate on both sides. Instead, my point is that he puts all of that invective in the mouth of the historical Jesus after having earlier recorded him—the new Moses giving a new law from a new Mount Sinai—as solemnly forbidding anger, insult, and name-calling (5:21–22) and demanding, "Love your enemies and pray for those who persecute you" (5:44). I ask, as before for John's Gospel: *Did Jesus change his mind, or did Matthew change his Jesus?*

Examples such as these four could be multiplied across our extant Gospels, as rhetorical invective gives back what it receives. As slowly, but surely, more and more Jews decline and oppose the Messianic/Christian Jewish option, its proponents respond by counterinvective, not just from themselves in oral disputes, but from the historical Jesus in written texts.

Hence that same question, but in an even broader context: *Did Jesus change his mind, or did the Gospels change their Jesus?* Unfortunately, that escalating rhetorical violence in the Gospels is only the first of two stages in which the nonviolence of Jesus morphs first into rhetorical and then into physical violence. I turn now to that second and even more serious stage.

"Blood as High as a Horse's Bridle, for Two Hundred Miles"

THE BOOK OF REVELATION, the last and climactic book of the Christian Bible, concludes with a vision as magnificent as any of those eschatological vistas that we saw toward the end of Chapter 8. It imagines Earth's consummation as a great wedding between divinity and humanity, Heaven and Earth, with "the holy city, the new Jerusalem, coming down out of heaven from God, prepared as a bride adorned for her husband" (21:2). It celebrates not Earth's destruction, but its transformation, not the world's evacuation, but its transfiguration:

> See, the home of God is among mortals.
> He will dwell with them;
> they will be his peoples,
> and God himself will be with them;
> he will wipe every tear from their eyes.
> Death will be no more;
> mourning and crying and pain will be no more,
> for the first things have passed away. (21:3b–4)

You will recall all of that from the opening of this book in Chapter 1. But for Revelation, how exactly would the world reach that moment of perfect consummation? What about, not the *end*, but the *means*?

We will reach that wedding celebration by wading through "blood . . . as high as a horse's bridle, for a distance of about two hundred miles" (14:20) and only after another and very different type of feast:

Then I saw an angel standing in the sun, and with a loud voice he called to all the birds that fly in midheaven, "Come, gather for the great supper of God, to eat the flesh of kings, the flesh of captains, the flesh of the mighty, the flesh of horses and their riders—flesh of all, both free and slave, both small and great." (19:17–18)

We have come a long way indeed from that feast of God promised to all humanity in Isaiah 25:6–8 (see Chapters 1 and 8). Now the vultures feast on all humanity—free and slave, small and great, "all the birds were gorged with their flesh" (19:21).

Furthermore, Christ is the "Lamb standing as if it had been slaughtered" (5:6) or "the Lamb that was slaughtered" (5:12), and the "blood of the Lamb" (7:14; 17:11) refers to Christ the crucified. But the Lamb is also Christ the conqueror: "the Lamb will conquer them, for he is Lord of lords and King of kings" (17:14). In the great final battle against "the kings of the Earth" with their earthly armies, Christ is identified as "Faithful and True," is named "The Word of God," and has a name inscribed as "King of kings and Lord of lords" (19:11–16). The slaughtered Lamb has become the slaughtering Lamb.

Finally, the weapon of Christ is identified inaugurally as a "sharp, two-edged sword" (1:16; 2:12) and thereafter specified as the "sword of" or "sword that came from" his mouth (2:16; 19:21). That sounds rather symbolic or parabolic, but what results from this metaphorical sword? "From his mouth comes a sharp sword with which to strike down the nations, and he will rule them with a rod of iron; he will tread the wine press of the fury of the wrath of God the Almighty" (19:15). If, for Christ, the sword of his mouth is metaphorical, the slaughter it produces appears all too realistic.

Indeed, Revelation is filled, repeatedly, relentlessly, and ruthlessly, with metaphors for actual, factual, and historical violence to come. Think, for example, of those infamous four horsemen. Those riders on white, red, black, and green horses are all symbolic, to be sure, but they are symbols for conquest, war, famine, and pestilence, and such events promise realities, not more metaphors.

Revelation's promise of a bloodthirsty God and a blood-drenched Christ represents for me the creation of a second "coming" to negate the first and only "coming" of Christ; the fabrication of violent apocalypse to deny nonviolent incarnation; and the invention of Christ on a warhorse to erase the historical Jesus on a peace donkey. Jesus's nonviolent resistance to evil is replaced by Christ's violent slaughter of evildoers. The challenge was never the Jesus of history versus the Christ of faith but the Jesus Christ of nonviolence versus the Christ Jesus of violence.

Still, for me, Revelation's worst aspect is not its gleefully venomous presumption of an avenging God nor even its ferociously violent description of an avenging Christ. The worst aspect appears when you compare the Kingdom's consummation in the writings of Paul of Tarsus and in that of John of Patmos. Compare, then, the metaphorical model that each of these authors uses to portray that climactic event.

When Paul imagined the cosmic consummation, his metaphorical model for Christ's advent was the peaceful, nonviolent, and celebratory visitation (*parousia* in ancient Greek) of the emperor or an imperial legate to one of Rome's great eastern cities. Indeed, by the 50s CE, after eighty years of the Pax Romana, who could even remember any other sort of imperial advent, any other meaning for an official *parousia* but a joyful greeting (*apantēsis*) and a communal celebration for a job well done?

For Paul, therefore, Christ returns to celebrate the successful consummation of the Kingdom of God (1 Thess. 2:10; 3:13; 4:15; 5:23) and to hand it over to the God of Kingdom (1 Cor. 15:23–28). That was not, however, the metaphor or model by which John of Patmos imagined his consummation.

First, the focus of Revelation's attack is "Babylon" (14:8; 16:19; 18:2, 10, 21), which quite clearly means Rome because, as the Babylonian Empire destroyed Israel's first Temple in 586 BCE, so the Roman

Empire destroyed its second Temple in 70 CE. But Rome-as-Babylon includes *everything* Roman, from the empire as globalized commerce to the emperor as divinized ruler.

Rome is built atop its famous seven hills—the "seven mountains on which the woman is seated" (17:9), and that woman "is the great city that rules over the kings of the earth" (17:18). But, says Revelation, Rome-as-Babylon-as-woman is the "mother of whores and of earth's abominations" (17:5).

Second, when, amid all its rampant and polyvalent symbolism, Revelation refers metaphorically to one very precise and specific historical factor, hearers or readers are warned with this clause: "This calls for wisdom . . . with understanding" (13:18), and again, "This calls for a mind that has wisdom" (17:9). What, in those twin locations, is the historical feature that must be interpreted wisely and with understanding?

Revelation 13 takes the three great beastlike empires/emperors in Daniel 7:1–7 (discussed in Chapter 8) and combines them in the beastlike Roman super-empire/emperor (13:1–2). But one particular emperor is specified as having "been wounded by the sword and yet lived" (13:14), and then comes the warning: "This calls for wisdom: let anyone with understanding calculate the number of the beast, for it is the number of a person. Its number is six hundred sixty-six" (13:18). Who is that person?

It is the Emperor Nero, who ruled from 54 to 68 CE. He was named NRON QSR (Nero Caesar) in transliterated Hebrew lettering. The numerical values of those seven Hebrew letters adds up to 666. But why is Nero also described as "wounded by the sword and yet living"?

Later, Revelation warns once again that what follows "calls for a mind that has wisdom" (17:9) and then catalogs seven kings, "of whom five have fallen, one is living, and the other has not yet come; and when he comes, he must remain only a little while" (17:10). The most plausible scholarly guess is this: the five dead or "fallen" emperors are Caligula, Claudius, Nero, Vespasian, and Titus (37–81 CE);

the present "living" one is Domitian (81–96 CE); and the short-ruling one to come is Nerva (96–98 CE). (This, by the way, dates Revelation to the time of Domitian and Nerva at the end of the first century BC.)

After those seven emperors, another is described as "the beast that was and is not, it is an eighth but it belongs to the seven, and it goes to destruction" (17:11). This is, once again, the ruling Nero of 54–68 CE and is therefore one of the seven just cited from 37 to 98 CE but is also imagined as an "eighth" beast-ruler, that is, as the once and future king, as what you might call a returning Nero.

Why is Nero singled out for such special emphasis with those two demands for wise interpretation? He was, of course, the persecutor who brutalized Roman Christians and was charged, by some historical accounts, with initiating the Great Fire of 64 CE. But it is not to a *persecuting* Nero but to a *returning* Nero that Revelation points with those twin warnings of the need for wise interpretation. What, then, is the legend of returning Nero, and why is Revelation so interested in it?

It often happens that populist rulers who die under uncertain circumstances with unfinished programs have supporters who generate legends claiming that they are not dead and buried, but asleep and hidden away only to return (hence "returning") at some future catastrophic or climactic moment. (Think of the English Arthur or the German Frederick Barbarossa as once and future kings.)

So it was with Nero, despised in the West but divinized in the East where, for example, he had made honorable peace with the Parthians in 63 CE and freed Greece from the requirement to pay tribute money at the Isthmian Games in 66 CE. In the East, therefore, the legend developed that Nero had not died but instead had fled beyond the Euphrates, from where he would return at the head of Parthian armies to destroy the Roman Empire.

You can read that anti-Roman legend from the East in those Jewish *Sibylline Oracles* mentioned at the end of Chapter 8. Here, for example, is returning Nero portrayed as a transcendental and apocalyptic figure in *Sibylline Oracles* 5, from the end of the first century CE around the same time that Revelation was written:[12]

> He [Nero] will destroy every land and conquer all. . . . He will destroy many men and great rulers and he will set fire to all men as no one ever did. . . . Blood will flow up to the banks of deep-eddying rivers. . . . For fire will rain on men from the floors of heaven, fire and blood . . . and destruction in war, and a mist over the slain will destroy at once all kings and noble men. (5.365–380)

In that whole section, returning Nero is no longer a historical, even if legendary, anti-Roman attacker but an anticosmic eschatological destroyer before the establishment of God's rule on earth (5.381–385). The book of Revelation is especially interested in that returning Nero legend, but again, why?

First, recall Paul's model for Christ's "coming" as the experience of a peaceful imperial *parousia* during the Pax Romana. Revelation, however, never uses that now-peaceful word *parousia* but speaks only of Christ's "coming" throughout the book. Think, for example, of this triple repetition as the book's climactic conclusion: "See, I am coming soon!" . . . "See, I am coming soon" . . . "Surely I am coming soon" (22:7, 12, 20). And the climactic response "Amen. Come, Lord Jesus!" (22:20).

Second, where, under that Pax Romana, could Revelation find any viable model for Christ's imperial "coming" as violently vengeful? Where else but in the returning Nero legend? Returning Nero is "the beast that . . . was, and is not, and is about to ascend from the bottomless pit and go to destruction" (17:8), but in its place comes returning Christ, "who is and who was and who is to come" (1:4, 8; also see 4:8).

Not Nero but Christ will destroy the cosmic Roman Empire, the divine Roman emperor, and all of Roman imperial theology—but with a violence far more overwhelming than anything Rome or Romanization can muster to defend itself. In a terrible, terrible, terrible irony, Revelation replaces returning Nero and his Parthian martial forces with returning Christ and his angelic hosts. This is Revelation's worst libel against God and worst slander against Jesus. It is also, to finish that trinitarian round, the worst sin against the Holy Spirit.

Where Are We Now and What Comes Next?

THE RHYTHM OF ASSERTION-AND-SUBVERSION that patterns the Christian Bible is also applied to the historical Jesus's here-and-now-present Kingdom of God as nonviolent resistance to the normalcy of civilization in its contemporary Roman incarnation.

Jesus is changed first into the rhetorically violent Christ within the Gospels and then into the physically violent Christ of Revelation. In that book, in a complete reversal of character, Jesus is given a "coming" where violence is symbolically portrayed as brutally vengeful and metaphorically described as utterly destructive.

At this point, I can almost rest the case I lay out in *How to Read the Bible and Still Be a Christian*: accept and follow the *assertion* of the nonviolent historical Jesus as the image and revelation of a nonviolent God; understand and reject the *subversion* that changes him across two stages, first into rhetorical and then into physical violence. In other words, I already have the solution to the challenge of *How to Read the Bible and Still Be a Christian*—for those who have eyes to see—within the Christian Bible itself: if the biblical Christ is the norm, criterion, and discriminant of the Christian Bible, then the historical Jesus is the norm, criterion, and discriminant of the biblical Christ.

Still, I have a few more chapters to go because they confirm for me all that we have already seen. We conclude by witnessing the Apostle Paul subjected to exactly the same process of affirmation-and-negation, assertion-and-subversion. The vision of Paul on the radicality of God in Jesus will be muted, again in two stages, back into the normalcy of human civilization and Roman culture.

CHAPTER 12

Rome and the Challenge of Caesar

The other gods are far away, or do not have ears,
or do not exist or do not heed us at all, but you we see present,
not of wood or stone but real.

ATHENIAN HYMN TO DEMETRIOS I POLIORKETES (290–291 BCE)

PEOPLE IN GREEK AND Roman antiquity believed that an eternal God or Goddess could appear on earth in any guise desired—mineral, vegetable, animal, or human. But of course, even in a case of the divine becoming human, that humanity was but a transient apparition and a temporary convenience—rather like a Halloween costume.

The opposite, however, was also possible: the case of a human becoming divine, an actual, factual, mortal person who was divinized and taken up among the immortals after death. How and why and when did such an apotheosis happen?

In Greco-Roman antiquity a human who became divine was a historical person who had done something of such extraordinary value or transcendental benefit for the human race that it revealed the power of the immortal deities by manifesting divinity incarnate. That, however, confronts our post-Enlightenment minds with a pre-

Enlightenment culture. And so we presume that such was all simply standard politics disguised as insincere religion or court protocol presented as false flattery.

Surely more was involved when a living human received divine names, titles, inscriptions, statues, altars, temples, libations, sacrifices, festivals, and celebratory games were dedicated to or held in honor of that human being.. Despite our post-Enlightenment secularism, we cannot dismiss antiquity's claims of a divine human as irrelevant propaganda. We must ask again what was intended religiously and theologically or achieved socially and politically by such titles and such claims.

Specifically, I ask, can we denigrate as polite ruler-cult or prudent emperor-worship the fact that Octavian became Augustus and Augustus became God incarnate? Is that an adequate explanation when Roman imperial theology grounded conquest in prophecy, victory in sanctity, imperialism in destiny, and Augustan ascendancy as Rome's awaited Golden Age, the reign of the God Saturn?

"Peace Established on Land and Sea"

ROME HAD LONG BEFORE rejected rule by a dynastic monarch in favor of two aristocrats, or consuls, in office for only one year. The Roman Republic was a strong enough institution to recover from and then defeat the imperial threat from Hannibal's Carthaginians between approximately 250 and 150 BCE. But, saved from tyranny, the republic succumbed instead to anarchy. What went wrong?

Athens invented a democracy, acquired an empire, and discovered that one could not have both for long. Rome invented a republic, acquired an empire, and learned the same lesson. What went wrong was that the cooperating consuls became competing warlords. Twenty years of savage civil war with battle-hardened legions on both sides continued across three major rounds (Octavian is Augustus-to-be):

FIRST ROUND   Julius Caesar, who goes west and conquers Gaul
               (modern France), versus Gnaeus Pompey, who
               goes east and conquers Syria.
      Result Caesar defeats Pompey at Pharsalus in central
               Greece (48 BCE).
      Finale Pompey is assassinated (48 BCE) and then Caesar
               is assassinated (44 BCE).

SECOND ROUND   Caesar's defenders, Octavian Caesar and Mark
               Antony, versus Caesar's assassins, Brutus and
               Cassius.
      Result Defenders defeat assassins at Philippi in
               northeastern Greece (42 BCE).
      Finale Assassins commit suicide and Antony marries
               Octavia, sister of Octavian (40 BCE).

FINAL ROUND   Octavian and his admiral Agrippa versus Mark
               Antony and his ally Cleopatra.
      Result Octavian and Agrippa defeat Antony and
               Cleopatra off Cape Actium in northwestern
               Greece (31 BCE).
      Finale Cleopatra and Antony commit suicide and
               Octavian acquires Egypt (29 BCE).

Rome had squandered the hundred-year aftermath of its Carthaginian triumphs in social conflict between the Optimates (the "haves" led by "haves") and the Populares (the "have-nots" led by "haves"). The social unrest culminated in the decades of civil war from approximately 50 to 30 BCE.

Finally, return for a moment to Octavian and Agrippa's victory over Cleopatra and Antony at Actium. After he pursued them to their double suicide at Alexandria, Octavian erected a memorial Nicopolis, or Victory City, north of Cape Actium. But a special and separate victory monument was also erected with an altar and completed by 29 BCE.

That special memorial included a row of thirty bronze attack rams captured from Antony's defeated warships. Above them was a long inscription in which Octavian dedicated the memorial in the name of religion to Mars and Neptune in gratitude for the war he had fought and the victory he had won, and the subsequent peace. The result was, in lapidary Latin, PACE PARTA TERRA MARIQUE ("peace established on land and sea"). Already in 29 BCE, Roman imperial theology was structured around this quite clear and explicit sequence: religion, war, victory, peace, or, in briefest summary as mantra and motto: *Peace Through Victory*.

There is, however, one striking aspect of that huge memorial. It was erected on the site of Octavian's battle tent, "from which," says that inscription, "he set forth to attack the enemy" that fateful morning of September 2, 31 BCE. Octavian's bed had become sacred ground. Peace through victory was not so much established by Octavian as incarnated in Augustus.

Civil war had not only threatened Rome's survival, it had devastated the Mediterranean. (Notice, for example, that those three climactic battles were fought in Greece.) But now, war was over, peace was restored, the empire was safe, and Octavian would be decreed "Augustus" by the Senate in 27 BCE. The syllogism was set: only Gods give victory; but Augustus gave victory; therefore, Augustus was—a? or the?—God.

Furthermore, Octavian-become-Caesar-become-Augustus was Rome's redeemer from sin. The poet Horace pondered Rome's civil wars and wondered, "Does some blind frenzy drive us on, or some stronger power, or fault [*culpa*]"? Is Rome doomed by its original sin, by "the crime [*scelus*] of a brother's murder, ever since blameless Remus's blood was spilt upon the ground, to be a curse upon posterity"? Were Romans "an impious generation, of stock accursed" [*Epode* 7]?

Rome's inaugural sin was repeated in the murder of Julius Caesar and the consequent fratricidal civil war. Once again, Horace asked: "Our children made fewer by their parents' sins . . . to whom shall Jupiter assign the task of atoning for our guilt?" It is, of course, assigned to Caesar the Augustus, "right ready to be called the avenger of [Julius] Caesar." Horace prays for Augustus: "late may you return to the skies and long may you be pleased to dwell among the Romans; and may no untimely gale waft you from us angered at our sins" (*Ode* 1).

Keep all of this in mind as I turn next to another Augustan inscription, this time on a temple dedication in Turkey.

"To Emperor Caesar, Son of God, God Augustus"

PRIENE, ONCE A CLASSIC Greek port city about twenty miles south of Ephesus, is today, thanks to seismic shifts, a ruin reclaimed by pines some eight miles inland off the Aegean coast of Turkey. The city climbed the lower southern slope of Mount Mykale in a terraced triumph of classical grid over natural terrain. The oldest, most beautiful, and most important temple was for the Goddess Athena Polias, patron and protector of the city.

When it was begun in 323 BCE, the temple was dedicated to Athena Polias by Alexander the Great; but when it was finally finished in 27 BCE, the rededication was to Athena Polias and Augustus. The inscription, from the architrave, or main beam, above the entrance now sits in four large chunks on the ground where it fell. Translated, it says in two lines:

> THE PEOPLE TO ATHENA POLIAS AND
> TO EMPEROR CAESAR, SON OF GOD, GOD AUGUSTUS

This is the standard English translation, but since the original is in Greek, four terms require some more detailed explanation. They are: God, Augustus, Son of God, and Emperor.

First, the term "God." The human being Octavian was actually four ways divine: by ancestry, conception, adoption, and decree of the Roman Senate.

Augustus was divine by ancestry. The Goddess Aphrodite-Venus conceived a son, Aeneas, with the Trojan shepherd Anchises more than a thousand years before the time of Julius Caesar and Augustus

Caesar. Later, the Goddess guided the warrior Aeneas, with father Anchises on his shoulder and son Julus by his hand, from the doomed city of Troy to found the Roman race and the Julian line in Italy.

Augustus was divine by conception. His mother, Atia, was impregnated by the God Apollo while she was asleep in his temple in 63 BCE. Furthermore, the God appeared as a snake because Alexander, the Greek conqueror of Darius's Persians, and Scipio Africanus, the Roman conqueror of Hannibal's Carthaginians, had also been conceived by a similar divine manifestation.

Augustus was divine by adoption. Julius Caesar, his maternal granduncle, adopted Augustus as his son and heir in his official will, which was read publicly after he was assassinated in 44 BCE. That gave Augustus the still glorious, but also now dangerous, family name of Caesar. A comet streaking across the sky was interpreted as Caesar's soul ascending to take its place among the Gods, and immediately, Augustus became *divi filius*, son of the divine Julius Caesar.

Augustus was divine by decree. On his death in 14 CE the Roman Senate officially declared his divinity. That decree was helped and hastened by a well-rewarded official who claimed that he saw Augustus's soul rise heavenward from the funeral pyre. That made him, of course, divinely equal to Julius Caesar, or as was said in Egypt, he was now "God from God."

Next, the term "Augustus." The Latin title "Augustus" is "Sebastos" in Greek, and that Priene inscription calls him God Sebastos. The Latin term is quasi-divine, semidivine, or divine-by-association, but the Greek Sebastos is much stronger and more direct. It comes from the verb "to worship" and means the worshipful one or the one to be worshipped.

Does, then, "God Sebastos" designate Augustus as the one God especially, primarily, or even exclusively to be worshipped? Of course not, put like that. But the great power of Roman imperial theology was how much was, on the one hand, stylized and uniformly depicted and how much was, on the other hand, left to imagination and interpretation.

Then, the term "Son of God." Latin distinguished between a *divi filius*, the son of a deified human being (an "Immortal") and *dei filius*, the son of a God or Goddess (an "Eternal"). Greek makes no such distinction but has only a single phrase for both options: *theou huios*. (That is Jesus's relationship with God throughout the New Testament, as proclaimed, for instance, by the Roman centurion in Mark 15:39.) In any case, Augustus was both *dei filius* from Apollo by conception and *divi filius* from Caesar by adoption.

Finally, the term "Emperor." We already know that Octavian became a Caesar by adoption into that family. But what about "emperor"? The Latin term behind our English word is *imperator*, and the Greek—as at Priene—is *autokrator* (hence our word "autocratic"). What does *imperator* mean?

For Rome, "imperium" was the legal right to command legions in battle, and *imperator* was the titular battlefield acclaim from victorious legions to their victorious general. (That was the prime condition for requesting a triumphal procession in Rome.)

Eventually, all such acclaims and any such triumphs were restricted to Augustus or his imperial heirs so that *imperator* became his own first and main title. All other titles, even or especially divine ones, depended on that prime one. We should translate it as something like "World-Victor" or the "All-conquering One." In other words: no victory, no divinity.

Once again, as with "Sebastos" and "Augustus," the Greek *autokrator* is stronger than the Latin *imperator*. The Greek word *kratos* means strength, power, force. English words ending in "-crat" explain the source of such power: from people for a democrat, from elites for an aristocrat, from wealth for a plutocrat, from science for a technocrat, from God for a theocrat—but from *himself* for an autocrat. *Autokrator* has shades of transcendence not explicitly present even in *imperator*.

As I turn to the next question, keep in mind all that titular content packed into the Greek dedication of Priene's main temple to Augustus. What did Augustus do to obtain and deserve such transcendental accolades? My answer comes from another and later Priene inscription as a commentary on that temple dedication. As we proceed, keep always in mind that inaugural title of *imperator* as supreme victor or even world conqueror.

"A New Look to the Whole World"

WE ARE STILL AMONG the ruins of Priene but slightly to the southeast of that temple to the divine couple Athena and Augustus. The city's Agora, or Forum, has a long *stoa* along its northern side, a covered colonnade providing welcome shade from the implacable southern arch of the Mediterranean sun. Behind the *stoa* was the religiopolitical heart of the city.

From east to west, the first edifice was the *Prytaneion*, site of the city's sacred hearth, eternal flame, executive council, and ambassadorial venue. Next to it was the *Bouleuterion*, the city's council chamber, multitiered on three sides around its central altar. Then, continuing in a row to the west, were fifteen small shrine rooms. I focus here on a two-part inscription originally preserved in one of those rooms and thence removed to the off-limits basement of Berlin's Pergamon Museum.

Around 29 BCE, the proconsul Paulus Fabius Maximus, governor of Asia Minor (now western Turkey), wrote a letter offering a golden crown to the person who submitted the best proposal for adequately honoring Augustus in that Roman province of Asia Minor. About twenty years later he awarded that prize to himself. His letter was then carved on a block of blue limestone and solemnly displayed in that shrine room at Priene:

> [It is a question of whether] the birthday of the most divine
> Caesar is more pleasant or more advantageous, the day which
> we might justly set on a par with the beginning of everything,
> in practical terms at least, in that he restored order when ev-

erything was disintegrating and falling into chaos and gave a new look to the whole world, a world which would have met destruction with the utmost pleasure if Caesar had not been born as a common blessing to all. For that reason one might justly take this to be the beginning of life and living, the end of regret at one's birth. . . . It is my view that all the communities should have one and the same New Year's Day, the birthday of the most divine Caesar, and that on that day, 23rd September, all should enter their term of office.

This is quite clear. New Year's Day will be changed to the birthday of Caesar Augustus for all the cities of Asia Minor. That is certainly an honor, but the reason for it is theologically quite profound.

Augustus's birth was itself a cosmic new creation, "in practical terms at least." It had saved from chaos and disintegration not just Rome, Italy, and the Mediterranean, but "everything"—"the whole world." Since his birth started a new world, his birthday should start a new year. A new way had been discovered "to honor Augustus that was hitherto unknown among the Greeks, namely to reckon time from the date of his nativity." How did the League of Asian Cities respond to the governor's suggestion?

Their reaction was also carved as the second part of the two-part inscription found at Priene. It is a fascinating summary of Roman imperial theology, but as you read it, replace "Caesar" or "Augustus" with "Jesus" or "Christ," and you can understand Pauline Christian theology as counterpoint to and confrontation with Roman imperial theology.

Since the providence that has divinely ordered our existence has applied her energy and zeal and has brought to life the most perfect good in Augustus, whom she filled with virtues for the benefit of mankind, bestowing him upon us and our descendants as a savior—he who put an end to war and will order peace, Caesar, who by his epiphany exceeded the hopes of those who prophesied good tidings [*euaggelia*], not only out-doing benefactors of the past, but also allowing no hope of greater benefactions in the future; and since the birthday of the God first brought to the world the good tidings residing in him. . . . For that reason, with good fortune and safety, the Greeks of Asia have decided that the New Year in all the cities should begin on 23rd September, the birthday of Augustus . . . and that the letter of the proconsul and the decree of Asia should be inscribed on a pillar of white marble, which is to be placed in the sacred precinct of Rome and Augustus.

Notice all those key claims about Caesar Augustus: "perfect good," providential "virtues for the benefit of mankind," "savior," war-ender and peace-bringer, "epiphany," prophecy, greatest bene-factor of all time, "the God." But I look in detail at just one phrase: "good tidings."

This is where translation falters a little. Our terms "good news" or "glad tidings" are plural terms that lack a singular: we do not speak of a single "good new" or single "glad tiding." But Greek can make that distinction: *euaggelion* is a Greek singular, while *euaggelia* is a Greek plural, both combining two roots, *eu* for "good" and *aggelion/a* for "message/s."

The Romans announced imperial victories, dynastic successions, and even Augustus's world-changing birthday as *euaggelia* (plural), or "good messages." But Paul, for example, and indeed the entire New Testament, always used *euaggelion* (singular) or "the good message." It is always the one and only *good news* that is the historical Jesus himself.

All we have seen so far reaches its climax when the Augustan Age is proclaimed to be the expected Golden Age of the world. Israel's vision of a transfigured earth and a transformed world was the King-dom of God as a future advent in linear time. Rome's was of the reign of Saturn as a future return to a primordial state in cyclical time.

In both cases, it was to be the Golden Age of fertility and prosperity, justice and peace. Also, in both cases, from Augustus to Nero and from Jesus to Paul, eschatological transformation was proclaimed not as indolent relaxation, but as active collaboration. Finally, in both cases, that Golden Age, that final, climactic, last, or eschatological era presumed atonement achieved for the sin that had postponed its advent.

I conclude this chapter, therefore, with how the Roman poet Virgil saw that golden eschaton in Augustus. Then, in the next chapter, we can compare how the Jewish prophet Paul countersaw it in Christ.

"A Golden Age Springs Up Throughout the World"

IN HIS *Eclogues* FROM 40 BCE, Virgil imagined the coming reign of Saturn as *unlabored* human prosperity in a world where "cattle will not fear huge lions" and "any lingering traces of our guilt shall become void" (4.13–22). By 29 BCE, when he published *Georgics*, that reign of Saturn was envisaged as *labored* rural fertility—far away from urban worries, commercial hazards, and military adventures (1.132–134; 2:495–540).

Between 29 BCE and his death in 19 BCE, however, Virgil created his epic masterpiece, the *Aeneid*. There he equated the Golden Age with the Augustan Age and the reign of Saturn with the reign of Caesar. The travels and travails of Aeneas (remember, from above, his Venus-guided flight from Troy) initiated and foreshadowed those of Augustus. Furthermore, that the Golden Age would be the Augustan Age was divinely decreed in heaven, prophetically foretold on Earth, and magnificently accomplished by Augustus.

First, in heaven, Jupiter assures his worried daughter Aphrodite-Venus about the destiny of her Trojan family:[13]

> For these I set no bound in space or time, but have given
> empire without end . . . the Romans, lords of the world, and

nation of the toga. Thus it is decreed. . . . From this noble line shall be born the Trojan Caesar [Augustus], who shall extend his empire to the ocean, his glory to the stars, a Julius, name descended from great Julus! Him in days to come, shall you [Venus], anxious no more, welcome to heaven, laden with Eastern spoils; he, too, shall be invoked in vows. (1.279–290)

Rome's destiny and Augustus's divinity were ordained from the beginning by Jupiter, and nothing would stop that heavenly decree from its fulfillment. Augustus, as the new Aeneas, was predestined to "bring all the world beneath his laws" (4.231).

Next, that destiny was prophetically foretold by twin proclamations from a dead father to a living son, with one from the Trojan start and the other from the Latin end of the story. The spirit of the dead Anchises tells Aeneas:

Glorious Rome shall extend her empire to earth's ends, her ambitions to the skies. . . . This in truth is he whom you so often hear promised you, Augustus Caesar, son of a God [*divi genus*], who will again establish a Golden Age in Latium amid fields once ruled by Saturn. (6.781–794)

As this prophecy continues, the new vision of the reign of Saturn's Golden Age is summed up in these overquoted lines: "You, Roman, be sure to rule the world (be these your arts), to crown peace with justice, to spare the vanquished and to crush the proud" (6.851–853).

That ended Book VI of the *Aeneid*. Then, as Book VII begins, we get another prophecy of Rome's destiny, but this time at the Italian end of the journey from Troy. The spirit of Faunus, the "prophetic sire" of King Latinus, tells Aeneas:

Strangers shall come, to be your sons, whose blood shall exalt our [Latin] name to the stars, and the children of whose race shall behold, where the circling sun looks down [from east to west] on each ocean, the whole world roll obediently beneath their feet. (7.98–101)

You will notice two major points in Rome's destiny: it is decreed by God, and it is cosmic in scope—as befits, of course, the Golden Age or the reign of Saturn. It is about the whole Earth and the entire world.

Finally, Venus asks her divine husband, the God Vulcan, to create weapons for Aeneas. On the shield he shows "the history of Italy and the triumphs of Rome" (8.626). This allows Virgil to depict the climax of that triumphant history as "the Battle of Actium":

On the one side, Augustus Caesar stands on the lofty stern, leading Italians to strife, with the senate and the people, the Penates [Gods] of the state, and all the mighty gods; his auspicious brows shoot forth a double flame, and on his head dawns his father's star.

On the other side comes Antony with barbaric might and motley arms, victorious over the nations of the dawn and the ruddy [Indian] sea, bringing in his train Egypt and the strength of the East and farthest Bactra; and there follows him (oh, the shame of it!) his Egyptian wife. (8.678–688)

But that battle is more than Augustus Caesar and his admiral Agrippa against Antony and his wife, Cleopatra. It is more than Italy against Egypt, or even West against East. It is this: "Monstrous Gods of every form and barking Anubis wield weapons against Neptune and Venus and against Minerva" (8.698–699). The grand finale in 29 BCE is "Caesar, entering the wall of Rome in triple triumph" (8.714–715) for his victories in Dalmatia, off Cape Actium, and at Alexandria.

In conclusion, I return to an earlier question. As our post-Enlightenment eyes read the texts, view the artifacts, or survey the ruins of Roman culture, we can ask, did some people, most of them, or all of them across the Roman Empire take Rome's imperial theology literally or metaphorically?

They knew that distinction, of course, but seldom confused—as we so often do—the literal/metaphorical divide with the real/unreal one. You might, far example, have lived if you told Augustus his divinity was metaphorical but probably not if you told him it was unreal. Regardless of how literally those titles of Augustus were taken, we know that they were taken seriously, practically, functionally, programmatically—and really. That is also, by the way, how Christians took them for Christ. And it was enough.

Think about it this way. Cleopatra had a son with Julius Caesar nicknamed Caesarion. She also had twins with Marc Antony named Helios and Selene. Caesar was Octavian's adoptive father and Antony was his sworn enemy. You would think that Augustus would destroy the children of his defeated enemy and protect the child of his deified father.

But he did exactly the opposite. Augustus took the twins to Rome, where they were reared by Octavia, sister of Augustus and rejected wife of Antony. But he had Caesarion murdered because there could be only one *divi filius*, son of the deified Caesar. (I wonder, as the killers prepared to strangle Caesarion, did the teenager protest, "I am only a metaphor"?)

Where Are We Now and What Comes Next?

THROUGHOUT THIS BOOK WE have seen again and again how the matrix of time, place, and situation slowly but surely subverts assertions of divine radicality back into claims of human normalcy. In Chapters 9–11 we saw this happen to John the Baptist and Jesus of Nazareth; in Chapters 12–14 it happens to Paul of Tarsus. But by then you will already know *How to Read* the Pauline tradition *and Still Be a Christian.*

I had a double purpose with this chapter. One, specifically for Paul, was to set the stage to correct erroneous accusations that Paul betrayed Jesus and Judaism, invented Christianity, used weird new terms, made weird new claims, was anti-Semitic and antimarriage, proslavery and propatriarchy. Much or all of those issues stem from ignorance of the terms and claims of Roman imperial theology and of how Paul proclaimed Jesus's vision of God's Kingdom both as a challenge to his fellow Jews and as a confrontation between Christ and Caesar. For that two-front struggle, his language was deliberately designed to be appropriate to the provincial capitals of the Roman Empire.

No betrayal of Jesus or Judaism was involved with Paul, who took Jesus's vision out of the villages of the Jewish homeland and accurately rephrased it for the great Roman cities of the Jewish Diaspora.

My other purpose was the more general one emphasizing the matrix of time, place, and situation to understand once again that biblical rhythm of affirmation-and-negation as we move from Pauline assertion in Chapter 13 to post-Pauline subversion in Chapter 14.

Finally, as we saw with the historical Jesus in Chapters 9–11 and will see again with the historical Paul in Chapters 12–14, beneath that seismic conflict of Christian Judaism and Roman imperialism was the grinding collision of history's two great tectonic plates: the normalcy of civilization's program of peace through victory against the radicality of God's program of peace through justice.

CHAPTER 13

Paul and the Radicality of Christ

To reserve for Christ the words already in use to worship . . . the deified emperors . . . [creates] a polemical parallelism between the cult of the emperor and the cult of Christ. [This] makes itself felt where ancient words . . . from the [Jewish] Septuagint . . . happen to coincide with solemn concepts of the Imperial cult. . . . [It is] a clear prophecy of the coming centuries of martyrdom.
ADOLF DEISSMANN, *Light from the Ancient East* (1908)

NERO WAS NOT YET seventeen years old when he became Roman emperor in October of 54 CE. The early honeymoon years of his reign inspired eschatological enthusiasm for a renewed Golden Age. Here, for example, is a medley from the long encomium to Nero as "the God himself" (*ipse deus*) in an eclogue, or pastoral idyll, by the poet Calpurnius Siculus:

Amid untroubled peace, the Golden Age springs to a second birth; at last kindly Themis [Justice] returns to earth; blissful ages attend the youthful prince. . . . While he, a very God [*deus ipse*], shall rule the nations, the unholy War-Goddess shall yield and have her vanquished hands bound behind her back. . . .

Fair peace shall come. . . . Peace in her fullness shall come; knowing not the drawn sword, she shall renew once more the Reign of Saturn in Latium . . . a kinder God [*melior deus*] will . . . displace the age of oppression . . . no presage of bloodshed. . . . Assuredly a very God [*ipse deus*] shall take in his strong arms the burden of the massive Roman state. (1.42–85)

That Latin phrase *ipse deus* or *deus ipse* could be translated as "God himself" (think of *ipse dixit* as used in the courtroom to mean "he himself has said it").

In another eclogue, the poet proclaimed Nero, "this youth . . . sent us from heaven," as "God in person [*deus ipse*]" and pleaded, "Caesar, whether you are Jupiter himself on earth in altered guise, or any other of the powers above concealed under an assumed mortal semblance (for you are very God) [*es enim deus*], rule, I pray you, this world, rule its peoples forever!" (4.137, 143–145).

At around the same time, the Apostle Paul wrote a rather different epistle to the various Christian communities at Rome. It proclaimed a divergent eschatological vision now already present, but in Christ rather than in Nero. The occasion was Paul's intention to visit Rome on his way from Jerusalem to Spain, from Roman East to Roman West, and from the Aegean to the Atlantic. He had, as you might expect, a different vision for the Golden Age of Earth.

"Buried with Him by Baptism into Death"

PAUL'S LETTER TO THE Romans turned out to be his last will and testament, a magnificent summary of who he was, what he was about, and how his Christian Judaism envisaged the destiny of the world. I begin with a quotation, and as you read it, notice how strange it is:

Do you not know that all of us who have been baptized into Christ Jesus were baptized into his death? Therefore we have been buried with him by baptism into death, so that, just as Christ was raised from the dead by the glory of the Father, so we too might walk in newness of life. For if we have been united with him in a death like his, we will certainly be united with him in a resurrection like his. (Rom. 6:3–5)

Paul writes to living Christians and tells them they have already died and risen with Christ by baptism. It is not a future and imminent happening, but a past and ongoing one. What does he mean by *having been* baptized into Christ's death and risen into Christ's resurrected life? It is certainly a metaphor, but what is the reality to which it points?

To understand Paul's meaning, we must move forward three hundred years to the post-Constantinian world in which Christianity's official basilica-churches needed to construct architectural baptismals and not just repeat Pauline texts. They either dug gravelike pits in the floor or built coffinlike structures on the floors of their baptistery buildings, and both were in cruciform shape with steps down into and up out of the water in the center. (Search online for "ancient baptismal fonts" for examples.)

Architecture finally mirrored and thereby illustrated theology, but putting text and structure together simply doubles and intensifies the problem. What did it mean to be baptized "into the death of Christ" by climbing into a cruciform coffin or descending into a cruciform grave?

Think about it like this: Rome had officially, publicly, and legally executed Jesus, but God had raised him from the dead. Jesus was therefore dead to Rome and alive to God. Similarly, in baptism, the followers of Jesus had died to the basic values of Rome's empire and been reborn to those of God's Kingdom. What, specifically, were those values? What else does Paul tell us about that baptismal death and rebirth?

Here are two texts that give specific examples of what happens in baptismal death. Neither cite, by the way, the central core of what is being negated without its framing elements because they are not concerned with differences outside the Christian community but with hierarchy inside that community:

> As many of you as were baptized into Christ have clothed yourselves with Christ. There is no longer Jew or Greek, there is no longer slave or free, there is no longer male and female; for all of you are one in Christ Jesus. And if you belong to Christ . . . (Gal. 3:27–29)
> For in the one Spirit we were all baptized into one body— Jews or Greeks, slaves or free—and we were all made to drink of one Spirit." (1 Cor. 12:13)

Notice the frames: baptism is *into* Christ, *with* Christ, *in* Christ, and *to* Christ; baptism is *in* one Spirit and *of* one Spirit.

In other words, Paul was saying that just as Christ was executed and was thereby dead *by* Rome, so Christians were baptized and thereby dead *to* Rome. They were dead, specifically, to Rome's four supreme values of patriarchy, slavery, hierarchy, and victory—especially violent victory on which those other three values depended.

Romans, by the way, could regularly see those core values enforced in free public entertainment as animals and gladiators were slaughtered on blood-stained sand while their own seating positions, from close-up to far-off, taught them their place in society. I now discuss how Paul negates those four basic values, basic for civilization in general and for his contemporary Rome in particular.

Patriarchy: "There Is No Longer Male and Female"

PAUL TAKES IT FOR granted that after baptism, women and men, wives and husbands are equal in the family, the community, and the apostolate.

First, with regard to equality in the family, in 1 Corinthians 7

Paul responds to a series of questions about abstinence, sex, marriage, virginity, and the Christian life. What is most striking in his every response is his very deliberate evenhandedness with regard to female and male or husband and wife. As for one, so for the other. Notice this process on each subject.

On abstinence: Paul was a permanent ascetic celibate—like those other Jewish celibates we know of from the desert south of Alexandria or west of the Dead Sea. (Indeed, those deserts are where that tradition passed eventually from Judaism into Christianity.) But Paul insists that temporary celibacy within marriage must be "by agreement for a set time" (7:5), and it involved husband/wife and wife/husband (7:3), wife/husband and husband/wife (7:4). Notice the even duality.

On divorce: Paul gives the following as his own advice rather than a command—and it is beautifully and humanely wise:

> If any believer has a wife who is an unbeliever, and she consents to live with him, he should not divorce her. And if any woman has a husband who is an unbeliever, and he consents to live with her, she should not divorce him. For the unbelieving husband is made holy through his wife, and the unbelieving wife is made holy through her husband. Otherwise, your children would be unclean, but as it is, they are holy. (7:12–14)

Notice, again, the even balance of wife/husband and husband/wife. Also notice the evenhandedness of "if she consents" and "if he consents."

On virginity: Paul applies virginity as an option for both men and women. There is no double standard, as if virginity were only for women: "Are you bound to a wife? Do not seek to be free. Are you free from a wife? Do not seek a wife. But if you marry, you do not sin, and if a virgin marries, she does not sin" (7:27–28).

On abstinence: Paul again advocates celibate asceticism instead of marriage for men (7:32) and women (7:34). Celibate asceticism is not a witness that sex, marriage, and family are evil but that normalcy is not inevitability, neither for sex nor for violence. It is a major witness (like martyrdom) that the normalcy of civilization is not the inevitability of human nature.

Next, with regard to equality in the community, one of the strangest outbursts from the historical Paul occurs in 1 Corinthians 11:2–16. There is no scholarly consensus on what exactly is the problem to which Paul responds so powerfully and unpersuasively. I offer, therefore, only my own interpretation on both the problem and the solution.

It clearly concerns head-covering for men and women, as each exercises leadership in the liturgical assembly. Notice, above and before all else, that Paul presumes that both sexes exercise communal leadership in prayer and prophecy: "Any man who prays or prophesies with something on his head disgraces his head, but any woman who prays or prophesies with her head unveiled disgraces her head—it is one and the same thing as having her head shaved" (11:4–5). Still, what is the problem, and why so much sound and fury over head-covering?

Here is my best guess. We know that there was a problem with temporary sexual abstinence within marriage at Corinth. It was, as seen above, their first question to Paul, and it asked whether "it is well for a man not to touch a woman" (7:1). Paul replied, yes, but only "by agreement and for a set time" (7:5). But what if certain wives were announcing temporary or even permanent celibacy against their husbands' wishes? And how would that be announced communally?

In Roman society, the hair (not face) of nubile virginal women was unveiled as a symbol of availability for marriage, but that of married women was veiled with the opposite symbolism. My guess is that some Corinthian wives were leading communal assembly with unveiled hair as a statement that they were now temporary or even permanent "virgins." That could lead, of course, to serious misunderstandings about them (available for marriage!) or serious consequences for them (divorce!).

In response, Paul, as we say today, loses it. He argues very badly against such unveiled female leadership from both scripture (7:7–12) and nature (7:13–15). You will notice, for example, how his argument that man "is the image and reflection of God; but woman is the reflection of man" (11:7) serenely contradicts how "God created humankind in his image, / in the image of God he created them; / male and female he created them" (Gen. 1:27).

In the end, as if to acknowledge the vacuity of his two arguments, Paul concludes that "if anyone is disposed to be contentious—we have no such custom, nor do the churches of God" (1 Cor. 11:16). Surely, if scripture and nature forbid something, custom for or against it is rather irrelevant.

All of this is, however, unfinished Christian business. During the following centuries, a series of texts such as the *Acts of Paul, Acts of Peter, Acts of John, Acts of Andrew*, and *Acts of Thomas* advocated celibate asceticism with the emphasis on wives against husbands. Sanctity by asceticism and martyrdom, or both, was equally available for women and men, wives and husbands, but it was also a fundamental challenge to a world of patriarchal power.

Finally, with regard to equality of the sexes in the apostolate, I return to where this chapter began—with Paul's letter to the Romans. Since he hoped, as we saw, to visit Rome on his way to Spain, he ended the letter with greetings to both Roman immigrants he knew and others about whom he had only heard.

First, the letter carrier is a woman, "our sister Phoebe, a deacon of the church at Cenchreae, so that you may welcome her in the Lord as is fitting for the saints, and help her in whatever she may require from you, for she has been a benefactor of many and of myself as well" (16:1–2). Phoebe would have to be able to deliver, read, and explain the letter to the various Christian communities in Rome.

Then, of the twenty-seven individuals Paul mentions specially to "greet," ten are women and seventeen are men. In terms of those singled out for special comment, five are women (Mary, Tryphaena, Tryphosa, Persis, and an unnamed mother) and six are men (Epaenetus, Ampliatus, Urbanus, Stachys, Apelles, and Rufus). But only four, all women—Mary, Tryphaena, Tryphosa, and Persis (16:6, 12)—get the special accolade of having "worked hard" (*kopiaō*) for Christ, elsewhere expressed by Paul only of himself (Gal. 4:11; 1 Cor. 15:10).

One name in this final greeting created a problem that would be funny if it were not ridiculous, and comic if it were not tragic. Junia, who apparently was in prison with Paul, is a female name, so we know that this is a woman who was "prominent among the apostles" (Rom. 16:7). But to obviate that unorthodoxy, for the past thousand years Junia has been declared to be short for the masculine name Junianus. Needless to say, no such masculine abbreviation existed in antiquity.

Paul takes it for granted that a woman could be an apostle, that is, a person sent (from the Greek *apostellein*, "to send") by God or Christ to found a new Christian community. If you do not like that, Paul would have said, get over it, or take it up with God.

Slavery: "There Is No Longer Slave or Free"

WHAT WAS PAUL'S VIEW on slavery and the slave economy of the Roman Empire? Did he agree with the fourth-century BCE Greek philosopher Aristotle that slavery was natural because "some men are by nature free, and others slaves" (*Poetics* 1.5)? Or with the first-century CE Jewish philosopher Philo that slavery was unnatural because "nature has created all men free, but the injustice and covetousness of some men who prefer inequality, that cause of all evil, having subdued some, has given to the more powerful authority over those who are weaker" (*On the Contemplative Life* 9.70)?

The best and clearest answer comes rather incidentally from a very specific case in Paul's letter to Philemon. You previously caught a glimpse of this letter as an "exploratory probe" in Chapter 2, but I explore it here again in greater detail. Paul, as you recall, was imprisoned, chained nightly to a guard in the barracks, when he wrote that personal letter to Philemon and also the communal letter to the Philippians. The location was, most likely, the governor's jail at Ephesus (1 Cor. 15:32; 2 Cor. 1:8–9).

Philemon's slave Onesimus, in serious trouble with his owner (punishment? death?), fled, as was acceptable under Roman law, to his owner's superior friend Paul to seek intercession and obtain forgiveness. We know, for example, that Pollio's slave "fled to Caesar [Augustus's] feet" to avoid death (Seneca, *On Anger* 3.40) and that Pliny the Younger interceded with his friend Sabinianus when "your freedman . . . threw himself at my feet" (*Letters* 9).

With Paul, Onesimus converts to Christianity, and Paul sends him back to Philemon with the letter because, as he says, "I am appealing to you for my child, Onesimus, whose father I have become during my imprisonment" (v. 10). What is the "appeal," and why does it take twenty-five verses to explain in this one-chapter letter?

First, the letter is a masterpiece of Greco-Roman rhetorical persuasion because, although it is a personal letter, it is not at all a private one. Paul addresses it not just to Philemon, but to two named others and all in his house-church (vv. 1b–2). And it comes not just from Paul, but from five other Christians helping him in prison (vv. 1, 23).

Next, the persuasive process works in the alternating rhythm of good-cop Paul (vv. 1–7, 10–12, 14, 17, 20) and bad-cop Paul (8–9, 13, 15–16, 18–19, 21–22). Compare, for example, these two bad-cop statements: "Though I am bold enough in Christ to command you to do your duty, yet I would rather appeal to you on the basis of love" (v. 8), and "confident of your obedience, I am writing to you, knowing that you will do even more than I say" (v. 21).

Notice also the barb in the words, "I wanted to keep him with me, so that he might be of service to me *in your place* during my imprisonment for the gospel" (v. 13, italics mine). Or in this signed IOU: "If he has wronged you in any way, or owes you anything, charge that to my account. I, Paul, am writing this with my own hand: I will repay it. I say nothing about your owing me even your own self" (vv. 18–19).

Philemon and Onesimus constituted a perfectly specific text case: Can a Christian owner have a Christian slave? Can one be equal and unequal in Christ Jesus at the same time? Does that baptismal "no longer slave or free" apply only to the interior spiritual life or also to external social status? Paul's answer is absolutely clear, lest there be any ambiguity in Philemon's mind: "Perhaps this is the reason he was separated from you for a while, so that you might have him back forever, no longer as a slave but more than a slave, a beloved brother—especially to me but how much more to you, both in the flesh and in the Lord" (vv. 15–16).

Furthermore, there is this fascinating feature of the letter of Paul to Philemon when compared with the above-cited one from Pliny to Sabinianus. Paul calls Onesimus by his name and never refers to him as "your slave." Pliny never names the petitioner but simply calls him "your freedman."

Finally, why does the letter take so long to say, essentially: "Dear Philemon, Free Onesimus. Yours, Paul"? Because we see here another profoundly important aspect of Pauline theology. For Paul, the issue is not, and never was, that unreal disjunction of faith versus works, but the real one of faith with works versus works without faith. For Paul, you could never have faith without works, but you could, all too often, have works without faith.

Paul must, paradoxically, command Philemon to free Onesimus freely. Philemon must do it because he believes in it (faith with works) and not just because Paul commands it (works without faith): "I preferred to do nothing without your consent, in order that your good deed might be voluntary and not something forced" (v. 14).

It is clear, then, that the baptismal commitment of "no longer slave or free" is neither hyperbole nor hypocrisy but program and platform. It means that Christians cannot own Christians.

Hierarchy: "There Is No Longer Jew or Greek"

IT IS IMPORTANT THAT the phrase "there is no longer Jew or Greek" (Gal. 3:28) never be quoted except within its Christian frame. It does not deny the ongoing existence of Judaism by rhetorical holocaust or supersessionist delusion. It states that whether you come into the Christian community from Jewish monotheism or Greco-Roman polytheism, you are now equal in Christ. There is no superiority of either over the other. Jews and Greeks now "drink of one Spirit" (1 Cor. 12:13).

This touches on the oft-made accusation that Paul was anti-Semitic and thereby betrayed both Jesus and Judaism. Paul believed, of course, that Jesus was the Messiah/Christ and wanted all Jews to become Messianic/Christian Jews, but that made him, from his point of view, pro-Semitic, not anti-Semitic.

First, Paul insisted again and again that he himself was a devout Jew and, indeed, a fervent Pharisee. He describes himself as "circumcised on the eighth day, a member of the people of Israel, of the tribe of Benjamin, a Hebrew born of Hebrews; as to the law, a Pharisee . . . as to righteousness under the law, blameless" (Phil. 3:5–6). And hear him again, in this medley, especially with its climactic statement of his love for his own people:

> I advanced in Judaism beyond many among my people of the same age, for I was far more zealous for the traditions of my ancestors. (Gal. 1:14)
>
> Are they Hebrews? So am I. Are they Israelites? So am I. Are they descendants of Abraham? So am I. (2 Cor. 11:22)
>
> I myself am an Israelite, a descendant of Abraham, a member of the tribe of Benjamin. (Rom. 11:1)
>
> I am speaking the truth in Christ—I am not lying; my conscience confirms it by the Holy Spirit—I have great sorrow and unceasing anguish in my heart. For I could wish that I myself were accursed and cut off from Christ for the sake of my own people, my kindred according to the flesh. They are Israelites, and to them belong the adoption, the glory, the covenants, the giving of the law, the worship, and the promises; to them belong the patriarchs, and from them, according to

the flesh, comes the Messiah, who is over all, God blessed forever. Amen. (Rom. 9:1–5)

For Paul, in other words, "the gifts and the calling of God are
irrevocable" (Rom. 11:29). He himself is a Messianic/Christian Jew,
but as such, there is no hierarchy of Jew over Gentile or of Gentile
over Jew within that Messianic/Christian community.

Victory: "Be Subject to the Governing Authorities"

THE SECTION ON OBEDIENCE to "the governing authorities" in
Romans 13:1–7 has been quoted out of context across two thousand
years as justification for obedience to almost anything ever commanded by government. I look at it here in a fuller context, and especially in terms of that supreme Roman value of violent victory.

First of all, the full context runs from 12:14 through 13:7 and is
where Paul comes closest to quoting Jesus almost verbatim. Compare, for example, 12:14–31 with what we call the Sermon on the
Mount (better: the new law from the new Moses on the new Mount
Sinai) in Matthew 5:39–48 = Luke 6:27–37.

The subject, for both Jesus and Paul, is to love your enemies and
practice nonviolence toward them no matter what they do to you.
For example, Jesus says, "Love your enemies and pray for those who
persecute you" in Matthew 5:44, or "Love your enemies, do good to
those who hate you, bless those who curse you, pray for those who
abuse you" in Luke 6:27–28. Paul says, "Bless those who persecute
you; bless and do not curse them" in Romans 12:14.

Continue now from that prologue and watch how Paul changes
emphasis. Jesus says, "Do not resist an evildoer" in Matthew 5:39.
Paul says, "Do not repay anyone evil for evil" (Rom. 12:17); "Do not
be overcome by evil, but overcome evil with good" (12:21); and finally,
climactically, with a triple use of the word "resist," "whoever resists
authority resists what God has appointed, and those who resist will

incur judgment" (13:2). I focus on that word "resist": Does it forbid resisting violently or also resisting nonviolently? Does it enjoin complete passivity? Those are key questions.

The Greek verb "to resist" in Matthew 5:39—*anthistēmi*—means, in that context, to resist violently. The major Greek lexicon, by Liddell and Scott, translates *anthistēmi* as "to set up in opposition" or "to stand against, especially in battle, to withstand, oppose." What Jesus forbids is violent resistance against evil.

So also with another Greek verb for "to resist"—*antitassō*—in Romans 13:2. It means exactly the same—but even more emphatically so. For Liddell and Scott, once again, *antitassō* means "to set opposite to, range in battle against" and also "to set oneself against, meet face to face, meet in battle." It comes from *anti*, which means "against," and *taxis*, which means "a drawing up, the order or disposition of an army . . . array, order of battle . . . a single rank or line of soldiers . . . to be drawn up a few lines deep . . . a body of soldiers, a squadron" and other such military dispositions for battle. (Our English word "tactics" comes from that Greek root.)

We can now see Paul's concern in 13:1–7 when it is placed within its fuller context of 12:14–13:7. It does, of course, command the payment of taxes and revenues to Rome, but even more specifically it forbids refusing them violently. Paul's fear is the specter of violent tax revolts among Christians at Rome in the transition from Claudius to Nero. It is something that appalls him so much that, in rather a rhetorical panic, he makes some very unwise and unqualified statements with which to ward off that possibility.

Paul is afraid, not that Christians will be killed, but that they will kill, not that Rome will use violence against Christians, but that Christians will use counterviolence against Rome. In that, the Christian nonviolent reaction to evil from Jesus through Paul is the most basic denial of Rome's core value of peace through violent victory. For Rome, and indeed for the normalcy of civilization, what underlies and justifies all other hierarchies is that of victor over vanquished, conqueror over conquered, empire over colony.

One final and unfortunate point. As we saw earlier, Jesus grounds human nonviolence in the nonviolence of God (Matt. 5:43–48 and Luke 6:27–36). But Paul grounds human nonviolence in divine violence:

> Beloved, never avenge yourselves, but leave room for the wrath of God; for it is written, "Vengeance is mine, I will repay, says the Lord." No, "if your enemies are hungry, feed them; if they are thirsty, give them something to drink; for by doing this you will heap burning coals on their heads." (Rom. 12:19–20)

Those two quotations are from Deuteronomy 32:35 and Proverbs 25:21. But while negating all human violence is certainly a magnificent injunction, presuming its replacement by divine violence rather than locating its source in divine nonviolence is not the vision of the historical Jesus. That is an unfortunate and unusual subversion by Paul of an assertion by Jesus.

Where Are We Now and What Comes Next?

I THINK THAT BY now, you can write this section for yourselves. You have already heard repeatedly throughout this book about that Biblical Heartbeat of expansion-and-contraction, affirmation-and-negation, assertion-and-subversion. So you expect what happens to Paul—just as it did to Jesus.

Furthermore, I gave you a preview of that process in the "exploratory probe" on Paul in Chapter 2. We saw there how the post-Pauline letter to the Colossians subverted and denied the Pauline letter to Philemon on slavery. That was an early warning of how Pauline radicality on certain basic values would be de-radicalized back into Roman normalcy.

Still, even though we expect that by now, it is sad how swiftly the New Testament returned to Roman acculturation in preparation for Constantine. We can at least lament the consequent sufferings of all those who never learned *How to Read the Bible and Still Be a Christian*, especially when it involved reading Christ against pseudo-Christ and Paul against pseudo-Paul. Finally, then, I focus on what happened to Paul.

CHAPTER 14

Paul and the Normalcy of Empire

The toga was everywhere . . . and they classed as civilization
what was but part of their enslavement.
TACITUS, *Agricola* (98 CE)

WRITING TO THE PHILIPPIANS in the early 50s CE, Paul told them
to "work out your own salvation with fear and trembling" (1:12b). If
you stop there, it seems that he is warning about divine retribution
for failure. Be afraid, he seems to say, of the avenging God's retributive justice. But now read the entire context (always, by the way, a
good idea): "Work out your own salvation with fear and trembling;
for it is God who is at work in you, enabling you both to will and to
work for his good pleasure" (2:12b–13).

Wait a minute: What is there to fear from God for failure if God
supplies both "will" and "work"? Then you see it: work out your salvation with fear and trembling not because *God* will punish you if
you fail, but because *Rome* will punish you if you succeed. As always,
of course, Rome was the normalcy of civilization—the first-century
Mediterranean version.

This warning explains why the oft-seen biblical pattern of
assertion-and-subversion as God's radicality is regularly dialed back

toward civilization's normalcy throughout the Christian Bible. So, therefore, as we already found with Jesus, so also here with Paul. How exactly was Paul de-radicalized back into Roman normalcy? Where do we see it most clearly?

"There Are Some Things in Them Hard to Understand"

THE CHRISTIAN NEW TESTAMENT has twenty-seven books. Of those, about half involve Paul: thirteen letters are attributed to him, and half of the Acts of the Apostles are about him. There is, however, a strong scholarly consensus about those thirteen letters, as we saw in Chapter 2: seven were certainly written by Paul; three were probably not written by him; and three were certainly not written by him.

That consensus is the basis of this chapter, as the division of the letters into three groups is based on cumulative differences within them in time and place, style and format, content and theology. But this raises even more important questions: What is the purpose of someone writing letters in Paul's name after Paul's death? What is the intention of the post-Pauline and pseudo-Pauline letters?

The most traditional answer is that Paul's disciples or even a collective Pauline "school" wrote letters in his name to discuss new problems that rose after his death. Their sense would be, If Paul were here today, this is what he would have written. This is a persuasive explanation, as long as you do not make the mistake of actually reading all thirteen of the letters.

If you were to do that, another answer becomes possible. Those six letters not written by him are not just post-Pauline and pseudo-Pauline letters but are actually *anti*-Pauline letters. They represent the subversion of which the seven authentic letters were the assertion. Jesus, as we saw, was subverted over two stages—by rhetorical violence in the Gospels and by physical violence in Revelation.

This happened similarly with Paul: he was de-radicalized and re-Romanized in two stages.

The seven authentic letters (1 Thessalonians, Galatians, Philippians, Philemon, 1 and 2 Corinthians, and Romans) represent the *radical* Paul. The three "probably not" letters (2 Thessalonians, Colossians, and Ephesians) represent an initial de-radicalization into a *conservative* "Paul." And the three "certainly not" letters (1 and 2 Timothy and Titus) represent a final de-radicalization into a *reactionary* "Paul." Only the first seven letters were written by the historical Paul, but the other six are equally important for confirming how to read those seven. You cannot de-radicalize someone who is not already a radical.

Think, for example, of this section's title. Here is the full text: "our beloved brother Paul wrote to you according to the wisdom given him, speaking of this [peace] as he does in all his letters. There are some things in them hard to understand, which the ignorant and unstable twist to their own destruction, as they do the other scriptures" (2 Pet. 3:15b–16).

But is Paul (like Jesus) hard to understand or only hard to follow? Is Paul (like Jesus) very easy to understand but terribly hard to imitate? Maybe twisting the scriptures could be another name for what I call assertion-and-subversion. In any case, in this chapter I focus on slavery and patriarchy to see how post-Pauline and pseudo-Pauline are actually anti-Pauline letters.

"Tell Slaves to Be Submissive to Their Masters"

WE SAW IN BOTH Chapter 2 and Chapter 13 that as far as the original, radical, and historical Paul was concerned, Christians could not own Christian slaves. But, to expand here on that glimpse in Chapter 2, the post-Pauline letters to the Colossians and Ephesians take for granted, without any discussion, that of course Christians could and did own Christian slaves.

I call the post-Paul of those two letters "conservative" because, although he contradicts the radical Paul on slavery, there are certain aspects to which a traditional Roman paterfamilias would have objected. Indeed, that paterfamilias might well have found post-Paul not nearly conservative enough, or maybe even far too liberal:

> Slaves, obey your earthly masters in everything, not only while being watched and in order to please them, but wholeheartedly, fearing the Lord. Whatever your task, put yourselves into it, as done for the Lord and not for your masters, since you know that from the Lord you will receive the inheritance as your reward; you serve the Lord Christ. For the wrongdoer will be paid back for whatever wrong has been done, and there is no partiality. Masters, treat your slaves justly and fairly, for you know that you also have a Master in heaven. (Col. 3:22–4:1)
>
> Slaves, obey your earthly masters with fear and trembling, in singleness of heart, as you obey Christ; not only while being watched, and in order to please them, but as slaves of Christ, doing the will of God from the heart. Render service with enthusiasm, as to the Lord and not to men and women, knowing that whatever good we do, we will receive the same again from the Lord, whether we are slaves or free.
>
> And, masters, do the same to them. Stop threatening them, for you know that both of you have the same Master in heaven, and with him there is no partiality. (Eph. 6:5–9)

There are some important aspects worth noting in these twin texts. First, post-Paul speaks separately to both slaves and masters with direct address to each, but with slaves getting, not unexpectedly, more attention. Second, he also invokes mutual and reciprocal obligations of each to each. A Roman paterfamilias might growl: How dare you tell *my* slaves about *my* obligations to them, and by the way, do not dare to address my slaves directly rather than through me.

You can see how all of this changes when we turn to the reactionary pseudo-Paul in the letter to Titus. Here is the text in question:

Tell slaves to be submissive to their masters and to give satisfaction in every respect; they are not to talk back, not to pilfer, but to show complete and perfect fidelity, so that in everything they may be an ornament to the doctrine of God our Savior. (2:9–10)

Apart from the concluding "God our Savior," any Roman paterfamilias would nod approval to this injunction. Obligations are from slaves to masters, with nothing said about any reciprocal ones from master to slave. Furthermore, slaves are not addressed directly but only through owners: "Tell slaves . . . "

Finally, that clash between real-Paul and pseudo-Paul on slavery clarifies how we should read an ambiguous comment in one of Paul's authentic letters. Here he is speaking to Christian slaves of non-Christian owners and wishes to reassure them that they are not thereby second-class Christians: "Were you a slave when called [by Christ]? Do not be concerned about it. But if also you gain freedom, *rather use it*" (1 Cor. 7:21, translation and italics mine).

The italicized phrase is as ambiguous in the Greek original (*mallon chrēsai*) as in my literal English translation. What is the "it" to be used? Does it mean, stay as a slave and use your slavery for Christ? That is how the NRSV text interprets the advice: "Were you a slave when called? Do not be concerned about it. Even if you can gain your freedom, *make use of your present condition now more than ever.*"

Or should we go with the NRSV note: "*Avail yourself of the opportunity of freedom*" and rather use it all the more for Christ? In the light of the above contradiction of real-Paul by pseudo-Paul, I read it to mean, take your freedom and use it all the more for Christ. Besides, could a Roman slave actually refuse an owner's offer or command of emancipation? All this discussion is, unfortunately and tragically, millennia too late for millions of Christian slaves with Christian owners.

"I Permit No Woman to Teach or to Have Authority over a Man"

AS FOR SLAVERY, SO for patriarchy: real-Paul is flatly contradicted by post-Paul. We move once again across the trajectory from radical Paul to conservative and reactionary anti-Paul in almost exactly the same manner. Watch as the historical Paul of baptismal theory in Galatians 3 and baptismal practice in Romans 16 (from Chapter 13) is de-radicalized and re-Romanized, first into the conservative and finally into the reactionary Paul.

I call post-Paul "conservative" about wives and husbands because, in Colossians and Ephesians, both parties are addressed directly and have reciprocal obligations—as we saw already with slavery (that might, once again, be much too liberal for a traditional Roman paterfamilias): "Wives, be subject to your husbands, as is fitting in the Lord. Husbands, love your wives and never treat them harshly" (Col. 3:18–19).

Notice that each party gets one verse apiece. Previously we saw that slaves and owners received, respectively, four verses and a single verse in both Colossians and Ephesians. But that balance shifts heavily here:

> Wives, be subject to your husbands as you are to the Lord. For the husband is the head of the wife just as Christ is the head of the church, the body of which he is the Savior. Just as the church is subject to Christ, so also wives ought to be, in everything, to their husbands.
>
> Husbands, love your wives, just as Christ loved the church and gave himself up for her, in order to make her holy by cleansing her with the washing of water by the word, so as

to present the church to himself in splendor, without a spot or wrinkle or anything of the kind—yes, so that she may be holy and without blemish. In the same way, husbands should love their wives as they do their own bodies. He who loves his wife loves himself. For no one ever hates his own body, but he nourishes and tenderly cares for it, just as Christ does for the church, because we are members of his body. "For this reason a man will leave his father and mother and be joined to his wife, and the two will become one flesh." This is a great mystery, and I am applying it to Christ and the church. Each of you, however, should love his wife as himself, and a wife should respect her husband. (Eph. 5:22–33)

You can see that, while wives now get three verses, husbands get nine. They apparently have even greater or harder responsibilities. There is obviously a similar hierarchy in that wives are to "be subject" while husbands are to "love," but there is, I think, almost an attempt to overcome that hierarchy on a more profound level.

For example, the citation of Genesis 2:24 in which a husband leaves his ancestral home for that of his wife is not how patriarchy normally worked in the biblical tradition. It is certainly much better for the wife—who would be married around first menses at about thirteen years of age—to have the husband move into her extended family than for her to enter his family system. (Some stories in the book of Judges reflect the bloody transition as culture changed from the wife's home to the husband's home at marriage.)

Furthermore, that "great mystery" of husband/wife and Christ/church provides space for thought. Christians as "members of his body," that is, the body of Christ, accurately reflects the radical Paul: "Do you not know that your bodies are members of Christ? Should I therefore take the members of Christ and make them members of a prostitute? Never! . . . Now you are the body of Christ and individually members of it" (1 Cor. 6:15; 12:27).

That is sometimes called the "mystical body of Christ," but it is an enfeebled phrase. Paul imagines actual, factual, living Christians as the *physical* eyes and ears, hands and feet, hearts and minds of Christ, still and always operational on earth, still and always transformational of the earth. Better to term Christians as communally and corporately the physical body on earth of the mystical Christ in heaven.

Be that as it may, any possible ambiguity with the conservative anti-Paul in Ephesians on women in the family disappears completely with the reactionary anti-Paul on women in the apostolate:

> Let a woman learn in silence with full submission. I permit no woman to teach or to have authority over a man; she is to keep silent. For Adam was formed first, then Eve; and Adam was not deceived, but the woman was deceived and became a transgressor. Yet she will be saved through childbearing, provided they continue in faith and love and holiness, with modesty. (1 Tim. 2:11–15)

This is clearly reactionary, as one would hardly forbid what had never happened. And we saw, of course, with the radical Paul (in Chapter 13) that both women and men were equal inside the community as ministers (1 Cor. 11:5) and outside it as apostles (Rom. 16:7). Furthermore, if Adam were actually in charge of Eve, he should simply have refused her temptation. The one in charge is the one most responsible for what happens.

There is, however, one very serious objection to the preceding analysis. It goes like this: 1 Timothy 2:11–15 on silencing women in community ministry is simply a repetition of what the allegedly radical Paul said himself in 1 Corinthians 14:33b–36:

> (As in all the churches of the saints, women should be silent in the churches. For they are not permitted to speak, but should be subordinate, as the law also says. If there is anything they desire to know, let them ask their husbands at home. For it is

shameful for a woman to speak in church. Or did the word of God originate with you? Or are you the only ones it has reached?)

You notice the similarities: silence not speech for women; submission/subordination for women (the same Greek root is used); home not church for women. But you also notice that the NRSV puts that whole paragraph in parentheses—as does the official Greek New Testament. Why?

First, the entire section is found at different locations among the earliest extant manuscripts of the letter. Some have it here, and others have it after 14:40—that is, at the end of the chapter. The best explanation for this discrepancy is that it was not originally part of the letter; that a copyist wrote it in the margin as his own version of 1 Timothy 14:33b–36, and later copyists inserted it from the margin into the text at two different places.

Second, the immediate context of 1 Corinthians 14:26–40 is about speech or silence in the church assembly. On the one hand, then, it was a good place to slip in a comment about women being silent and against women speaking in church. But on the other hand, here is the specific context:

> If anyone speaks in a tongue, let there be only two or at most three, and each in turn; and let one interpret. But if there is no one to interpret, let them be silent in church and speak to themselves and to God. Let two or three prophets speak, and let the others weigh what is said. If a revelation is made to someone else sitting nearby, let the first person be silent. (1 Cor. 14:27–30)

The very specific context is about glossolalia ("a tongue") and prophecy ("interpretation"). Glossolalia (from Greek *glossa*, tongue; and *lalein*, to speak) is uttering nonlanguage easily, fluently, and at length while in an ecstatic trance. In the specific context from

14:26–40, Paul is insisting that prophecy—that is, the ability to interpret unintelligible ecstatic vocalization as intelligible discourse—must accompany glossolalia. And, in any case, individuals must always take turns and not speak at the same time.

In other words, 14:33b–16 is a post-, pseudo-, and anti-Pauline insertion in an authentic Pauline letter. Such a claim, by the way, is protected from the accusation of special pleading and political correctness only if there is such objective manuscript dislocation as found in the present case. That is the primary argument. Contextual disharmony is only a secondary and confirming argument.

"They Forbid Marriage and Demand Abstinence from Foods"

ALTHOUGH PAUL WAS A celibate ascetic, he also knew that celibacy was an individual Christian grace and in no way a general Christian rule: "each has a particular gift from God, one having one kind and another a different kind" (1 Cor. 7:7). Hold on to that concept as I return once more to 1 Timothy and Titus.

We have seen how these two letters rejected the radical Paul on the subjects of slavery and patriarchy. But they also reacted against him on the issue of celibacy with the same process of de-radicalization and re-Romanization. Leaders in the church had to be men, and never women. Though masculinity is necessary, it is not in and of itself enough for leadership:

> A bishop [literally: an overseer] must be above reproach, married only once. . . . He must manage his own household well, keeping his children submissive and respectful in every way. . . . Let deacons be married only once, and let them manage their children and their households well. (1 Tim. 3:2, 4, 12)
>
> . . . appoint elders in every town, as I directed you: someone who is blameless, married only once, whose children

are believers, not accused of debauchery and not rebellious. (Titus 1:5b–6)

Leaders, be they overseers, elders, or deacons, must not only be male, but be married and fertile—no married celibacy here!

Bluntly, the Christian leader is to look externally just like the Roman paterfamilias at his best. This implicit criticism of acetic celibacy is confirmed by this explicit and rather virulent indictment:

Now the Spirit expressly says that in later times some will renounce the faith by paying attention to deceitful spirits and teachings of demons, through the hypocrisy of liars whose consciences are seared with a hot iron. They forbid marriage and demand abstinence from foods, which God created to be received with thanksgiving by those who believe and know the truth. For everything created by God is good, and nothing is to be rejected, provided it is received with thanksgiving; for it is sanctified by God's word and by prayer. (1 Tim. 4:1–5)

We know, of course, that Paul never forbade marriage and never said that all had to be celibate, but he did say that it would be very good if all were: "I wish that all were as I myself am" (1 Cor. 7:7). But Paul was far too wise to think celibacy could be established by rule and mandated as necessity for anyone, even or especially for Christian leaders, female or male.

Finally, certain Roman moralists would have agreed with Paul's opinions against slavery and patriarchy. And, of course, female Vestal Virgins were part of Rome's sacred landscape. But advocating both male and female celibate asceticism would have been an affront to Roman patriarchy and would witness to another and different world clashing bodily and physically, socially and politically with Roman normalcy.

"A License for Women's Teaching and Baptizing"

I CONCLUDE THIS CHAPTER with something that also would have appalled Rome's patriarchal presumptions that young women would be passed from a father's to a husband's control with very little say of their own. It also would have appalled the anti-Paul writer of 1 Timothy, who commanded that women be silent in the assembly.

By the early second century CE, as we have just seen, Christian leaders had to be men rather than women *and* married parents rather than ascetic celibates. What, then, about Saint Thecla of Iconium, who was both a female leader and an ascetic celibate in that same century?

At that time, Thecla was more important than even Mary, mother of Jesus, and devotion to her spread all around the Mediterranean. Her story is told in the *Acts of Thecla*, which is probably still extant only because it was included among the first chapters of the *Acts of Paul*.

Around 200 CE, the North African theologian Tertullian complained, "The writings which wrongly go under Paul's name [that is, the *Acts of Paul*] claim Thecla's example as a license for women's teaching and baptizing" (*On Baptism* 17). In 2001, Stephen Davis's book *The Cult of St. Thecla* was subtitled *A Tradition of Women's Piety in Late Antiquity*. In other words, Thecla was never simply about Thecla alone. She was a programmatic model and normative exemplar for other women. When 1 Timothy and Titus react against female leaders, Thecla and/or her disciples would have been perfect cases in point.

Thecla was a nubile virgin, a teenager soon after first menses around thirteen years of age. As such, she was often depicted with breasts uncovered and hair unveiled; also, in these images we see that she listened to Paul's ideal of celibate asceticism not in public outside her home, but in private, inside, from her window. She decided to reject her fiancé and remain celibate. That, however, was not mere domestic disobedience to family plans but a complete rejection of patriarchal dictates.

Accordingly, in these tales she was not simply confined to her room but condemned to die in the arena. But no matter what mode of execution was attempted against her—being burned alive or torn apart by wild bulls—God always saved her miraculously. Two features are of very special, if not extraordinary, importance among those stories.

First, since Paul had refused to baptize her, she cast herself into a huge vat of water filled with lethal sea creatures. She baptized herself, and God approved by destroying the dangerous marine animals.

Second, there occurs one scene, not of early Christian femin-ism but of early Christian female-ism. The arena crowd splits into two, for and against Thecla, but not into Christians for her and pagans against her. It splits into women for her and men against her. Even the animals sent to kill her do the same:

> Lions and bears were set upon her, and a fierce lioness ran to her and lay down at her feet. And the crowd of the women raised a great shout. And a bear ran upon her, but the lioness ran and met it, and tore the bear asunder. And again a lion trained against men, which belonged to Alexander, ran upon her; and the lioness grappled with the lion, and perished with it. And the women mourned the more, since the lioness which helped her was dead. (*Acts of Thecla* in *Acts of Paul* 3)

Later, the women attempt to confuse and distract other wild animals by tossing their perfumes down into the arena.

When an adolescent stands up to an empire, when a teenager chooses celibate asceticism rather than patriarchal control, when non-Christian women defend that teenager in the arena and Christian women follow her in the community, something extraordinary has occurred. And no matter how much is fact and how much is fiction, how much is history and how much is parable, the extraordinary legacy of the tale of Thecla persists.

When we debate today about whether Paul was pro-woman or

anti-woman, it might be instructive to remember what a second-century woman and her female followers thought about that historical Paul. Apparently, they found him useful; they knew he was on the Way with them and not in the way of them. Still, even granted that, the *Acts of Thecla* is about the Apostle Thecla, and not about the Apostle Paul.

Where Are We Now and What Comes Next?

PAUL WAS NEVER TERRIBLY hard to understand on the theoretical and theological levels. Instead, he was terribly hard to follow on the social and practical levels. The same goes for Jesus before him: easy to understand, difficult to follow. Paul's lordship of Christ was Jesus's Kingdom of God taken from Jewish homeland across Jewish Diaspora in language that was crystal clear against the matrix of Roman imperial theology.

This chapter has presented post-Paul and pseudo-Paul as the anti-Paul subversion of the historical Paul's assertion on the issues of slavery, patriarchy, and violent human victory presented in Chapter 13.

That, of course, is exactly the same process of negation we saw for John the Baptist and Jesus himself in Chapters 10 and 11. The historical Baptist's original vision of God's advent as the divinely nonviolent Return from Babylon (in Mark and John) was changed later into the divinely violent Exodus from Egypt (in the Q Gospel as used by Matthew and Luke). So also with Jesus as his proclamation of God's nonviolent Kingdom became God's violent Apocalypse.

Both those processes were more difficult to discern than the case of Paul. There at least we had clearly distinct letters that could be separated into three groups that depicted a sequence from radical through conservative to reactionary. Assertion and subversion almost jumped out at you there even if all those letters were explicitly attributed to Paul.

All of that biblical tradition, however, from Old Testament through New Testament, from Torah and Prophecy through Jesus and Paul, portrays the same process repeated throughout the Christian Bible as the radicality of God is brought back into the normalcy of civilization. At the end, the Roman Empire is no more and no less than the normalcy of civilization robed in a toga.

To Outsoar the Shadow of Our Night

First, I find the center point.
HUGH OF SAINT VICTOR,
The Mystic Ark (1125–1130)

THE PROBLEM OF THE Christian Bible is that its God is portrayed both nonviolently and violently; its Christ, proclaimed as the human image of that God, is also portrayed both nonviolently and violently; and therefore Christians are called to a life of political confusion at best, or religious hypocrisy at worst. (Suspect the peace donkey, expect the warhorse.)

The solution offered in this book is not one invented externally by a clever author but one discovered internally from within that Christian Bible itself. In fact, nobody has ever deconstructed the Christian Bible externally as well as it deconstructs itself internally. Here, in summary, are the steps by which I finally recognized what was there all along.

Matrix

I BEGIN BY REPEATING the fundamental supposition I brought to both that problem and its solution in this book. Like any presupposition, it must be judged by whether it explains more than it obfuscates, and whether it is ultimately adequate to ancient intentions and respectful of past purposes.

My foundational presupposition, a very general but very basic one, concerns how to read anything, ancient or modern, biblical or nonbiblical. That process demands awareness of matrix; that is, anything spoken or written must first be understood within its own time and place. Matrix is the background you cannot skip, the context you cannot avoid. (For example, as mentioned at the beginning of this book, the matrix for Gandhi is British imperialism, and that for Martin Luther King Jr. is American racism.) The cross-haired coordinates of matrix are communal tradition and individual vision as well as specific time and particular place. And, whether we like it or not, matrix is destiny, for speaker and writer as for hearer and reader.

The alternative to matrix meaning is Rorschach reading or inkblot interpretation, which is when an ancient text means whatever your modern mind decides it means. But under matrix discipline we should never respond with either agreement or disagreement, belief or disbelief, until we know what was intended in its original situation then, as we understand that situation now.

This concept of matrix is neither new nor esoteric. It is simply common sense. We operate easily and readily on this principle every day of our lives because we know our own time and place, our own situation, our own contemporary environment. Normally we take matrix for granted, since we swim in it like fish in water.

The past, however, is a foreign country, and we must enter its matrix and at least try to hear with its ears and see with its eyes. We do that by reading its texts slowly, studying its artifacts fully, and walking its ruins thoughtfully. This process is neither totally objective nor fully subjective, but it is necessarily interactive between now and then, present and past, us and them.

For the Christian Bible, therefore, matrix means the millennia between the Sumerians and Romans for time and the land from the Mesopotamian plain to the Mediterranean Sea for place. My emphasis in every case is on both adoption and adaption. We must pay equal attention both to what a biblical text or tradition adopts from its cultural and imperial matrix and to how it adapts it to its own vision. Does it do that incompetently, inadequately, incompletely, or brilliantly?

We have just seen, for example, the matrix of Jesus and Paul as Roman imperial theology in the Jewish homeland or Jewish Diaspora. If you hear or read, for example, that Jesus is Divine, Son of God, or God Incarnate, that he is Lord, Redeemer from Sin, and Savior of the World, it is absurd, I claim, to accept or reject those titles without first asking what they meant when first uttered within the matrix of Judaism under Rome and Rome under Augustus.

Within that matrix, all those titles belonged not just potentially to the Jewish Messiah, but to the Roman Emperor. Any exclusive use of such titular claims for anyone other than the emperor represented *majestas*—that is, high treason. Only after you discern what it meant to transfer those titles from emperor to peasant and Palatine Hill to Nazareth Ridge *then*, can you assert either belief or disbelief *now*.

Metaphor

THIS BOOK'S SOLUTION ON *How to Read the Bible and Still Be a Christian* developed downward through three major levels, as in an archaeological dig, with each level summarized in a major metaphor.

The first and surface level of the Christian biblical tradition is one that most people recognize only too well. It presents that rather bipolar God of nonviolent rewards and violent punishments. Furthermore, it is emphatically clear that God's nonviolence promises distributive justice, while God's violence threatens retributive justice.

My metaphor for that surface level is the Biblical Express Train. I imagine the Christian biblical tradition thundering along on the parallel tracks of both a transcendentally nonviolent rail and a transcendentally violent one. Apologists and polemicists may imagine alternative monorails, but my first metaphor is that of a train operating on not one, but two tracks.

The second and deeper level of this biblical tradition challenges the adequacy of that surface glimpse. When you actually read the entire text from start to finish, you notice that those just-seen bipolar characteristics of God are more successive than simultaneous, and more alternating than parallel.

Furthermore, those alternations involve a repeated pattern of "yes" and "no" in which God's radical divine vision of justice and liberation is regularly muted or turned back into the normalcy of civilization's injustice and oppression. The radicality of peace through nonviolent justice is repeatedly affirmed and then negated by the normalcy of peace gained through violent victory. Divinity proposes, but humanity disposes—from Torah and prophecy to Jesus and Paul.

Below, before I suggest a second metaphor for that second and deeper level of the Christian Bible, is a diagram that sums up this dynamic visually.

The diagram has two axes and four quadrants. But two of the quadrants are of primary importance to my understanding of this second level of the Christian Bible.

One axis is the Axis of Justice, with distributive justice and retributive justice as its two terminuses. But always remember that, as seen in Chapter 1, those terminuses are not equal, as distribution is the basis even for retribution. Used without qualification, therefore, justice should be presumed to concern distribution.

The other axis is the Axis of Power, and for me, this is never a negative term. Its terminuses are nonviolent power (persuasion) and violent power (force). Used without qualification, therefore, power can be either nonviolent or violent. (This book is an act of power— but it could not and should not be one of force—only of persuasion.)

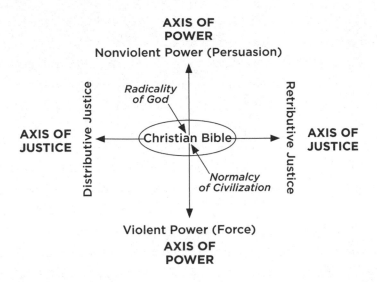

The transverse line from the top left to the bottom right quadrant diagrams the rhythm I propose for the Christian Bible (also, of course, for the actual Christian church and the practical Christian life). The central oval indicates that the Christian Bible is the textual arena where the struggle between God's radicality and civilization's normalcy occurs.

My second metaphor, therefore, changes from the Biblical Express Train to the Biblical Heartbeat and thereby indicates a rhythm of expansion-and-contraction, affirmation-and-negation, declaration-and-retraction. That constant alternation means that the heartbeat of the Christian Bible is a rhythmic sequence of assertion-and-subversion between God's radicality and civilization's normalcy.

You will recall these two examples: Torah's assertion that land cannot be acquired permanently by buying and selling begets the subversion that it can be obtained by loans and foreclosures. Paul's assertion that Christians cannot own Christian slaves generates the subversion that they can do so, but with kindness.

Granted, however, both that diagram and that metaphor, we are still caught in a biblical impasse. Since both assertion and subversion are equally attributed to God or Torah, Jesus or Paul, how should we as Christians decide between them? Maybe, after all, the biblical God prefers the normalcy of civilization?

The answer takes us down to the third and deepest level of the Christian biblical tradition where it internally solves it own internal problem. We will also need a third metaphor for that foundational layer.

Since the Christian Bible proclaims that Jesus of Nazareth is the Messianic Son of God, he cannot be but one more beat in that rhythm of assertion-and-subversion. (By the way, in a patriarchal world of male primogeniture where the firstborn or beloved son gets family farm and dynastic throne, "son" simply means "heir.")

You could even translate John's opening words like this: "In the beginning was the *Assertion*, and the *Assertion* was with God, and the *Assertion* was God. . . . And the *Assertion* became flesh and lived among us" (1:1, 14a). But to stop the immediate subversion of Christ within the Christian biblical tradition, it itself offers us this ultimate solution:

> *The norm and criterion of the Christian Bible is the biblical Christ*
> *but*
> *the norm and criterion of the biblical Christ is the historical Jesus.*

This is almost obvious when, as mentioned earlier, you consider that Christianity does not count time moving forward to a climactic and apocalyptic consummation but moving down to and up from the arrival of the historical Jesus. Jesus is for us Christians imagined religiously and theologically as the hinge of our history, the center of our time, and the norm of our Bible.

I repeat and thereby emphasize strongly that I am not invoking that antiquated distinction of the Jesus of history versus the Christ of faith. Whether the historical Jesus was or was not Christ, the Messianic Son of God is not the present debate—that is a matter of faith. Instead, the debate is whether the historical Jesus, whether accepted or rejected as Christ and Messianic Son of God, was or was not invoking nonviolent or violent resistance against Rome—that is a matter of history.

What is at stake here for us Christians is theologically quite evident. Whether Jesus accepted, advocated, or used nonviolent or violent resistance against the violence of oppression and injustice determines how we Christians are to imagine the very character of our God. That also determines our religious, theological, and ecclesiastical processes as well as our economic, social, and political lives.

In the light of my two accurate but ultimately inadequate metaphors—twin-railed Biblical Express Train and rhythmically patterned Biblical Heartbeat—what is the appropriate third metaphor? What is the best model for this third and deepest level of the Christian biblical tradition, for its normative criterion revealed internally as the historical Jesus, that nonviolent embodiment of the nonviolent Kingdom of the nonviolent God? What best portrays a narrative whose meaning is in the middle, not the end, and whose climax is in the center, not the conclusion?

Those first two metaphors of train and heartbeat jumped out at me immediately, but imagining an adequate third one was extremely difficult. In fact, it was only during the final editing process of this book that it came to me. At that time, I was also working on early Christian art involving the integrated narrative iconography of Old and New Testament scenes—from Creation to Pentecost. In fresco and mosaic, on ivory and parchment, the viewer's eye is usually guided toward a central scene among all the others. I give you just one example, because it was where I finally found my third metaphor.

In early September 2014, my wife, Sarah, and I along with our friends Anne and Alan Perry spent a morning among the magnificent frescoes of the Benedictine Basilica of the Archangel Michael, Sant'Angelo in Formis, high above Capua in Italy. The frescoes are from around 1072 and are similar to those painted on Monte Cassino's contemporary abbey church of Saint Benedict. They are the most complete integrated bitestamental fresco cycle still extant in Europe.

When you stand just inside the entrance of the basilica, facing forward, the biblical scenes swirl around you in one continuous narrative sequence from creation to ascension. That spiral sequence has four layers, one for the Old Testament on the outer walls of the side aisles framing three for the New Testament on the inner walls of the nave.

On your left the outer Old Testament story moves toward you from creation through Eden to Cain and Abel, and on your right it continues away from you through Abraham, Isaac, and Jacob to Gideon (counterclockwise). The New Testament story is then picked up again from front right toward you to front left away from you but descending through three layers—top, middle, and bottom—on the parables and healings, the life, death, and resurrection of Jesus (clockwise). In other words, that fourfold spiral starts and ends at the apse so that your eye is directed by architecture and narrative to the climactic image of Christ in majesty that dominates the apse.

On one hand, of course, this is not exactly the historical Jesus in everyday garments from Galilee. Instead, he is seated and robed like a Byzantine emperor. On the other hand, his halo is cruciform and he is barefooted. It is Christ as Jesus even more than Jesus as Christ. The four evangelists appear, two on each side. They are in symbolic and winged form, each holding his closed book and with their eyes fixed not on their texts, but on the one named "Jesus Christ." (By the way, Latin artists miscopied the Greek name CHRIST by reversing its two-letter abbreviation from XC to CX.)

Christ also holds a book on his left knee and raises his right hand in traditional blessing style. He is not reading the book because he is its norm, criterion, and discriminant. Instead, it is opened toward the viewer and proclaims in Latin, "I am the Alpha and the Omega, the first and the last" (Rev. 22:13a). That is not the book speaking, but the norm of the book. That was where I finally found my third metaphor.

Indeed, once I saw it there that morning, I could immediately recall it from all those Christian narrative cycles, from fresco to mosaic, from ivory reliquary boxes to silver gospel-covers, where narrative images from both Old and New Testaments surround one of Jesus that is both central for them, larger than them, and normative to them.

I also realized that my first two metaphors of *Biblical Express Train* and *Biblical Heartbeat* were metaphors of time, as was appropriate for reading a text from beginning to end and recognizing the recurrent themes within it. But my third and ultimate metaphor had to be a metaphor of place. It had to be focal rather than kinetic; locational rather than chronological; simultaneous, visual, and spatial rather than successive, temporal, and terminal. It is a metaphor of place, not a metaphor of time.

I call that third metaphor *Biblical Iconic Focus*, and thereby apply the experience of visual narrative to verbal narrative. In visual narrative, from tiny icon to great basilica, your architectural eye and your artistic eye are focused centrally rather than terminally, are directed to that central core that is the deliberate norm, the intended criterion, and the didactic discriminant of the entire composition.

In summary, here is the way to *Read the Christian Bible and Still Be a Christian*: Do not just read it as a book and expect the meaning at its end, but view it as an image and expect the climax in the center. Read it verbally, but picture it visually.

Meaning

THE LONGER I LOOK at the central "Christian Bible" oval of the diagram above, the more I see other contents that could appear there with equal validity. The diagram would work as well for "General Christian History" or for "Individual Christian Life" as for the Christian Bible. It might even work just as well for "American History"; but in the light of the words "endowed by their Creator with certain unalienable Rights" from the Declaration of Independence or "liberty and justice for all" from the Pledge of Allegiance, we might have to admit that for us, subversion preceded assertion.

Furthermore, if you find the term "God" or "civilization" distracting, I suggest you look at that diagram as simply the clash between a radical and a normal vision for the future of human life on earth. The radicality of nonviolent resistance versus the normalcy of violent oppression, and the radicality of peace through distributive justice versus the normalcy of peace through victorious force seem to apply equally to the first century then, our twenty-first century now, and all the centuries in between.

But there is one terrible and fateful change across those centuries, and it gives us our current rendezvous with destiny. Escalatory violence now directly threatens the future of our species and indirectly undermines solutions to other survival problems such as global warming, overpopulation, and resource management. This was not true of first-century violence: try an iron sword against an olive tree and see who wins.

If, therefore, you agree with this book that there are no divine punishments but only human consequences (apart, of course, from natural disasters and random accidents), then the challenge to our species is clear. Governed not by chemical instinct but by moral conscience, can we control escalatory violence before it destroys us? Can we abandon violence as civilization's drug of choice? Can we opt deliberately for peace gained through justice and abandon, as a fatally bankrupt option, that mantric chant of peace gained through victory?

I come back one final time to this book's title. I ask ultimately, with that third metaphor established and *Biblical Iconic Focus* directed on the historical Jesus, what it means to Still Be a Christian? How now is that historical Jesus the norm of your Christian faith?

This book has talked repeatedly of the biblical tradition's emphasis on distributive justice: that is, on justice as primarily about the fair and equitable distribution of God's world for all God's people. But that God is both a "God of justice" (Isaiah 30:18) and a "God of Love" (1 John 4:8, 16), so to be a Christian must involve both justice and love. But how exactly do justice and love correlate with one another?

I begin with an immediate negative, which I hope is quite unnecessary at this stage. I reject absolutely any response claiming that the Old Testament depicts a God of justice as vengeance and the New Testament one of love as mercy. As you know by now, that works well as long as you do not make the mistake of actually reading the Christian Bible all the way to its climactic violence in the book of Revelation. What, then, is the positive relationship between justice and love in the Christian Bible?

We live within a world of visible externals and invisible internals. (If I were sure enough of what Albert Einstein meant by the terms, I might say a world of "mass" and "energy.") From the tiny ant to the expanding universe, everything has, let us say, a visible outside and an invisible inside. Take, for example, our human self. We are body and soul, flesh and spirit. But when they are separated from one another, we do not get both—we get neither; we get a physical corpse. So it is with justice and love.

Justice is the body of love, and love is the soul of justice. Separate them and you do not get both—you get neither; you get a moral corpse. Justice is the flesh of love, and love is the spirit of justice. Think about this for a moment.

Why, on one hand, do individuals or groups who set out with the highest ideals of distributive justice so often end up in bloody slaughter—especially of "the unjust"? Why, on the other hand, is "love" a word so empty of content that it can be used at the same time for our favorite candy bar and the soulmate of our life, for our favorite sports team and God Almighty?

It is because we have separated what cannot be separated if each term is to retain its full power. Justice without love may end in brutality, but love without justice must end in banality. Love empowers justice, and justice embodies love. Keep both, or get neither.

My title for this epilogue adapted a line from Percy Bysshe Shelley's "Elegy on the Death of John Keats," and I revert to Keats in conclusion. He ended his "Ode on a Grecian Urn" by having that vase proclaim that "Beauty is truth, truth beauty,—that is all / Ye know on earth, and all ye need to know." Imagine, instead, or as well, an "Ode on a Biblical Urn" in which that urn proclaims, "Justice is love, love is justice. That is all we know on earth, and all we need to know."

NOTES

1. The full text of the Code of Urukagina is in Samuel Noah Kramer, *The Sumerians: Their History, Culture, and Character* (Chicago: University of Chicago Press, 1963), 317–19. His commentary on it is in *History Begins at Sumer: Thirty-Nine Firsts in Man's Recorded History*, 3rd ed. (Philadelphia: University of Pennsylvania Press, 1981), 45–50.
2. Translations of Sumerian texts are taken from the Electronic Text Corpus of Sumerian Literature (ETCSL), by the Faculty of Oriental Studies of the University of Oxford in England. I cite texts by the title and number used in that collection at http://etcsl.orinst.ox.ac.uk.
3. Translation, along with introduction and notes for both versions are taken from Stephanie Dalley, *Myths from Mesopotamia: Creation, the Flood, Gilgamesh, and Others*, rev. ed. Oxford World Classics (New York: Oxford University Press, 2000), 39–153.
4. These three titles for this text are from, respectively, Noah Kramer, *History Begins at Sumer*, 136; ETCSL 4.08.33; and *Ancient Near Eastern Texts Relating to the Old Testament* [*ANET*], 3rd ed., ed. James B. Pritchard (Princeton, NJ: Princeton University Press, 1955), 41–42.
5. Robert Alter, *Genesis: Translation and Commentary* (New York: Norton, 1996), 17 and 20.
6. Alter, *Genesis*, 20.
7. Dalley, *Myths from Mesopotamia*, 20–30.
8. The full text is in *ANET*, 203–205. When I count lines below, they are only rough comparisons based on that English translation. Other Hittite suzerainty-vassal examples are on 205–206 and 529–30.
9. The full texts are in *ANET*, 534–42; and, with introductory details, in Donald J. Wiseman, "The Vassal-Treaties of Esarhaddon," *Iraq* 20 (1958), 1–99, with Plates I–XII.

10. In general, on divine distributive justice, see Hosea 4:1–3; 5:10; 12:7–9; Isaiah 5:7b–9; 33:14–15; Micah 2:1–2; 3:1–3; 6:10–12; 7:2; Jeremiah 22:3; Ezekiel 18:5–9; 45:9–1. In particular, for the poor, see Amos 2:6–8; 5:11–12; 8:4–7; Isaiah 3:14–15; Jeremiah 22:13–17; for widows and/or orphans, see Jeremiah 5:26–28; 22:3; Zechariah 7:9–10; for the resident alien, see Jeremiah 7:7–5; 22:3; Zechariah 7:9–10.

11. John J. Collins, "Sibylline Oracles," Vol. 1, *The Old Testament Pseude-pigrapha*, ed. James H. Charlesworth, 2 vols., (Garden City, NY: Doubleday, 1983–1985), 317–472. See 478–79.

12. Collins, "Sibylline Oracles." For the legend of returning Nero, see 3.63–74; 4.119–124, 137–139; 5.28–34, 93–105, 137–154, 214–224, 361–380. The Roman historians Tacitus (*Histories* 2.8) and Suetonius (*Nero* 57) even describe imposters claiming to be returning Nero.

13. Virgil, *The Aeneid*, trans. Henry Rushton Fairelough, 3rd ed. rev. G. P. Gould, 2 vols., Loeb Classical Library (Cambridge: Harvard University Press: 1999).

Scripture Index

SUBJECT INDEX

Israel *(continued)*
148–52; hope for Kingdom of God
and, 132, 133–35; invasion and defeat of, 118; Kingdom of God for,
196–97; kings, good vs. bad and
Deuteronomic tradition, 95–98;
"lost tribes of," 106; Maccabean
Revolt, 127; Mesopotamia theology
and, 53, 54, 56, 57, 67; messianic
hopes of, 153–55; northern/south-
ern split, 89; Priestly tradition,
24, 69, 75, 76, 80, 87, 88, 94, 98;
Psalter as prayer book of, 110; Rabbinic tradition, 18–19; the Return
(from Babylon), 160, 161–62, 171,
232; Romanization of, 148–52;
Roman rule, 143–56; Roman rule,
armed revolts against, 143–44, 150,
155–56; Roman rule, nonviolent
protests against, 144–48, 150, 151,
155–56; Syrian persecution, 127,
129; Torah and, 53; Yahwist tradition, 69

Jenkins, Jerry, 14
Jerusalem, 89; Caligula's intention to
place his statue in the temple, 144,
146–48; deliverance from Assyrian threat, 105–7; destruction of
the First Temple (by Babylon), 12;
destruction of the Second Temple
(by Rome), 12; eighth century
BCE, 9; Hadrian and, 144; Jesus in
the Temple incident, 8–9; in Left
Behind series, 14–15; Messiah on
a donkey entering, 29–30; Nero's
destruction of, 143; Pilate and, 144;
Romanization of, 149
Jesus: assertion-and-subversion pattern in portrayal of, 173–85, 220;
baptism of, 158, 204–5; Barabbas
and, 169–70; beatitudes, 164–65;
Christ/church mystery, 225; conversation with Pilate, 170; on divorce, 152; entering Jerusalem on
a "peace" donkey, 30, 35, 36, 37,
56, 181, 235; escalatory violence
and acculturation of historical
Jesus, 173–85, 232; execution of,
168; "good news" and, 196; histor-

ical, 5–7, 29, 163, 167, 196, 201;
historical, as the biblical Christ,
35, 36–37, 171, 185, 240–41;
hypocrites and snakes and, 178; in
Jerusalem, Holy Week, 169; John
the Baptist and, 157, 158–59, 166;
Kingdom of God for, 158, 164–71,
185; martyrdom of, 169; matrix
of eschatology, nonviolence, and
martyrdom, 157–58, 163; nonviolence of, 7, 8–9, 15, 16, 19, 28, 29,
167–70, 171, 181, 215, 216; normalcy of civilization and, 173–85,
232; passion of, 5–6; program of,
164–71; Q Gospel and escalatory violence depicted in, 174–79;
radicality of God vs. normalcy of
civilization and, 30–31; reaction to
rejection, 175; request for miraculous sign from, 175–76; resistance
to Rome and, 151; response to the
Pharisees, 164; resurrection of,
205; Roman matrix of, 143–53,
163, 200, 237, 242; second coming of, 9; Sermon on the Mount,
9, 16, 19, 29, 214; as Son of God,
171, 192, 237; as Son of Man, 158,
165; true Jesus of the Incarnation,
30–31, 36; violent Christ of *Chronicles of Narnia*, 15; violent Christ
of Revelation, 9–13, 19, 28, 29, 35,
37, 181; "weeping and gnashing
of teeth" and, 176–78; "a whip of
cords" and, 7–9
Jewish Antiquities (JA) (Josephus),
143, 144, 145, 147, 148, 150, 159,
163, 168
Jewish Diaspora, 136, 139, 201, 232
Jewish War (JW) (Josephus), 143, 144,
145–46, 147, 148, 149
Jezebel, Queen, 24
Job, 89, 97–98, 121, 126
Joel, 28–29
John, The Gospel According to:
favorite Christian quotation from,
35; Jesus's reaction to rejection in,
175; opening words, 240; parable
of conversation between Pilate and
Jesus, 170; parable of nonviolent
Kingdom of God vs. violent Em-